LITERARY RELATIONS

Literary Relations

Kinship and the Canon
1660–1830

JANE SPENCER

OXFORD
UNIVERSITY PRESS

OXFORD
UNIVERSITY PRESS

Great Clarendon Street, Oxford OX2 6DP

Oxford University Press is a department of the University of Oxford.
It furthers the University's objective of excellence in research, scholarship,
and education by publishing worldwide in

Oxford New York

Auckland Cape Town Dar es Salaam Hong Kong Karachi
Kuala Lumpur Madrid Melbourne Mexico City Nairobi
New Delhi Shanghai Taipei Toronto

With offices in

Argentina Austria Brazil Chile Czech Republic France Greece
Guatemala Hungary Italy Japan Poland Portugal Singapore
South Korea Switzerland Thailand Turkey Ukraine Vietnam

Oxford is a registered trademark of Oxford University Press
in the UK and in certain other countries

Published in the United States
by Oxford University Press Inc., New York

© Jane Spencer, 2005

British Library Cataloguing in Publication Data

Data available

Library of Congress Cataloging in Publication Data

Spencer, Jane.
Literary relations : kinship and the canon, 1660-1830 / Jane Spencer.
p. cm.
Includes bibliographical references and index.
ISBN 0–19–926296–9 (alk. paper)
1. English literature—History and criticism—Theory, etc. 2. Influence (Literary, atristic, etc.)
3. Authors, English—Family relationships 4. Mentoring of authors—Great Britain. 5. Women
and literature—Great Britain. 6. Kinship in literature. 7. Family in literature. 8. Canon
(Literature). I. Title.
PR408.I57S66 2005 820.9–dc22 2005019765

Typeset by Laserwords Private Limited, Chennai, India
Printed in Great Britain
on acid-free paper by
Biddles Ltd, King's Lynn, Norfolk

ISBN 0–19–926296–9 978–0–19–926296–0

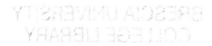

For my parents, my sister and brother,
and my daughters

Acknowledgements

Some material in Chapter 2 appears in my article 'The Mighty Mother: Pope and Maternity', in *Studies in the Literary Imagination*, Copyright Georgia State University Press, 2005, and is reproduced here by permission of the Editors.

I am grateful to the Arts and Humanities Research Board for a Research Leave Award in 2001–2, and to Exeter University School of English for the matching funding that allowed me to take up this award and have two semesters' leave.

I'd like to thank all those students, colleagues, and other scholars who have listened to me deliver various papers on this work in progress. Their insights and suggestions have been of enormous help. The anonymous readers at Oxford University Press offered beautifully constructive criticism. Many people have read some part of the work in progress, helped me think through my ideas, or saved me from errors: grateful thanks to Marilyn Butler, Regenia Gagnier, Adeline Johns-Putra, Thomas Keymer, Colin MacCabe, Robert Mack, Sarah Prescott, Jacquie Rawes, Rick Rylance, George Rousseau, Peter Sabor, Ashley Tauchert, and Min Wild. Remaining errors, of course, are mine.

Kate and Eleanor Spencer have been a constant source of joy. Many others as well, family and friends, have helped me through a difficult time. You know who you are: thank you.

J.S.

Contents

Introduction   1

1. Fathers and Mentors   18

2. The Mighty Mother   73

3. Brothers, Sisters, and New Provinces of Writing   131

4. Women in the Literary Family   188

Bibliography   231
Index   255

Introduction

In 1808 Walter Scott, Edinburgh lawyer and man of letters, editor of the collection *Minstrelsy of the Scottish Border* and author of *The Lay of the Last Minstrel* and *Marmion*, published an eighteen volume edition of the works of John Dryden. His efforts to make the work of Scots balladeers known as a part of the British literary tradition were thus complemented by a work of homage to an admired English predecessor whose critical work had done a great deal to establish confidence in an illustrious national literary history. The experience of editing Dryden brought Scott full up against the burden of past poetic achievement. Referring to Dryden's time, he wrote to his friend and fellow poet, Anna Seward: ' "in these days were giants in the land" and we are but dwarfs beside them'.[1] He echoed the concerns of Dryden himself, for whom Shakespeare and Jonson belonged to 'the Gyant Race, before the Flood'; and, like Dryden, he thought of his giant predecessors as fathers.[2] One of the problems he

---

[1] *Letters of Sir Walter Scott*, ed. H. J. C. Grierson (London: Constable, 1932), i. 354. Scott alludes to Elijah Fenton's 1711 'Epistle to Southerne', which, itself recalling Dryden's treatment of literary ancestors, compares modern writers unfavourably with Shakespeare, Jonson, Beaumont, and Fletcher: 'Few Moderns in the Lists with these may stand, | For in those Days were Giants in the land'. *Poems on Several Occasions* (London: Bernard Lintot, 1717), 70. For Scott, Dryden himself belongs with Chaucer and Spenser, the giants of the past.

[2] John Dryden, 'To my Dear Friend Mr. Congreve, on his Comedy, call'd The Double-Dealer', *The Works of John Dryden*, iv. *Poems 1693–1696*, ed. A. B. Chambers and W. Frost (Berkeley and Los Angeles: University of California Press, 1974), 432.

faced in his edition was what to do with the indecent passages that, in his politer age, were not considered suitable to print in volumes that might be read by the young. Advised by the antiquary George Ellis to produce an expurgated version, Scott reacted strongly:

> I will not castrate John Dryden. I would as soon castrate my own father, as I believe Jupiter did of yore. What would you say to any man who would castrate Shakespeare, or Massinger, or Beaumont and Fletcher? I don't say but that it may be very proper to select correct passages for the use of boarding schools and colleges.... But in making an edition of a man of genius's works for libraries and collections ... I must give my author as I find him.[3]

Scott's reverence for the genius whose immortal body must be preserved entire is mingled here with an undercurrent of Bloomian anxiety of influence in the remark on Jupiter (who dethroned his father, Saturn, and became supreme among the gods). Behind his words lies an implicit question: is Scott to be just an editorial son or will he take over the father's poetic authority? In thinking of his duty and his dilemma as those of a son in relation to a powerful father, Scott is making use of a metaphor that has helped constitute the literary tradition with which he is so concerned.

So Scott could be thought of as Dryden's son. Whether Anna Seward, whom he invited to look back with him at past poetic giants, might be Dryden's daughter, is a more complicated question. Shortly after Scott's edition of Dryden was published, the problem of women's relation to a literary tradition understood as a genealogy and an inheritance was raised by Lucy Aikin in *Epistles on Women*. This poem was ambitious in its historical and anthropological scope—it was intended 'to mark the effects of various codes, institutions, and states of manners' on human virtue and happiness—and in its political aim, to redress the neglect of women's history. 'I sing the Fate of Woman', Aikin announces, for while 'man to man | Adds

---

[3] *Letters of Sir Walter Scott*, i. 264–5.

praise, and glory lights his mortal span', woman, with no one to praise her after death, 'sinks, and leaves no vestige of her birth'. It was ambitious, too, in its claim to epic form. Like Milton before her, she echoes and alters the Virgilian epic opening; and like Milton, she treats the story of Genesis, altering the great English epic in her insistence on the prelapsarian equality of Adam and Eve, 'Alike the children of no partial God'. Bold in following Milton at all, bolder in revising him, Aikin not surprisingly has something to say about the possibility of cultural inheritance from the opposite sex. Her introduction moves through the obligatory early-nineteenth-century denial of a Wollstonecraftian or Revolutionary adherence to the Rights of Woman into an appeal for recognition of women's humanity. 'Nothing . . . could, in my opinion, be more foolish than the attempt to engage our sex in a struggle for stations that they are physically unable to fulfil', she assures us. In today's words, 'I'm not a feminist, but':

> but let not sex be carried into every thing. Let the impartial voice of history testify for us, that, when permitted, we have been the worthy associates of the best efforts of the best of men; let the daily observation of mankind bear witness, that no talent, no virtue, is masculine alone; no fault or folly exclusively feminine; . . . that there is not an endowment, or propensity, or mental quality of any kind, which may not be derived from her father to the daughter, to the son from his mother. These positions once established, and carried into their consequences, will do every thing for woman. Perceiving that any shaft aimed at her, must strike in its recoil upon some vulnerable part of common human nature, the Juvenals and Popes of future ages will abstain from making her the butt of scorn or malice. Feeling with gratitude of what her heart and mind are capable, the scholars, the sages, and the patriots of coming days will treat her as a sister and a friend.[4]

---

[4] Lucy Aikin, *Epistles on Women, Exemplifying Their Character and Condition in various ages and nations* (London: J. Johnson, 1810), pp. vii, 3, 12, v–vi, vi; ellipses in original.

This moderate plea for women is based on the claim that women belong in the human family—an obviously reasonable idea, and one that was likely to command especially sympathetic approval in the early nineteenth century, with its glorified understanding of family life. In the context of her poem's epic pretensions, though, Aikin's plea is also, and more radically, about *literary* kinship and inheritance. If Scott could see himself openly as a son of Dryden, Aikin is implicitly claiming to be a daughter of Milton.

What of her maternal literary inheritance? The implied criticism of Wollstonecraft may suggest that it is being repudiated; but in aiming for an alternative to Wollstonecraftian rights she is also following her aunt, Anna Letitia Barbauld, who had done the same in her poem 'The Rights of Woman'. Aikin, who later edited Barbauld's works, was certainly conscious of her inheritance from female poets. What most interests me about the passage I have quoted, though, is her claim that qualities are inherited across the sexual divide—from father to daughter, from mother to son—as well as from the parent to the child of the same sex. It seems a common-sense enough position for her own day and has since been given all the support it needs from advancing genetic knowledge. Yet our most commonly used metaphors of literary inheritance still tend to assume a kind of sexual apartheid. In the paradigmatic inheritance metaphor, which lies unremarked behind most accounts of literary tradition, the father transmits that tradition to his sons. Feminist criticism has created alternative traditions in which daughters inherit from their mothers. What may come 'from her father to the daughter' has received some critical attention; what may be passed on 'to the son from his mother' much less. In this study, I have tried to give full weight to literary relations between women and men, as well as those between men and between women.

At the time Scott and Aikin were writing, the national literary tradition was a well-defined one. Between the age of Milton and Dryden and their own time, the canon of British writers was consolidated, and new writers, and new literary traditions, were absorbed into it (or dropped from it) as it was continually being generated and contested.

Shakespeare was crowned the nation's playwright, Milton its sublime poet. Fielding and Richardson were rapidly canonized as its rival great novelists. Anthologies of poetry, essays of criticism, and historical surveys of dramatists, poets, and novelists were published. The timing of the canon's creation has been a bone of critical contention.[5] I agree with Richard Terry that canon-making began early, and can be traced in the sixteenth and seventeenth centuries, but that the post-Restoration period is important for the increase in attention given to the literary past.[6] The period from 1660 to the early 1800s is also important, of course, as a time of growing commercialization of literature, the professionalization of authorship, and the immense growth—slow at the beginning of the period, rapid by its end—of women's writing.

The argument of this book is that kinship relations between writers played a central part in the process of building the national literary tradition. I mean kinship here in a number of senses, from the figurative to the literal. At the rhetorical level, kinship metaphors were an organizing principle of literary history. Literary tradition was understood as a genealogy in which individual writers figured as fathers and sons, and if writers were to be remembered after their deaths, to be incorporated into the literary histories that were now being produced, they needed to find, or be granted, a place within the family of literature. At the biographical level, literary kinship worked differently. A writer might look to Chaucer, dead and distant, as a literary father, or he might find himself hailed as a son by a living writer, as Congreve was by Dryden. Such a literary relationship was still metaphorical, but it was mixed with the experience of a kind of paternal mentoring, protection, or injunction. The father was not just a symbol within literary history but an active participant in the

---

[5] See the debate among Richard Terry, Thomas P. Miller, Clifford Siskin, Howard Weinbrot, Barbara M. Benedict, Robert Crawford, J. Paul Hunter, Thomas Bonnell, and Jonathan Brody Kramnick in the two-part 'Forum: Literature, Aesthetics, and Canonicity in the Eighteenth Century', *Eighteenth-Century Life*, 21 (Feb. 1997), 80–107; 23 (Nov. 1997), 79–101.

[6] Richard Terry, *Poetry and the Making of the English Literary Past 1660–1781* (Oxford: OUP, 2001).

construction of the son's place within it. Moving even further along the scale from the metaphorical to the literal, biological kinship between writers played a significant part in their lives as a context for their writing, and affected the ways they connected themselves to literary tradition. A writer might find, as Sarah Fielding did, that her brother in life was also her literary brother, sharing with her in the development of a new kind of writing. My discussions, therefore, range over metaphorical and biological kinship relations, and I am especially interested in those cases where the two intersect.

Other kinds of metaphors, beside kinship ones, were used to conceptualize authorship and writers' relations to their works and each other. The developing role of literature as a commodity in the market led to a legal and rhetorical interest in literary property and literary theft. Writers understood themselves as borrowing from other writers, as building up literary debts which should be repaid by acknowledgement. The unacknowledged use of others' writings was increasingly condemned as theft. These understandings of literary property have received emphasis in recent studies of the commercialization of literature, which are themselves part of the current historical interest in the modernity of eighteenth-century culture, its place in an expanding capitalist economy.[7] It is not surprising if kinship relations have been given less attention in this context. Historians have described the movement from pre-industrial to industrialized society as one in which economic, political, and social relations became less closely tied to the structures of kinship.[8] The eighteenth-century literary market seems at first glance a good example of the new commercial, contract-based, individualist culture.

Nevertheless, I find kinship relations and kinship metaphors crucial both to the literary lives of writers from the Restoration

---

[7] Martha Woodmansee, *The Author, Art and the Market: Rereading the History of Aesthetics* (New York: Columbia University Press, 1994); Laura J. Rosenthal, *Playwrights and Plagiarists in Early Modern England* (Ithaca, NY: Cornell University Press, 1996); Paulina Kewes, *Authorship and Appropriation: Writing for the Stage in England, 1660–1710* (Oxford: Clarendon Press, 1998).

[8] Linda J. Nicholson, *Gender and History: The Limits of Social Theory in the Age of the Family* (New York: Columbia University Press, 1986), 122–9.

to the Romantics, and to the creation of the canon. First, while the long-term account of the separation of kinship and economy is justified, the extent to which kinship was in decline in the period under discussion can easily be exaggerated. Capitalist organization did not necessarily mean that the family group lost its economic role. Leonore Davidoff and Catherine Hall, in a classic study, showed how important family businesses were to the expanding economy of the late eighteenth and early nineteenth centuries, and Richard Grassby's large empirical study of London business families in an earlier period concludes that the business world, organized around kinship relations, can be described as a world of 'familial capitalism'.[9] These historians offer helpful ways of thinking about writers working together in the eighteenth century. People did not only compete in the literary market as isolated individuals. For the married couple Richard and Elizabeth Griffith, who published their premarital correspondence as *Letters of Henry and Frances*, or sisters Harriet and Sophia Lee, who ran a school together and collaborated on a volume of fictional tales, or the several generations of Sheridans who worked in various literary genres, writing was a kind of family enterprise. How a family setting for literary life nurtured and constrained writers, and how it affected their sense of themselves as authors and the ways they were received (or not) into the developing canon, will be a part of my focus in the following chapters.

Secondly, even when there are significant changes in economic and social organization, older ways of cultural understanding retain a great deal of their power, and show themselves in commonly used metaphors. Kinship metaphors are a particularly strong example of this, for while kinship has lost ground as a structuring principle for trade and industry, and individuals today are less likely than those of 300 years ago to centre their lives in their families of origin, the psychological importance of primary kinship relations remains.

[9] Leonore Davidoff and Catherine Hall, *Family Fortunes: Men and Women of the English Middle Class 1780–1850* (London: Hutchinson, 1987); Richard Grassby, *Kinship and Capitalism: Marriage, Family, and Business in the English-Speaking World, 1580–1740* (Cambridge: Woodrow Wilson Center Press and CUP, 2001).

8   *Introduction*

The importance of the idea of paternal generation and authority is evident in the common habit of referring to inventors as fathers of their inventions, artists and writers as fathers of movements and traditions, or scientists as fathers of different specialisms.[10] Kinship metaphors can even be understood as a fundamental kind of metaphor, because we understand all kinds of resemblance 'in terms of kin relation and family resemblance', ideas which therefore underlie our patterns of language and cognition.[11] This is not to say, though, that the ideas that necessity is the mother of invention and J. Robert Oppenheimer was the father of the atomic bomb express universal truths. Current anthropological thought is moving away from the view that kinship is transhistorically, cross-culturally central to all societies. Rather, it is the huge importance of kinship within Western views of the world that has led Western anthropologists to impose it as a pattern for understanding societies which understand themselves in quite different terms.[12] The centrality of the concepts of generative literary fatherhood, mythical literary motherhood, and

[10] Robert K. Merton lists the fathers of pathology, palaeontology, electrotechnics, mathematical physics, histology, protozoology and bacteriology, preventive medicine, modern acoustics, scientific pedagogy, experimental psychology, biometry, 'and, of course, Comte, the Father of Sociology': his names, he points out, are selected from a much longer list of generally acknowledged fathers. See 'Priorities in Scientific Discovery: A Chapter in the Sociology of Science', in Bernard Barber and Walter Hirsch (eds.), *The Sociology of Science* (New York: Free Press of Glencoe, 1962), 447–85. For a discussion of the sinister implications of the modern competition for scientific paternity see Brian Easlea, *Fathering the Unthinkable: Masculinity, Scientists and the Nuclear Arms Race* (London: Pluto Press, 1983).

[11] Mark Turner, *Death is the Mother of Beauty: Mind, Metaphor, Criticism* (Chicago: University of Chicago Press, 1987), 11. Turner classifies a number of 'basic' metaphors dependent on parenthood and siblinghood, and notes the gender prejudices implicit in them, e.g. in metaphors in which 'a female state generates a male activity' (ibid. 56). For the cognitive linguistic view of metaphor, which sees metaphors not as arbitrary rhetorical devices but as rooted in sensorimotor experiences, see Mark Johnson, *The Body in the Mind: The Bodily Basis of Meaning, Reason and Imagination* (Chicago: University of Chicago Press, 1987), and Zoltán Kövecses, *Metaphor: A Practical Introduction* (Oxford: OUP, 2002).

[12] The challenge to the anthropological consensus on kinship is found in David Schneider, *A Critique of the Study of Kinship* (Ann Arbor: University of Michigan Press, 1984). For a discussion of current trends in kinship studies see Ladislav Hóly, *Anthropological Perspectives on Kinship* (London: Pluto Press, 1996).

competitive and co-operative literary brotherhood and sisterhood, to
the creation of the British literary tradition should be seen as part
of a culturally and historically specific (though widespread and long
lasting) complex of ideas about kinship relations.

One important part of this complex in the Britain of the seventeenth to nineteenth centuries was, of course, the notion that an
individual's social status derived from his or her familial descent.
As social mobility increased, the symbolic importance of genealogy remained. Even—or rather especially—in a commercial world
where hacks of low birth could sell their writing, authors aspiring
to lasting literary fame needed to prove their worth by establishing
their place in a metaphorical pedigree of writers. The main way of
doing this was for a writer to present himself as the son of past
authors, and eventually to become in turn understood as the father
of a new generation or even a new form. This emphasis on a literary
patrilineage depended on a number of closely related ideas about
reproduction, creativity, kinship, and inheritance. These were rooted
in ancient customs and systems of thought, at the same time as they
were inflected by the particular concerns of their time and place.

A biblical understanding of creation and genealogy was central to
the understanding of culture. In Genesis, God the Father as the sole
Creator of all life becomes the paradigm for human fatherhood and
creativity. The line of humanity descended from Adam is described
in long genealogies in which fathers beget sons (with mothers rarely
mentioned). Carol Delaney argues that the story of Abraham's
willingness to sacrifice his son Isaac in obedience to God establishes
him as a conduit for divine power and the father of nations. The
authority of God over man and the father over the son is established
and 'the power to procreate, imagined as a divine power, transforms
a merely patrilineal system into a patriarchal one'.[13] This notion
of divine procreative power, applied to artistic creativity, produced

[13] Carol Delaney, 'Cutting the Ties that Bind: The Sacrifice of Abraham and
Patriarchal Kinship', in Sarah Franklin and Susan McKinnon (eds), *Relative Values:
Reconfiguring Kinship Studies* (Durham, NC: Duke University Press, 2001), 457.

the view of poetry as a spirit inhabiting the poet and passed on to his literary sons. This common and long-lived notion of poetry as a divinely ordained patrilineage took on a sharpness of significance in the late seventeenth century. Traditional patriarchal views basing king's and father's authority on God's had been shaken in the English Revolution and reaffirmed in the Restoration, and Dryden's establishment of a patrilineage for the English poetic tradition, discussed in Chapter 1, can be seen as attempting to underpin the political return to legitimate patriarchal succession with a patriarchy in the literary realm.

Another ancient source for literary patrilineage was Aristotle's theory of reproduction. Aristotle held that the father alone was the true parent of the child, because his semen provided the form and spirit that shaped and animated the essentially inert matter provided by the mother. The male was the agent of generation, the female its passive receptacle. In his dualized hierarchy, female was to male as passive to active, as matter to form, as imperfection to perfection. It is easy to see that a view of artistic creativity based on this idea of human reproduction would understand men as the true creators, and the father–son relation as the central literary relationship. Aristotle's theory had been challenged by Galen, who held that male and female both contributed seed; and in the revolution of scientific thought and experimentation that occurred between the sixteenth and nineteenth centuries, many rival new reproductive theories were put forward. Some attributed life-giving force to the sperm alone, some to sperm and ovum, some even to the ovum alone. While this controversy contained the potential to encourage a revision of notions of the gender of creativity, the Aristotelian theory remained symbolically powerful long after its biological accuracy was exploded. As a mental framework, Aristotelian theory continued to influence both new reproductive theories and the more general cultural understanding of creativity.[14]

---

[14] For accounts of new reproductive theories in this period see Londa Schiebinger, *The Mind Has No Sex? Women in the Origins of Modern Science* (Cambridge, Mass:

Both the biblical account of creation and Aristotle's account of reproduction emphasize the analagous hierarchies of male over female, mind over body, spirit over matter. Under the influence of these accounts women, understood as closer to and more confined in the body than men, are not expected to be artistic creators in the highest or spiritual sense. Nor do they have a clear place in literary genealogies. Kinship, in the Western world, is the organizing principle for inheritance, and the trope of inheritance is central to the idea of literary history. The patrilineal model of inheritance, based on ancient sources and still influencing cultural ideas today, has obviously made women's place within literature problematic, to say the least. One of my aims in this book is to illuminate the question of women's place within the canon. It has often been observed that women writers are in many cases recognized and indeed highly praised during their lifetimes, but are very rarely given a lasting place in literary history after their deaths. One explanation that has been advanced for this is that women are simply not interested in the kind of competition men engage in to transcend their own time and place. I don't think this is essentially the case. Rather I think that the powerful cultural myths I have just outlined have meant that women have not been understood either as the natural generators of a literary tradition, or as its inheritors. In a previous study I have explored some of these ideas in relation to Aphra Behn, who represented, I argue, a rejected mother in the national literary tradition, leaving an inheritance that was richly influential but more often denied than acknowledged.[15] Here I widen the argument to encompass a range of writers and literary relationships from the Restoration to the Romantic period, in an attempt to show how cultural understandings of the relations of fathers, mothers,

---

Harvard University Press, 1989), emphasizing their potential to challenge ancient views of female passivity, and Maryanne Cline Horowitz, 'The "Science" of Embryology before the Discovery of the Ovum', in Marilyn J. Boxer and Jean H. Quataert (eds.), *Connecting Spheres: Women in the Western World, 1500 to the Present* (Oxford: OUP, 1987), 86–94, focusing on the way Aristotelian paradigms continued to influence new ideas.

[15] Jane Spencer, *Aphra Behn's Afterlife* (Oxford: OUP, 2000).

daughters, sons, sisters, and brothers stood at the heart of the emerging literary canon.

Cultural myths about a masculine spiritual inheritance and the bodily nature of women are immensely powerful, but I do not share the view, implicit in some feminist accounts of literary tradition, that they have succeeded in excluding women from canons altogether. April Alliston, in a fine study of the suppressed matrilineage of women's fiction in the eighteenth century, points out that the idea of literary tradition is based on the 'paradigm of patrimonial inheritance', and argues that where the literary tradition is represented as a patrimony, 'women's writings are both exiled and disinherited; they become everywhere and always improper'.[16] Laura Mandel, who sees the anthology as the eighteenth century's central canon-making form, argues that the association of women and women's writing with the merely bodily allowed men's writing to be seen as transcendent. Miscellaneous collections were full of women authors, but anthologies claiming to be representative of national literary history included very few women. According to Mandel, 'representing women poets as forgotten is integral to the anthology medium: they took up the burden of representing the material body in order to help solve the difficult problem of establishing the poet as one who has an immortal body that transcends time'.[17] These studies deal in demonstrable processes and point to real tendencies in canon-formation, but their own tendencies are towards the abstraction and universalizing of what they describe. Their theories would not account for the successful entry of Jane Austen into the company of the (admittedly novelistic rather than poetic) immortals. Cultural myths, however powerful, are always being contested, and people notice it when lived experience seems to contradict them. The literary tradition whose development I am describing here may have been understood as a symbolically male affair, but women's efforts to be part of it were not entirely in vain.

[16] April Alliston, *Virtue's Faults: Correspondences in Eighteenth-Century British and French Women's Fiction* (Stanford, Calif.: Stanford University Press, 1996), 7, 8.

[17] Laura Mandel, *Misogynous Economies: The Business of Literature in Eighteenth-Century Britain* (Lexington, Ky.: University of Kentucky Press, 1999), 112.

Modern studies of literary relations have been dominated by the Bloomian model of influence, based on a Freudian reading of the son's Oedipal struggle with his literary father. Poets are oppressed by the anxiety of influence when they cannot transcend the greatness of past poets, and Milton figures as the 'Great Inhibitor' for Romantic poets, the too-powerful father who induces despair.[18] Fathers also appear in other guises, however: as enabling figures who provide the writer with a legitimate precedent for his work, or as paternal mentors offering him or her a helpful or unhelpful guide. One reason for my double focus on kinship as metaphor and writers' lived experiences of kinship relations is that it allows for an understanding of the variety of meanings that the father–son and other kinship relations can bear for writers. As well as considering the vertical, parent–child relations, I also consider the horizontal relations of brother and sister. My four chapters deal respectively with fatherhood, motherhood, sibling relations, and women's place in what I am calling the family of the British literary tradition. I approach the dynamics of literary relations through a number of case studies. The first of these is of Dryden, because the father–son metaphor was central to his way of critical thinking, and he established it as the popular way of understanding the native canon; and the final one is of Austen, because she is such an important special case: the earliest woman writer whose membership of the canon has remained undisputed since the nineteenth century.

While I argue for the persistent symbolic importance of certain ideas about kinship and inheritance, I also take account of ways in which historical changes in the understanding of kinship roles affected writers and literary tradition. Kinship in this period has been the focus of much historical debate. Historians have described broad changes in Western kinship patterns from medieval to modern times, involving a move from extensive kinship networks as a basis of social and economic life to a much more individualistic

---

[18] Harold Bloom, *The Anxiety of Influence: A Theory of Poetry* (2nd edn., New York: OUP, 1997).

society in which only the closer kinship relations are important. The extent and timing of these changes has been much disputed. The change from extended to nuclear families, once seen as a decisive modern break, has been challenged by studies that contend that the nuclear family was important as early as the medieval period, and conversely, that extended kin networks played an important social and economic role well into the nineteenth century.[19] Arguments for the growth of close family affections during the seventeenth and eighteenth centuries, with the development of companionate marriage and the increase of parental affection, have been challenged both by those arguing for evidence of enduring marital and parental affection in early periods, and by others arguing that the eighteenth-century rhetoric of domestic affection was merely a new cover for patriarchal domination.[20] Changes in inheritance patterns and the laws governing inheritance have also received a good deal of attention. It has been shown that from the seventeenth century in England, changes in inheritance law led to a greater use of the system of male primogeniture, and a corresponding loss of the equal division of inheritance.[21] Ruth Perry has recently argued that there was a shift in the definition of the primary kin group during the eighteenth century, moving from a notion of kinship based on consanguineal ties to one based on conjugal bonds: 'the biologically given family into which one was born was gradually becoming secondary to the chosen family constructed in marriage'. This change, she contends,

[19] See Ralph A. Houlbrooke, *The English Family 1450–1700* (London: Longman, 1984), and David Cressy, 'Kinship and Kin Interaction in Early Modern England', *Past and Present*, 113 (1986), 38–69.

[20] The rise of affective individualism and companionate marriage was argued by Lawrence Stone, in *The Family, Sex and Marriage in England 1500–1800* (London: Weidenfeld and Nicolson, 1977). His thesis has been much challenged: for a study that places affective individualism as early as the middle ages see Alan Macfarlane, *Marriage and Love in England: Modes of Reproduction, 1300–1840* (Oxford: Basil Blackwell, 1986). For the growth of affective individualism as a reinscription of patriarchal rule, see Anthony Fletcher, *Gender, Sex and Subordination* (New Haven: Yale University Press, 1995).

[21] Amy Louise Erickson, *Women and Property in Early Modern England* (London: Routledge, 1993).

combined with changes in inheritance law, led to a loss of female power and influence, 'the dispossession of daughters in the new capitalist dispensation'.[22]

Some changes in family organization or the ideology of the family can certainly be seen to have affected the way people understood literary kinship. Fraternal relations, whether or not they were decreasing in importance over the eighteenth century, were certainly more important within most people's lives than they are today. Brothers and sisters were much more likely than they are now to remain close throughout their lives, and even to live together; and this led to brother-and-sister writing partnerships, two of which will be discussed in Chapter 3. Connections can be made between historical developments and individual cases of literary relations: between Dryden's political commitment to Stuart authority and his stress on creating legitimate literary successions, or between Johnson's mentoring of Burney and the late eighteenth-century sentimentalization of paternal authority. But I am not offering a narrative in which literary kinship and inheritance follow a clear line of historical development. The literary use of kinship metaphors did not necessarily change at the same rate, or even in the same direction, as changes in kinship relations. The metaphor of patrilineal inheritance has remained, overall, remarkably resilient, implicitly informing our ideas about literary tradition long after patrilineal succession became less socially and economically important. Conversely, while women were losing some legal inheritance rights during the eighteenth century, the idea that they might share in the metaphorical inheritance of literary tradition was growing at the same time. Ideas about literary kinship and inheritance were complex and contested; very different ideas coexisted in the same period about what it might mean, for instance, for a poet to look back to a mother figure. There is a broad story here, about the development of the national literary canon as a mainly masculine affair, in which women's place was problematic. Within

---

[22] Ruth Perry, *Novel Relations: The Transformation of Kinship in English Literature and Culture 1748–1818* (Cambridge: CUP, 2004), 2, 76.

that broad outline are many different narratives—about different
genres, different movements, and about many individual writers and
groups of writers. They do not add up to a simple story of historical
progress or decline; and I have told only a selection of them here.

A discussion of writers' relations to their real or imagined fathers
and mothers, daughters and sons, sisters and brothers, raises questions
about psychoanalytical readings of these relationships. This is not a
psychoanalytical study, though it does draw on psychobiographical
work. Studying a range of writers, for whose lives we have very varied
sets of evidence, I have necessarily been uneven in my treatment of
psychological factors. The very large body of material for studying the
lives, thoughts, and feelings of William Wordsworth or of Frances
Burney makes plausible psychobiographical speculation much easier
in their cases than in those of Sarah and Henry Fielding. Still, the
general questions psychoanalytic critics raise about the relation of
language to subjectivity are always relevant to my account. There is
now a good deal of critical work built on the Lacanian theory that the
infant's entry into language is dependent on moving away from the
undifferentiated closeness to the mother and submitting to the Law
of the Father.[23] Kristeva's development of this view gives the prelinguistic relation with the mother an added importance as the source
of those disruptions to symbolic order that for her are necessary to
the formation of poetic language.[24] I have never found the Lacanian
account of the infant's access to language convincing (for one thing,
it would seem to predict that girls would learn to speak later and
with more difficulty than boys, while the opposite is the case).[25]
However, the idea of the maternal as prelinguistic force has very

[23] A representative selection of Lacan's theories is found in Jacques Lacan and the école
freudienne, *Feminine Sexuality*, tr. Jacqueline Rose, ed. Juliet Mitchell and Jacqueline
Rose (London: Macmillan 1982). See 'Introduction II', by Jacqueline Rose, for a helpful
discussion of the Lacanian account of woman's relation to language.

[24] Julia Kristeva, *Revolution in Poetic Language*, tr. Margaret Waller, introd. Leon
S. Roudiez (New York: Columbia University Press, 1984). For a good selection of
Kristeva's work see *The Kristeva Reader*, ed. Toril Moi (Oxford: Basil Blackwell, 1986).

[25] For a feminist account of language that is critical of Lacanian versions and argues
for the importance of empirical accounts of language acquisition and use, see Deborah
Cameron, *Feminism and Linguistic Theory* (2nd edn., London: Macmillan, 1992).

clear resonances in *The Dunciad*, where the mother goddess Dulness destroys ordered language, and—differently valorized—in *The Prelude*, where the poet's mind develops through initial union with, and later separation from, maternal Nature. The Lacanian account seems to me not a way of explaining these poetic orientations towards the mother, but another version of the myth that they promulgate.

Myths about maternal nature joined the other myths that surrounded the national literary tradition: a tradition that was created in the image of a patriarchal family. The reproductive myth that the male was the active principle in generation made it seem natural for men, not women, to be authors of great works and the originators of tradition. The myth that the male represented spirit, the female the body, meant that words borrowed from a woman had a very different status and significance from those borrowed from a man. We can see these myths in action in critical responses to Richard Brinsley Sheridan's use of his mother's work, and in the prolific naming of literary fathers and the rare acknowledgement of literary mothers. Such myths are powerful and long lasting, but not omnipotent. For one thing, different and mutually contradictory myths meet and clash. The idea that woman is more confined than man to materiality coexists, in the eighteenth century, with the idea that the virtuous woman is in fact especially spiritual. For another, in their lives people don't only or simply follow cultural myths: rather, they engage with them critically. My reason for combining a study of the operation of kinship metaphors with close attention to writers' real-life relationships with their kin is to bring the myths into contact with the complexities and contingencies of lived experience as it is represented in journals, letters, biographical accounts, poems and fiction. I do not mean that this can bring simple 'myth' into collision with simple 'real life'; but it can show how myths both inform people's experience and are contested within it. The result of this interplay of real and metaphorical relationships, as I hope to show, was a literary canon that was predominantly masculine, and symbolically male, but in which women had always a marginal, shifting, and sometimes unsettling place.

1

Fathers and Mentors

Fathers and Sons: Dryden and Inheritance

'Milton was the poetical son of Spenser, and Mr Waller of Fairfax; for we have our lineal descents and clans as well as other families,' wrote John Dryden in his preface to *Fables Ancient and Modern* (1700), explaining a metaphor that had animated some of his poems and much of his critical writing over the previous thirty years. There was already a centuries-old tradition of conceiving relations among poets as paternal and filial, and Dryden's recent precursors had joined it. Ben Jonson had hosted suppers at the Apollo for the sons of Ben, and as Dryden remarked, 'Spenser more than once insinuates, that the soul of Chaucer was transfused into his body; and that he was begotten by him two hundred years after his decease'.[1] Part of the point of the metaphor of filial inheritance was that it was itself inherited. It was Dryden who, making extensive use of this metaphor, turned it into a popular and widespread way of understanding literary tradition. His critical writing, much of it in prefaces, dedications, and essays appended to his poetry and plays, famously intertwined discussion of literary principles and the practices of his predecessors with the defence and explication of his own works. As a result it delineated a modern, national tradition seen as the legitimate heir of classical writing, at the same time as staking Dryden's own claim to be a founder of that tradition. Through placing himself as a son, and later in his career also as a father, within an unfolding literary

---

[1] *Essays of John Dryden*, ed. W. P. Ker (Oxford: Clarendon Press, 1900), ii. 247.

inheritance made up of a series of different 'lineal descents and clans' in different genres, Dryden created his own position, accorded him by Samuel Johnson and enthusiastically endorsed by a recent scholar, as 'the father of English criticism'.[2]

The considerable body of work discussing paternal literary legacies is typically preoccupied with the question of whether the son's relation to his literary fathers should be interpreted in Freudian terms as one of Oedipal anxiety driven by desire to replace one's own father, or more kindly, in all senses of the word, as displaying a fundamental acceptance of and delight in the bonds of kinship. This is linked to the question of whether writers of Dryden's generation—and later ones—are oppressed by the greatness of past literature, or enabled by it. W. Jackson Bate's argument that from Dryden's time onwards, English writers have found 'the rich and intimidating legacy of the past ... the greatest single problem that modern art ... has had to face', was taken up by Harold Bloom, whose early work on influence concentrated on Milton's relation to the Romantics.[3] Bloom's discussion of the anxiety of influence did not include Dryden and Pope, and a number of critics have filled up this gap with a more positive assessment of the relations between literary sons and fathers, portraying a more helpful Milton who induced in his immediate successors 'a sense of detachment, friendly rivalry, and literary possibility',[4] or emphasizing the generosity, gratitude, geniality, and grace of Dryden's and Pope's responses to other predecessors.[5] Both kinds

[2] S. Johnson, *Lives of the English Poets*, ed. A. Waugh (London: OUP, 1961), i. 287; Michael Werth Gelber, *The Just and the Lively: The Literary Criticism of John Dryden* (Manchester: MUP, 1999), 1, 253.

[3] W. Jackson Bate, *The Burden of the Past and the English Poet* (London: Chatto and Windus, 1971), 4; Harold Bloom, *The Anxiety of Influence: A Theory of Poetry* (2nd edn., New York: OUP, 1997).

[4] Dustin Griffin, *Regaining Paradise: Milton and the Eighteenth Century* (Cambridge: CUP, 1986), p. ix.

[5] See C. Ricks, 'Allusion: The Poet as Heir', in R. F. Brissenden and J. C. Eade (eds.), *Studies in the Eighteenth Century III* (Canberra: Australian National University Press, 1976), 209–40. See also Earl Miner, 'Introduction: Borrowed Plumage, Varied Umbrage', and Jennifer Brady, 'Dryden and Negotiations of Literary Succession and

of argument have a point. Dryden's fear that earlier great writers may have made it impossible for his own generation to equal them is expressed too many times to be discounted. Dustin Griffin, even as he gives a generally positive view of Dryden's relation to Milton, notes the younger poet's disinclination to include this nearest and somewhat troubling forebear in the various literary lineages he traces.[6] At the same time, Dryden's incorporation into his poetry of a rich and varied legacy from classical and native sources, together with his praise for his fathers and his chosen literary son, makes it imperative to recognize how fundamentally enabling the metaphor of literary paternity was for him. I am concerned not with establishing whether Dryden, and other literary sons, are more anxious than they are grateful, or more freed than they are daunted, but with the way father–son relations have been made the basis for a literary tradition that in the process has been masculinized.

Among those who have commented on Dryden as literary heir and literary father, there has been very little discussion of the exclusively masculine terms of the metaphors, which are taken for granted. 'Dryden is pre-eminently the critic who conceives of poetic creation and influence as paternal,' explains Christopher Ricks in his rich essay on filial allusion in Augustan poetry. 'It is a natural way to speak.'[7] I argue on the contrary that the focus on all-male poetic parenthood and the assumption that poets father only sons, are not natural but were produced through various customs and systems of thought, some ancient, others particularly pertinent to this historical period. The silence about poetic mothers was not a simple matter of the lack of candidates. In fact, Sappho was considered significant as the ancient proof that there could be female poets, but there was only a very limited attempt to trace modern poetic descent from her in the way that it was extensively traced from Homer and

Precession', in R. F. Brissenden and J. C. Eade (eds.), *Literary Transmission and Authority: Dryden and Other Writers* (Cambridge: CUP, 1993), 1–26, 27–54.

[6] Griffin, *Regaining Paradise*, 142–3.   [7] Ricks, 'Allusion', 214.

Virgil.[8] An ancient female writer as mother of poets was unnecessary, even potentially a hindrance, for the poetic lineage derived from particular ways of construing the related systems of reproduction and inheritance as men-only affairs.

The idea of Homer and Virgil as classical, Chaucer as native, and Waller and Denham as recent, fathers of modern poetic sons, without the intervention of any maternal figure except in the form of an abstract quality[9] or the material ground of language,[10] was implicitly based on the Aristotelian notion that the father alone was the agent of generation. If Dryden was the father of English criticism, Aristotle was named 'the father of criticism' overall,[11] so it is fitting that literary critics have developed their ideas of literary parenthood by inheriting his reproductive theory, which has exerted such powerful cultural influence long after being discarded as literal explanation. The Aristotelian emphasis on the spirituality of paternity as opposed to the materiality of maternity aided the metaphorical extension of fatherhood into poetic fatherhood, because such metaphorical paternity is itself understood as a spiritual rather than physical relationship. Fathers were more spiritual than mothers; and poetic fathers were more spiritual than biological ones.

As for inheritance, it too figured in many imaginations as a male concern. The common-law system of male primogeniture, increasingly used in the seventeenth and eighteenth centuries, handed property down the male line and considered women as the conduits of property, not its owners. It was no more the only way of passing on

---

[8] One rare example of Sappho being treated as a source of a modern male poet's good qualities is found in Walter Hart's poem 'To Mr Pope' (1727): 'A thousand charms at once my thoughts engage, | *Sappho*'s soft sweetness, *Pindar*'s warmer rage, | *Statius*' free vigour, *Virgil*'s studious care, | And *Homer*'s force, and *Ovid*'s easier air'. John Barnard (ed.), *Pope: The Critical Heritage* (London: Routledge and Kegan Paul, 1973), 152.

[9] In 'A Discourse Concerning the Original and Progress of Satire' (1693), Dryden cites Dacier as saying 'that the mother of [poetry], in all nations, was devotion'. *Essays*, ii. 108, 48–9.

[10] In the Preface to *Fables Ancient and Modern* Dryden compares two of his father figures, Chaucer and Boccaccio, who 'Both writ novels, and each of them cultivated his mother tongue', ibid. 268.

[11] 'Life of Cowley', in *Lives of the English Poets*, ed. Waugh, i. 13.

property than Aristotle's was the only way of viewing reproduction, and as soon as we look beyond the aristocracy a variety of inheritance customs, many of them relatively egalitarian, are in evidence. Mothers made wills as well as fathers, and daughters inherited as well as sons, and often on equal terms, at least where moveable goods were concerned.[12] Land was more likely to be passed on to sons, however, and among the rich the increasing use of the strict settlement, which entailed an estate on the eldest son and prevented his father from selling it, was intended to protect large landed estates from dispersion. Land was a basis for political power and carried a strong symbolic value, and it is no surprise that males were considered its most suitable owners; and when the literary tradition was figured as property to be passed down the generations, it was in the form of a landed estate, a part of the nation. In *Of Dramatic Poesy*, Dryden's Neander worries that Shakespeare, Jonson, and Fletcher have spoiled the drama for later practitioners by using up all the plots, characters, and humours, so that there is nothing left to do. He figures this as a ruined inheritance: 'We acknowledge them our fathers in wit; but they have ruined their estates themselves, before they came to their children's hands.'[13]

On the basis of these assumptions about reproduction and inheritance, exclusively male poetic lineages were drawn up and popularized. For Dryden, Shakespeare's paternity was itself a reproduction of Homer's: he 'was the Homer, or father of our dramatic poets'.[14] Equally, Chaucer, 'the father of English poetry', was comparable to Homer the father of Greek, or Virgil the father of Roman poetry.[15] It followed that literary legitimacy and worth were to be gained through becoming the son of an illustrious father and inheriting from him. This applied not only to the individual poet but to particular literary genres and national traditions. In the late seventeenth

[12] Richard Grassby, *Kinship and Capitalism: Marriage, Family, and Business in the English-Speaking World, 1580–1740* (Cambridge: Woodrow Wilson Center Press and CUP, 2001), 343–52.
[13] Dryden, *Essays*, i. 99.   [14] 'Of Dramatic Poesy', ibid. 82.
[15] Preface to *Fables Ancient and Modern*, ibid. ii. 257.

century, Dryden's analogies between Homer and Virgil on the one hand, and Chaucer and Shakespeare on the other, had the effect of helping to elevate the native poetic tradition to a status commensurate with the Greek and Roman ones it emulated; while by the early nineteenth century, the rising status of prose fiction was indicated and furthered when Sir Walter Scott identified Henry Fielding as 'father of the English Novel', and himself, implicitly, as his son.[16] When Dryden was granted Charles II's patent in 1670, the elevation of the individual poet went hand in hand with that of the native line of poets. The patent identified

> him the said John Dryden, our POET LAUREAT and HISTORI-OGRAPHER ROYAL; giving and granting unto him the said John Dryden all and singular the rights, privileges, benefits, and advantages, thereunto belonging, as fully and amply as Sir Geoffrey Chaucer, Knight, Sir John Gower, Knight, John Leland, esquire, William Camden, Esquire, Benjamin Johnson, Esquire . . . had or received.[17]

The line of laureates was another line of fathers and sons, determined by royal decree. For the pro-Stuart Dryden, they represented in the poetic sphere the legitimate succession that was so crucial in the political one, and after the 1688 Revolution the true line was disrupted in both, as James II fled to France and Dryden's poetic office went to the Whig playwright Thomas Shadwell.

If the true poet is the legitimate son of an illustrious father, his counterpart is the false claimant. Literary antagonisms in Dryden's time were frequently expressed by denying an opponent his identity as son to his chosen father, and giving him a baser lineage. Dryden had plenty of detractors who, seeing the importance to him of the right paternal line, tried to take it from him. In *The Battle of the Books* Jonathan Swift mocked Dryden's claims as a poet in Virgil's line. Dryden translating the *Aeneid* is a 'weak and remote'

---

[16] *Lives of the Novelists* (London: J. M. Dent, 1820), 70.
[17] James Kinsley and Helen Kinsley (eds.), *Dryden: The Critical Heritage* (London: Routledge and Kegan Paul, 1971), 39.

voice emerging from a helmet nine times too large for him; and though, 'in a long Harangue', identified in a note to the text as his dedication to the *Aeneid*, he 'soothed up the good *Antient*, called him *Father*, and by a large deduction of Genealogies, made it appear, that they were very nearly related', he is unable to mount Virgil's horse or ride against him: he has not inherited his strength.[18] In *The Tory-Poets: A Satyr*, one of the many pieces of politically motivated invective published around the time of the Exclusion Crisis, Dryden the Tory playwright ('Bays' in mockery of his laureateship) figures as the son not of the ancients nor of Shakespeare, Jonson, or Fletcher, but of a nearer, and less illustrious father, Thomas Davenant, who preceded him as Poet Laureate. According to this poem, the only inheritance Dryden has gained from him is venereal disease:

> 'Tis wit in him, if he all Sense oppose,
> 'Twas wit in *D'avenant* too to lose his Nose;
> If so, then *Bays* is *D'avenants* wisest son,
> After so many claps to keep his on.[19]

After the publication of *The Hind and the Panther*, which defended his conversion to Catholicism, Dryden was ironically placed as a son of the Puritan pamphleteer William Prynne, the filial likeness in this case alleged on the basis of the forgetability of the writing: '*unjoynted, incoherent* Stuff', claimed Tom Brown, predicting that Dryden's '*Book-sellers* will dwell at the *South-side* of *Paul*'s, where his *Works* shall be bound up, as his *Forefather William Prynnes* were, in Trunks, Hatcases, and Bandboxes'.[20]

Dryden himself was master of the art of detraction through filial placement. *Mac Flecknoe* mocks Thomas Shadwell by making him the son of Richard Flecknoe, a Catholic priest and obscure writer whose main claim to fame was that he had been satirized by Andrew Marvell. Flecknoe hails Shadwell as his son in a parody of Augustus

---

[18] *Dryden: The Critical Heritage*, 247.   [19] Ibid. 156.
[20] 'Reflections on the Hind and the Panther' (1687), ibid. 189.

Caesar's attempt to 'settle the Succession' of Rome; the idea of true succession overshadows the false succession from one bad writer to another. Shadwell had criticized Dryden for showing too little appreciation of Ben Jonson and humours comedy, implicitly casting himself as Jonson's heir; Dryden denies him this status by fathering him on Flecknoe instead, and, in highly allusive verses, sets up his own claim to inherit truly from Jonson among many others.[21] The poem 'transfers all rights in Jonson to Dryden and gives [Shadwell] a debased succession',[22] while establishing Dryden as the true heir to a classical tradition that he denies to Shadwell:

> Nor let false friends seduce thy mind to fame,
> By arrogating *Johnson's* Hostile name.
> Let father *Fleckno* fire thy mind with praise,
> And uncle *Ogleby* thy envy raise.[23]

In this allusion to lines from the *Aeneid* in which Andromache prays that Ascanius will be inspired by his father Aeneas and his uncle Hector, Dryden proves himself a son of Virgil while relegating Shadwell to his position as son of Flecknoe.[24] Shadwell is equally found wanting when judged against Longinus' 'On the Sublime'; unable to write sublimely, he can only offer the grotesque. 'Swelled with . . . Pride' and 'big with Hymn', Shadwell's 'swollen

[21] In the Dedication to *The Virtuoso* (1676) which was the immediate occasion for *Mac Flecknoe*, Shadwell had charged Dryden with insufficient respect for Jonson, to whom he declared his own allegiance. Jonson was 'incomparably the best Dramatick Poet that ever was, or, I believe, ever will be; and I had rather be Authour of one Scene in his best Comedies, than of any Play this Age has produced'. Cited in James A. Winn, *John Dryden and His World* (New Haven: Yale University Press, 1987), 289. See ibid. 287–8 for a discussion of Shadwell's earlier attacks on Dryden.

[22] Brady, 'Dryden and Negotiations', 29.

[23] *Mac Flecknoe*, 171–4; *The Works of John Dryden*, ii. *Poems* 1681–1684, ed. H. T. Swedenberg, Jr. (Berkeley and Los Angeles: University of California Press, 1972), 58–9.

[24] See Ricks, 'Allusion', 211. The lines he refers to are *Aeneid*, iii. 342–3: 'ecquid in antiquam virtutem animosque viriles | et pater Aeneas et avunculus excitat Hector?' ('Does the old courage and manliness ever rise in him at the thought of his father Aeneas and his uncle Hector?') See David West, *The Aeneid, A New Prose Translation* (London: Penguin, 1990), 67. Dryden's mockery is compounded by the reference to Ogilby as Shadwell's uncle: in Dryden's view Ogilby was a poor translator of Virgil and so another failed heir to the classical tradition.

body, like that of Longinus's "man who has the dropsy", is the physical equivalent of the overblown style'.[25] Reduced to his physical largeness, Shadwell is implicitly feminized, denied masculine spirit. The lines suggest he is a pregnant body: later in the poem his writing is figured as failed childbirth, 'Pangs without birth, and fruitless industry', making him a failed imitation of Longinus' Pythian princess, who is impregnated by the divine and produces oracles.[26] This image of Shadwell as grotesque, failed mother has been cited as an example of an Augustan turn from positive to negative uses of childbirth imagery as a figure for creativity.[27] The same combination of physical grotesquerie and feminization works to strip Shadwell of any pretensions to be Jonson's son:

> Nor let thy mountain belly make pretence
> Of likeness; thine's a tympany of sense.
> A Tun of Man in thy Large bulk is writ,
> But sure thou 'rt but a Kilderkin of wit.
>
> (193–6; *Works*, ii. 59)

Dryden, alluding to Jonson's own rueful self-description as a 'mountain belly' and 'rocky face' unable to attract a young woman,[28] accomplishes several things at once: he asserts that Shadwell's likeness to Jonson is merely physical; conversely, he links Jonson's physical size to a greatness of wit and spirit; and he suggests through use of Jonson's own phrases that Dryden's is the real likeness to Jonson, a likeness achieved through wit and urbane humour.

In the treatment of Shadwell in *Mac Flecknoe*, Dryden exemplifies a principle that can be seen at work in all the literary uses of the father–son metaphor. If the son proves his title through resemblance to the father, it is intellectual or spiritual resemblance that counts,

[25] ll. 40–1, *Works*, ii. 55; Gelber, *Just and Lively*, 20.

[26] ll. 148, *Works*, ii. 58; Gelber, *Just and Lively*, 20.

[27] Terry Castle, 'Lab'ring Bards: Birth *Topoi* and English Poetics 1660–1820', *Journal of English and Germanic Philology*, 78/2 (1979), 201.

[28] Ben Jonson, 'My Picture Left in Scotland', *Complete Poems*, ed. George Parfitt (Harmondsworth: Penguin, 1980), 140.

not physical. Physical resemblance is feminized: it is inheritance of mere matter, a kind of inheritance figured in the maternal. It follows that imitation and translation are tricky matters. The son translating Virgil or emulating Jonson must be sufficiently like them to establish the relationship, but he will fail if he simply echoes their words without doing enough to prove that he is like them in skill and creativity. In his 'Discourse Concerning the Original and Progress of Satire' Dryden was to express his rejection of too-literal translation in terms of the body–spirit divide: 'A noble author would not be pursued too close by a translator. We lose his spirit, when we think to take his body. The grosser part remains with us, but the soul is turned away in some noble expression, or some delicate turn of words, or thought.'[29] One of the ways the Shadwell of *Mac Flecknoe* fails to be like Jonson is that, unlike Jonson, he slavishly imitates his contemporaries, using their work without being able to absorb it into the texture of his own:

> When did his Muse from Fletcher scenes purloin,
> As thou whole Eth'ridg dost transfuse to thine?
> But so transfus'd, as Oyl on Waters flow,
> His always floats above, thine sinks below.

> (183–6; *Works*, ii. 59)

The distinction between the false son's plagiarism and the true son's allusion is the difference between simply taking matter and demonstrating likeness of spirit.

The higher value placed on spiritual resemblance and inheritance also has consequences for the way relationships between poets are understood and remembered in literary history. It complicates relations of literary mentoring. The key relationship between poets being understood as paternal and filial, it is not surprising that the metaphor is used of a relationship between living writers where the ideal father is understood as the son's teacher and protector, bringing him up to take over the estate; and the ideal son is understood as preserving and

---

[29] *Essays*, ii. 112.

improving on what the father passes down, showing filial reverence
to his memory, making him live again in his own works. Ben Jonson
meant to cultivate just such relationships between himself and the
group of writers variously known as the 'sons' or 'tribe' of Ben. He
initiated them into the tribe in ceremonies at the Apollo; he composed poems welcoming them in; they wrote poems praising him as
the source of their own work, and they preserved his legacy by bringing out his collected works. Such a mentoring relationship would
clearly carry a particular significance (and impose a special burden)
where the poetic relationship coincided with a literal one—when a
father's bodily son attempted to become his poetic heir. On the one
hand, the high value placed on the father–son relationship might
encourage both literal and metaphorical fathers to act as mentors to
their sons. On the other hand, the spiritualization of the relationship meant that close physical connection—a real-life mentoring
relationship, and even more so, literal parenthood—between father
and son carried less cultural prestige than did physical separation
combined with spiritual relationship. It was rarely the biological
son, or even the chosen disciple, who was eventually recognized by
posterity as the true poetic heir. Dryden mocked old playgoers who
thought they could judge contemporary plays because they had seen
Jonson's at Blackfriars: 'The memory of these grave gentlemen is
their only plea for being wits. They can tell a story of Ben Johnson
[*sic*], and, perhaps, have had fancy enough to give a supper in the
Apollo, that they might be called his sons.'[30] The clear implication
is that John Dryden, without benefit of tavern companionship, was
Jonson's truer son. In his view Spenser was all the more Chaucer's
son for having been begotten after a 200-year gap.

John Dryden, Senior and Junior

The struggle between different kinds of son to become the poetic
heir was played out in Dryden's own life and afterlife, which were
marked by significant relationships with sons: his own sons, two

---

[30] 'Defence of the Epilogue', ibid. i. 175.

of whom wrote and published with him; his chosen poetic son, William Congreve, to whom he willed his dramatic inheritance; and Alexander Pope, identified in the eighteenth century as his true heir. Throughout this sequence we see how poetic filiation increases in prestige the more it is removed from literal fatherhood and physical proximity.

Dryden and his wife Elizabeth Howard had three sons, Charles (b. 1666), John (b. 1668), and Erasmus-Henry (b. 1669). Like their father, who converted in the 1680s, all three embraced Roman Catholicism.[31] Charles was elected to Trinity College, Cambridge, but did not take up his election, and entered the service of the earl of Middleton, one of the secretaries of state. John had a fellowship at Magdalen but was dismissed from it at the time when James II was attempting to regain public favour by restoring Fellows who had been ejected earlier for political opposition to him. All shared their father's difficult political position after the 1688 Revolution, which coming as it did while they were in their teens and early twenties, severely restricted their career choices. Charles and John eventually followed their younger brother to Rome, where Erasmus-Henry entered the priesthood. For a time in the late 1680s and early 1690s, though, the two elder sons were at home, and both turned to writing poetry under their father's guidance—an attempt which probably had as much to do with the difficulty of finding a livelihood in William and Mary's England as with a desire to take up the father's mantle.[32] Both of them contributed to the translation of the *Satires of Juvenal and Persius* which appeared together with the *Discourse on Satire* in October 1692 (by which time they had both gone to Italy). Dryden himself translated most of the Persius and five of the satires of Juvenal, while a number of men, including William Congreve, Nahum Tate, William Bowles, George Stepney, and Stephen Hervey, translated the other Juvenal satires. Charles Dryden contributed the

[31] Elizabeth Dryden may always have been Catholic, and it is possible her sons converted before her husband did. See Winn, *John Dryden*, 415.

[32] For Dryden's sons' careers see Charles E. Ward, *The Life of John Dryden* (Chapel Hill, NC: University of North Carolina Press, 1961), 221, 239, 248, 319.

seventh satire of Juvenal, while John Dryden, junior, translated the
fourteenth satire of Juvenal and was probably the son whom Dryden
credited with providing the first part of the second satire of Persius.[33]
The literary efforts of Dryden's sons are in fact one of a remarkably
small number of examples of the son following his literal father into
the literary profession, and they were immediately seen as significant.
Peter Motteux, announcing the future publication of the *Satires* in
the *Gentleman's Journal* for February 1692, commented that 'Poetry
is it seems Hereditary in [Dryden's] Family, for each of his Sons have
done one Satyr of Juvenal, which with so extraordinary a Tutor as
their Father, cannot but be very acceptable to the World'.[34]

John junior's experience of hereditary poetry, however, does not
seem to have been wholly encouraging. In the early 1690s he wrote,
and sent to his father from Rome, *The Husband His Own Cuckold*, an
unpleasant comedy which unequivocally celebrates the actions of Sir
John Crossit, who impersonates his wife's lover to prevent her from
committing adultery, and punishes her for the intention by scratching
and disfiguring her face. The misogyny is striking at a time when
other playwrights, notably Southerne, were writing plays dealing
sympathetically with the problems of unhappily married women,
and it may represent the attempt of a son overshadowed by a famous
father to establish his own position through a display of machismo.
When the play eventually reached the stage, its prologue, written
by William Congreve, also had a misogynist ring. Now that 'Ladies
and all, I faith' are writing for the stage, it has become a feminized
occupation on a par with fancy-work: 'Contriving Characters, and
Scenes, and Plots, | Is grown as common now, as knitting Knots.'
Dryden junior by contrast offers a (youthful, untried) masculinity by
virtue of his heredity, and it is on this basis that the public is begged to
'spare Young *Dryden* for his Father's sake'.[35] This rhetorical attempt
to clear the way for the father's son by sidelining the feminine is

[33] *The Works of John Dryden*, iv. *Poems 1693–1696*, 513–14.
[34] Cited ibid., 513.
[35] *The Husband His Own Cuckold* (London: J. Tonson, 1696), sig. A5ᵛ.

all the more noticeable coming from a playwright who in fact had a good record of helping women writers establish themselves at Lincoln's Inn Fields. The father in whose name young Dryden was put forward, however, was not very impressed by *The Husband His Own Cuckold*. When he read the manuscript he thought it 'the Essay of a young unexperienc'd Author', and not worth staging.[36]

The son went to his uncle, Sir Robert Howard, in search of alternative patronage, and obtained it. The play was staged at Lincoln's Inn Fields in 1696, and published with a dedication to his uncle and a preface by his father, both of which suggest the family tensions surrounding the performance and publication, and an uneasiness generated by the connection of real-life family relationships and literary inheritance. In becoming Howard's protégé, John junior was following in his father's footsteps in a way Dryden senior might not have wished to recall, since he had himself become established as a Restoration writer through Howard's patronage before becoming estranged from him both on political grounds and through literary rivalry and disagreement. The dedication expresses the young playwright's anxiety that he might be counted one of the too numerous upstart writers of the day, whose works are figured as illegitimate offspring, cheekily submitted to the patronage of great men:

> Plays are grown meer Foundlings, and generated so fast, that we find one or more laid at the door of every Noble-Man; and these impudent begetters are not satisfy'd that you give their unlawful Issue a maintenance and rearing, but have the Conscience also to expect a Reward for easing themselves on you of their ungodly burthen. Sir, I must confess I am little better than a lewd Sinner of this Order.

His choice of Howard as 'Foster-Father' for his play is fraught with anxiety related to his father's long-standing quarrel with his noble maternal uncle, the reason that John Dryden, junior considers 'my

---

[36] 'The Preface of Mr Dryden, to his Son's Play', ibid., sig. A3ᵛ.

very Name bears an accusation against me', and declares himself 'unluckily a Poet by descent'. He praises his uncle's writing, and claims his own literary relationship to the uncle as much as the father: 'I have the honour also to be related to the Muses by the Mothers side; for you your self have been guilty of Poetry, and a Family Vice is therefore the more excusable in me'.[37]

The staging and publication of *The Husband His Own Cuckold* were the occasion for a reconciliation between Dryden and his brother-in-law, who may have watched its rehearsals together and were on friendly terms thereafter. Nevertheless the tone of Dryden's preface indicates that he had felt some irritation, at least initially, at the approach to the uncle. He reports that his son 'in my absence from the Town last Summer, took the boldness to Dedicate his play to that Person of Honour, whose Name you will find before his Epistle'. Howard's 'Candor and Generosity' in receiving the play are praised, and then Dryden washes his hands of it: 'the Play was no longer in my power, the Patron demanding it in his own right', he explains, and adds that Howard revised the work, ordered it, and made it fit for the stage at a time when he himself was too ill to help (*Husband*, sig. A3ᵛ). Dryden certainly helped with the publication of the play, and according to James Winn, chose the title-page quotation 'Et Pater Aeneas, & Avunculus excitat Hector'. Dryden was working on his own translation of the Aeneid at the time, and this reference to himself as father Aeneas to his son's Ascanius is his strongest note of welcome to John junior as poetic son. All the same, the praise of the play is lukewarm, even allowing for the need to display public modesty about his son's achievements. The play 'may want Beauties, but the faults are neither gross, nor many', and if his son returns from Rome, he will 'inform him better of the Rules of Writing'. At least, 'if I am not partial', John junior has shown 'that a Genius is not wanting to him'. He ends by excusing his support of the play as a matter of paternal fondness: 'Farewell, Reader, if you are a Father you will forgive me, if not, you will when you are a Father' (sig. A4ᵛ).

---

[37] 'The Preface of Mr Dryden, to his Son's Play', ibid., sig. A2ʳ.

Being the son of Dryden obviously encouraged John junior's literary debut in certain ways, from his father's tutelage to favourable publicity. Equally clearly, this very help had its constricting aspects, implying as it did that the son would be always junior, worth reading only because of the indulgence of his father and a readership of fathers and potential fathers. The best that Dryden senior could say of *The Husband His Own Cuckold* was that 'it may pass amongst the rest of our new Plays; I know but two Authors, and they are both my Friends, who have done better since the revolution' (sig. A3ᵛ). These two friends are Southerne and Congreve; and the latter of these, especially, was already strongly identified as Dryden's literary heir. When Congreve contributed a prologue to assist in Dryden junior's stage debut, the father praised it above the play itself: 'both my Son and I are extreamly oblig'd to my dear Friend Mr. *Congreve,* whose Excellent Prologue was one of the greatest Ornaments of the Play' (sig. A4ᵛ). John Dryden, junior could be forgiven if he reflected that it was much better for a writer to be John Dryden's metaphorical son than his literal one.

Dryden and Congreve

Congreve had been hailed as Dryden's poetic son three years previously. Born in 1670, a year after Dryden's youngest son, by the age of 19 he was living in London and (he later claimed) beginning to draft his first play, *The Old Batchelour.* His early writing included the short novel *Incognita,* published early in 1692, and various translations. He had been introduced to Dryden by late 1691. At this time Dryden, though out in the cold politically as the deposed Stuart laureate, still had prestige within opposition culture as the grand old man of English theatre. Congreve was first associated with him in the 1692 translations of Junius and Persius, to which, like Dryden's two elder sons, he contributed a Junius satire (no. 11). He was more prominent than the rest of the young contributors because he also included a poem in praise of Dryden's translation of Persius. Here, while presenting Dryden as the son who so outsoars his classical father that Persius is 'Dead in himself, in you alone he lives', Congreve is

implicitly claiming his own place in the male chain.[38] By the time
the translations were published in October 1692, *The Old Batchelour*
had been accepted for the stage and was in rehearsal. In this process
the young playwright was receiving help from established writers to
an unprecedented degree. As Thomas Southerne later reported it,
Congreve was recommended by his cousins to a friend who 'engaged
Mr. Dryden in its favour, who upon reading it sayd he never saw
such a first play in his life ... the stuff was rich indeed, it only
wanted the fashionable cutt of the town'. Dryden, Southerne, and
Arthur Mainwaring read the play carefully and Dryden performed
the service his brother-in-law was later to give John Dryden, junior:
he 'putt it in the order it was playd'. Southerne got Thomas Davenant
to agree to let Congreve use the playhouse for six months before the
play opened, so that it was very thoroughly rehearsed—a privilege,
Southerne comments, that he 'never knew allowd any one before'.
No wonder 'it was playd with great success'.[39] Southerne crowned
this careful nurturing of his protégé with a poem 'To Mr. Congreve',
published in the first edition of *The Old Batchelour* in 1693, which
figures Dryden as absolutist monarch of poetry, ruling 'By Right
Divine' of Apollo's authority and now in age needing to choose
his successor. Wycherley and Etherege have neglected writing too
much to take Dryden's place, Lee and Otway are dead, but at last
'*CONGREVE* appears, | The darling, and last Comfort of his Years.' The
poem ends by looking to the future when Dryden, dying, will leave

> thee behind,
> (The natural Successor of his Mind)
> Then may'st thou finish what he has begun:
> Heir to his merit, be in Fame his Son.[40]

The man hailed so swiftly as Dryden's natural successor perhaps felt
some uneasiness about the help he had been given. Jennifer Brady has

---

[38] 'To Mr. Dryden, on his Translation of Persius', in Dryden, *Works*, iv. 809.
[39] Alexander Lindsay and Howard Erskine-Hill (eds.), *William Congreve: The Critical
Heritage* (London: Routledge, 1989), 59.
[40] Ibid. 61.

suggested that Congreve's second play, *The Double-Dealer*, expresses his anxiety about the shaping and ordering his first play had received from Dryden. The subplot concerning Lady Froth, who is being helped with her frothy attempt at a heroic poem, the 'Sillabub', by the sycophantic Brisk, is a satiric inversion of his own mentoring by Dryden, intended to distance Congreve's professional work and Dryden's sponsorship from the self-satisfied attitude and hopelessly amateur efforts of their surrogates in the play.[41] Lady Froth's careless writing, so different from his own perfectionism, allows Congreve to 'insist on the differences between himself and his targets, setting up hierarchical dualisms based on class and literary talent',[42] and, I would add, gender. Mockery of female pretensions to wit had been found in recent London plays and derives from Molière's *Les Femmes savantes*,[43] but Congreve, by making the female fop a writer, introduces an implicit comparison between the male author of the play and the female author he ridicules. Women writers were frequently seen as descended from Sappho, or, in the case of Anne Killigrew as she appeared in Dryden's panegyric, a reincarnation of her. Lady Froth, instead, gives the name Sappho to her daughter, a young child at nurse on whom she dotes, and whom she evidently sees as heir to her own talent: 'I swear she has a world of wit, and can sing a tune already'.[44] Congreve is entering the world of letters as the son of worthy fathers; Lady Froth is attempting to set herself up as originary mother to a female tradition. Her ridiculous matrilineal attempt highlights by contrast his legitimacy and the worth of the patrilineal tradition he is joining.

In his poem to Congreve on *The Double-Dealer*, Dryden explicitly endorses Congreve's implicit claim to be the heir of the fathers of

[41] Jennifer Brady, 'Dryden and Congreve's Collaboration in *The Double Dealer*', in Paul Hammond and David Hopkins (eds.), *John Dryden: Tercentenary Essays* (Oxford: Clarendon Press, 2000), 113–39.

[42] Ibid. 135.

[43] See J. C. Ross's introd. to *The Double-Dealer* (London: Ernest Benn, 1981), p. xviii, which points out that Congreve goes beyond his sources in making Lady Froth an authoress.

[44] Ibid. 68.

English drama. The influence of Jonson and Fletcher on Congreve's first two plays is interpreted here as a triumph for Congreve, a playwright in whom the modern age, at last, is able to outdo the strong 'Syres' who up to now have overshadowed it.[45] Dryden's anxiety that the cultivated wit of the Restoration stage represented skill gained at the expense of strength, that 'The second Temple was not like the first', recalls the sense of struggle with literary fathers expressed in some of his critical prose; Congreve's ability to combine the best of the last age and the present one means that he outperforms the fathers by absorbing them. Dryden places himself at first with Congreve's 'foil'd Contemporaries', outdone but not envious, and cites precedents for an older man's welcome of a young man's superiority:

> *Fabius* might joy in *Scipio*, when he saw
> A Beardless Consul made against the Law,
> And joyn his Suffrage to the Votes of *Rome*;
> Though He with *Hannibal* was overcome.
> Thus old *Romano* bow'd to *Raphael*'s Fame;
> And Scholar to the Youth he taught, became.
>
> (34–40; *Works*, iv. 433)

Through his praise of Congreve, then, Dryden can simultaneously honour 'the Gyant Race, before the Flood' and move on from its influence, at the price of placing himself too in the line of fathers to be superseded. The second half of the poem concerns itself with naming Congreve his son and passing on to him his poetic legacy:

> Oh that your Brows my Lawrel had sustain'd,
> Well had I been Depos'd, if You had reign'd!
> The Father had descended for the Son;
> For only You are lineal to the Throne.
>
> (41–4; *Works*, iv. 433)

---

[45] For Congreve's use of Jonson's influence in *The Old Batchelour* see Brian Gibbons, 'Congreve's *The Old Batchelour* and Jonsonian Comedy', in Brian Morris (ed.), *William Congreve* (London: Ernest Benn, 1972), 3–20. For the influence of Fletcher on *The Double Dealer* see John Barnard, 'Passion, "Poetical Justice", and Dramatic Law in *The Double-Dealer* and *The Way of the World*', ibid. 95–112.

Taking up the familiar imagery of royal succession, he refers to his own loss of the laureateship at the Revolution, when the wrong successor (Shadwell) was chosen in the poetic sphere just as William and Mary wrongly succeeded to the throne. In naming Congreve his heir, the poem undoes the Williamite curse on poetry through which '*Tom* the Second reigns like *Tom* the First',[46] and restores the true line. Congreve is now declared to have Shakespeare's genius, and the poem ends with an exhortation to him to go on as a poet and to protect the memory of his poetic father:

> Be kind to my Remains; and oh defend,
> Against Your Judgment Your departed Friend!
> Let not the Insulting Foe my Fame pursue;
> But shade those Lawrels which descend to You:
> And take for Tribute what these Lines express:
> You merit more; nor cou'd my Love do less.
>
> (72–7; *Works*, iv. 434)

This poem has delighted generations of critics who have found the expression of paternal feeling for the son intensely moving. Walter Scott, Edmond Malone, and Swinburne all singled out these closing lines for praise. One biographer of Congreve finds the poem's eulogy to the young poet overstrained but concludes that 'The last twelve lines ... are a noble appeal from father to son and'—therefore, no doubt—'have the ring of great poetry'.[47] Explicitly or implicitly, it is the masculinity of the father–son theme that has called forth such critical enthusiasm. The lines passing on the laurels to Congreve are, for Scott, Dryden's most moving: 'the interest is excited by means of masculine and exalted passion, not of those which arise from the mere delicate sensibilities of our nature', he explains, 'and to use a Scottish phrase, "bearded men" weep at them, rather than Horace's audience of youths and maidens'.[48] Edmund Gosse, delighted with

---

[46] Tom the second is Thomas Rymer, who had succeeded Thomas Shadwell as historiographer royal in 1692; see Winn, *John Dryden*, 461.

[47] D. Crane Taylor, *William Congreve* (New York: Russell & Russell, Inc., 1963), 55.

[48] Kinsley and Kinsley (eds.), *Dryden: Critical Heritage*, 360.

such an unprecedented example of 'full and generous praise of a
young colleague by a great old poet', describes the poem as 'seventy-
seven of Dryden's most muscular verses', which 'sealed Congreve
with the stamp of immortality'.[49] Dryden has often been celebrated
for the masculinity of his poetry; the praise heaped on his lines to
Congreve suggests that he acquired this aura of masculinity in part
from placing himself so firmly in his readers' minds in the guise of a
loving father.

Congreve was 23 when his second play called forth this tribute,
which matched the extravagant encouragement he had been given
with *The Old Batchelour*. For Dryden, Congreve's work promised
to join Southerne's in an attempt to 'revive and advance' the older,
Carolean mode of comedy in the 1690s, and both he and Southerne
were keen to sponsor the young playwright for this reason.[50] Howard
Erskine-Hill describes additional reasons why the deposed laureate
was so keen to adopt Congreve even before his first play was fit for
the stage. Potentially, he had more to gain from the association than
his young protégé had:

> He needed someone of the younger generation whom he could
> himself recognize and assist; one whose talent, with assistance,
> could not fail to win applause; and one, not of Dryden's own
> religion and loyalty, who would be acceptable to the new
> Orange establishment. This heir might then protect his 'father'
> and mentor, and defend his reputation after death. Such an
> heir might have been John Oldham, 'too little and too lately
> known' as Dryden said in his great elegy. Congreve, a young
> poet already known to him, now promised to be the candidate
> for fame he sought.[51]

As Brean Hammond puts it, it was less the young poet's promise
than 'the sense of a Congreve-shaped hole in the literary universe'

---

[49] Edmund Gosse, *Life of William Congreve* (London: Walter Scott, 1888), 56.
[50] R. D. Hume, *The Development of English Drama in the Late Seventeenth Century*
(Oxford: Clarendon Press, 1976), 382.
[51] Lindsay and Erskine-Hill (eds.), *Congreve: Critical Heritage*, 2.

that ensured his swift fame.[52] Once Dryden had hailed Congreve as his son, others quickly took up the metaphor. Joseph Addison's poem 'An Account of the Great English Poets' calls him 'the Muses other Hope', promising Dryden that '*Congreve* shall still preserve thy Fame alive | And *Dryden*'s Muse shall in his Friend survive.'[53] Charles Hopkins also expressed the hope that Congreve would take Dryden's place: 'Late, very late, may the great *Dryden* dye, | But when deceas'd, may *Congreve* rise as high'.[54] In 1697 Catharine Trotter, praising Congreve's tragedy *The Mourning Bride*, called him Dryden's 'greatest darling son', possessor of the stage now Dryden had left it.[55] The chorus of praise provoked a backlash. By 1698 an anonymous 'Session of the Poets' poem depicted Congreve as one who 'Thought without pleading the Laurel to get | Since by most he'd been told he was the best wit', and one poem of 1700 described his entrance: 'Stiff, as his Works, th'elab'rate Cong[re]ve came, | Who could so soon Preferment get, and Fame'.[56] Being Dryden's darling son had other drawbacks. The chosen son had not done the choosing. He had not, as Dryden had, made the poetic fathers his own, and was in danger of being seen rather as the father's mouthpiece. One of his most admired poems, 'The Mourning Muse of *Alexis*. A Pastoral', was praised in terms that gave much of the credit to Dryden. In these lines, Congreve is valued as a representation and reproduction of the elder poet:

> In *Congreve Dryden*'s ours, to Him we owe
> The tuneful Notes which from *Alexis* flow:
> He chose out *Congreve*, and inspired his Flame.[57]

---

[52] Brean Hammond, *Professional Imaginative Writing in England 1670–1740* (Oxford: Clarendon Press, 1997), 207.

[53] Published in the *Annual Miscellany* for 1694; Lindsay and Erskine-Hill (eds.), *Congreve: Critical Heritage*, 86.

[54] 'To Walter Moyle, Esq' (1694), ibid. 87.

[55] 'To *Mr* Congreve, on his Tragedy, The Mourning Bride', ibid. 102.

[56] Ibid. 164; Daniel Kenrick, 'A New Session of the Poets', ibid. 181.

[57] *The Mourning Poets* (1695), ibid. 87.

Exactly how far Congreve was inspired by his position as Dryden's choice is open to question. Certainly he had strong early theatrical ambitions, and in his short stage career he took Restoration comedy to new heights of wit and elegance in *Love for Love* and *The Way of the World*. However, Dryden expected more. Not only was Congreve supposed to guard the older writer's literary legacy and memory after his death, but in 1693 Dryden, praising his protégé's fragments of Homer, publicly encouraged him to embark on a full-scale translation of the *Iliad*: a work that, Dryden explained, would demonstrate the truth of his own long-held view that the present was 'a much better Age than the last' for 'Versification, and the Art of Numbers'.[58] Made in the Dedication of his *Examen Poeticum* to Lord Radcliffe, this suggestion amounts to a recommendation to Dryden's patron that in future he should support Congreve in a long-term literary project;[59] but this sponsorship came with some daunting expectations. In effect Dryden was asking Congreve to be the son who would join and complete his own efforts to found a modern literary tradition that would replace the work of the earlier fathers. Congreve did not show much interest in following Dryden to this extent, and no complete translation of the *Iliad* followed. While he took on such quasi-filial duties as using his legal knowledge to help Dryden deal with his bookseller, he did not take the expected public role of mourning son when Dryden died. Among the huge outpouring of literary tribute released on Dryden's death, one encomiast, bewailing his own unworthiness, urged that a greater genius should take his place: 'Let *Congreve* then in Deathless Song | His Father's Loss deplore', but Congreve did not oblige.[60] His public tribute came later: too little, too late, for many of his critics. Dryden's *Dramatick Works* were published in 1717 with a dedication by Congreve to the Duke of Newcastle, who had ordered a monument built to Dryden. Here Congreve writes that he has been 'sensibly touched' by Dryden's

---

[58] Dryden, *Works*, iv. 374.   [59] Brady, 'Dryden and Congreve', 122.
[60] John Froud, 'Upon the Death of John Dryden', in *Luctus Britannici* (London: Henry Playford and Abel Roper, 1700), 42; repr. in *Drydeniana XIV: On the Death of Dryden* (New York: Garland, 1975).

early plea to him to '*be kind to his Remains*', and implies that he feels the present edition a rather late fulfilment of the obligation. He refuses the role of son to the father critic by hardly discussing Dryden's writings at all. Instead he writes warmly of Dryden's personal qualities and pointedly claims no particular literary position in relation to him. His only excuse for taking it on himself to thank the Duke in this dedication, he insists, is 'that I loved Mr. *Dryden*'.[61]

Love is not enough, at least for a critical tradition that wanted him to emulate the father. This Congreve failed to do. Whether or not the loss of Dryden's 'incentive and example' had anything to do with it, it is noticeable that Congreve's literary and theatrical career tailed off after his mentor's death in 1700.[62] Images of death and burial abound in the biographical commentary on this change in Congreve's life.[63] Edmund Gosse considered that Dryden's 'funeral train might have been swelled by [Congreve's] own hearse, for now, at the age of thirty, he had ceased almost as completely as Dryden himself to be a living force in literature'.[64] Maximilian E. Novak notes 'some sense of relaxation of [literary] effort' in the summer of 1700, and concludes of Congreve that 'the greatest comic genius of his time buried his talent for three decades before his death'.[65] Many and various reasons have been given for Congreve's quitting the stage. Jeremy Collier's attack on the theatres, which targeted Congreve, put playwrights of the time on the defensive, and *The Way of the World* had only very moderate success at Lincoln's Inn Fields in 1700. Congreve, with income from his previous plays, and salaries from his political positions, had less reason than some writers had

---

[61] *The Dramatick Works of John Dryden*, Esq. (London: J. Tonson, 1717), i. A4^v, A6^r.

[62] Montague Summers, introd. to *The Complete Works of William Congreve* (Soho: Nonesuch Press, 1923), i. 56. See also Brady, 'Dryden and Congreve', who suggests the ending of the 'productive partnership' between the two writers as one of the reasons for Congreve's 'retreat from authorship' (138).

[63] Congreve did not completely stop writing: his post-1700 works include odes, the masque *The Journey of Paris*, the opera *Semele*, unperformed in his lifetime, and some part in the Molière adaptation *Monsieur de Pourcegnac*.

[64] Gosse, *William Congreve*, 140.

[65] M. E. Novak, *William Congreve* (New York: Twayne, 1971), 34, 167.

to continue writing for the stage in the face of this discouragement. He also suffered from ill health: he had a bad attack of gout as early as 1695, and his eyesight was impaired by cataracts. However, many other writers have continued in the face of illness or without financial imperatives, and some of the further explanations offered for Congreve's behaviour—that he wanted to be a gentleman rather than a writer, that he liked an easy life—suggest that he simply did not have a strong commitment to a literary career. I hesitate to add the pressures of being Dryden's chosen heir to the list of the factors contributing to his literary disinclination: after all, why should he have carried on writing? Literary critics and biographers rather too easily assume that writers ought to place literature first. Still we can conclude that in the long run, the identity of Dryden's son was not what Congreve wanted.

The disappointment of his biographers and critics is palpable. As well as the remarks on his premature literary decease, quoted above, there are criticisms of his love for idleness, and complaints that he was 'lazily indifferent' to the selection of poems for his *Collected Works*.[66] His 'poetry fell far short of the expectations raised by Dryden when he announced Congreve as his literary successor', and an 'even greater disappointment' than a 'slight' essay by Congreve in the *Tatler* is the equally 'slight' dedication to the 1717 edition of Dryden: he 'might have better performed the debt that he owed his benefactor'.[67] What literary critics and historians, from the eighteenth century to the twentieth, wanted from Congreve was a literary son who would take on the father's manliness, like Ascanius inspired by father Aeneas. Yet the father's own description of him suggested that he would provide something rather different. As Novak notes, Dryden praised Congreve for the tenderness and pathos of his early translations, which in this respect improved on Homer himself, who was better at 'exciting the Manly Passions, than those of Grief and Pity'.[68] Dryden

[66] Taylor, *William Congreve*, 162, 44.
[67] Novak, *William Congreve*, 165.
[68] Cited ibid., 27–8.

perhaps saw in this the potential for developing a literature that, in comparison to the rugged ancients, would be more inclusive of the feminine and therefore more suited to the modern world; but in retrospect it has been taken as part of the evidence against Congreve. Lazy, prone to illness, concerned about social status, author of slight pieces, better at the softer passions than the virile ones: Congreve evidently just wasn't man enough to be Dryden's son.

Dryden and Pope

Manliness was an important concern for the poet whom posterity has hailed as Dryden's true son: Alexander Pope. Physical deformity, small stature, and the recurrent attacks of illness resulting from his tuberculosis of the spine made Pope appear an effeminate figure to many of his contemporaries, and attacks on him frequently took the form of denials of manhood. The social and political disabilities he suffered as a Catholic in Hanoverian England also amounted to the imposition on him of a humiliating, unmanly identity.[69] Pope's early and sustained devotion to a poetic career can be seen as in part a consolation for his physical and social disadvantages. His inheritance from the classical poets brought him not only fame and fortune, and the public role that would have been otherwise denied him, but also the means of creating for himself a masculine identity through poetry. Homer's *Iliad*, with its concern for proper manly behaviour and for the virtues that pass from father to son—a concern intensified in the early modern critical tradition, which emphasized Greek manliness and Trojan effeminacy—was a particularly auspicious text for him.[70] As a child, he read it with delight in Ogilby's illustrated translation; and as a young man, he produced his own translation, not to become Ogilby's son, but Dryden's. Dryden's admirers had mourned the fact that the great translator of Virgil's epic had not translated Homer's; Dryden himself had made clear his hope that Congreve would take

[69] Maynard Mack, *Alexander Pope: A Life* (New Haven: Yale University Press, 1985), 43–4.
[70] Carolyn D. Williams, *Pope, Homer and Manliness: Some Aspects of Eighteenth-Century Classical Learning* (London: Routledge, 1993), 59, 61, 89, 93.

on the task of translating the *Iliad*. So when Pope published his translation in 1715, he was finishing the father's work, and by choosing the role of son, replacing the son who had been chosen. It is entirely fitting that he dedicated the work to his friend, William Congreve, 'One who has try'd, and knows by his own experience, how hard an undertaking it is to do justice to *Homer*', and who had performed only fragments of the task he himself had completed. [71]

If Pope became Dryden's son through their shared inheritance from the classical epic, he sustained the identity through his development of Augustan satiric modes. His great mock epic, *The Dunciad*, is treated in more detail in the next chapter. Here I want only to note that this poem, taking up Dryden's concern, in *Mac Flecknoe*, with the false lineage of bad poets, implicitly underlines Pope's position in the true line of which Dryden is part. Intricate networks of allusion help establish the filial claim; and by expanding *Mac Flecknoe*'s concern with poetic dullness into a wide indictment of Hanoverian culture, Pope also goes beyond Dryden in his satiric scope, taking on his inheritance by surpassing his father. He is not confined to one father, but like Dryden, claims an inheritance from a string of classical and native sires, among whom Milton is for both poets a particularly compelling figure.

Pope, unlike Congreve, was able to work out his own poetic relation to Dryden without any of the constraints and obligations imposed by being mentored and sponsored by him. His filial relation to Dryden was something achieved through his writing, not through personal contact. It is this disembodied, and hence hallowed, father–son relationship that has been honoured in literary history, making Pope 'of all the sons of Dryden the true heir'.[72] Yet the heir still felt the need for material tokens of his spiritual affinity, as his story of seeing Dryden in his childhood shows. 'I saw Mr Dryden when I was about twelve years old,' he told Joseph

[71] John C. Hodges (ed.), *William Congreve: Letters and Documents* (London: Macmillan, 1964), 233.
[72] Ricks, 'Allusion', 237.

Spence. 'I remember his face, for I looked upon him with the greatest veneration even then, and observed him very particularly.'[73] The idea of this meeting has fascinated Pope scholars: the spiritual son's encounter with his literary father.[74]

Father and Daughter: Johnson and Burney

If Pope emerged as Dryden's true poetic son, there was another candidate for the role of his son in criticism. Samuel Johnson, dubbing Dryden 'father of English criticism' in his biography of the poet, was simultaneously naming a tradition and implicitly claiming his inheritance of it. It was through his scholarly and critical writing—the *Dictionary of the English Language*, the edition of Shakespeare, the *Rambler,* and the *Lives of the Poets*—rather than through his poetry, that Johnson became what Frances Burney called him, 'the acknowledged Head of Literature in this Kingdom'. Dryden's critical son lived through very different literary conditions from those his father had experienced. By the mid-eighteenth century the burgeoning industry in educational, biographical, editorial, and critical writing meant that the role of the professional man of letters, still financially precarious, was expanding in range and growing in prestige. At the same time, the growing numbers and increasing respectability of literary women meant that in this period, for the first time, a man of letters might think seriously of leaving a legacy to literary daughters, as well as literary sons.

Dryden, of course, worked in a mixed-sex literary world, and his literary relations with women were varied. He commemorated Anne Killigrew in a famous ode; he commissioned Aphra Behn to contribute to his edition of Ovid, and praised her translation; and he sent out

[73] Joseph Spence, *Observations, Anecdotes, and Characters of Books and Men,* ed. James M. Osborn (Oxford: Clarendon Press, 1966), i. 25.

[74] See James M. Osborn's note, 'When did Pope see Dryden?', ibid. ii. 611–12, which points out that the meeting must have taken place before Pope's twelfth birthday. Pope's wish to establish connection with other literary fathers can be seen in the portraits he had painted, of himself in Chaucer's dress and of himself as Milton—his own features, with Milton's hair. See Griffin, *Regaining Paradise,* 157.

mixed signals to Elizabeth Thomas, praising her writing and advising
her to avoid Behn's licentiousness. Congreve, his chosen son, also
worked alongside women writers in the theatre, and encouraged
Catharine Trotter and Mary Pix at Lincoln's Inn Fields. However, as
Dryden's long and close concern with patrilineal inheritance indicates, this practical acceptance of women writers went along with a
symbolic exclusion of them from the English literary line. For Johnson, that exclusion was not so clear-cut. From his earliest days as a
writer he had been working alongside women, and in 1738 published
a poem in the *Gentleman's Magazine* celebrating Elizabeth Carter as
a successor to Pope, who could pluck laurels in his garden because
she was a worthy heir to his poetic crown.[75] Moreover, if poetry still
seemed by and large to have a male lineage, the century's upstart
genre, the novel, was a different matter. Several women novelists,
including Charlotte Lennox, Frances Sheridan, and Frances Burney,
received praise, encouragement, and, in the case of Lennox, sustained
help and patronage from Johnson. His encouragement of women
writers had its basis in a sense of sharing with them the difficult
position of professional writer, a position he thought women had as
much right as men to try and take up. His help, though, extended
to helping them to literary prestige, thus raising the status of female
writers and professional writing together. The famous supper at the
Ivy Lane Club, celebrating Lennox's first novel with an apple pie
stuck with bay leaves, was one of Johnson's efforts to crown a female
writer. His championship of the young Frances Burney was another.
In these relationships Johnson went beyond offering practical help
to struggling writers; he was supporting female attempts to join the
literary line.

   In Frances Burney's literary relations with Samuel Johnson, we can
see a new kind of mentoring relationship, one in which the woman
is granted a place as inheriting daughter within the male-owned
literary tradition. It is still not a relationship exactly analogous to
Dryden's with Congreve: Johnson does not hail Burney as the heir

[75] Norma Clarke, *Dr Johnson's Women* (London: Hambledon, 2000), 43–4.

who will continue his own line into the future. The case of Johnson and Burney reveals a great deal about the place of women in literary tradition. The long tradition of associating the female with matter, the male with spirit, makes it hard to conceive of the writing daughter as the spiritual heir to paternal tradition. The problems that paternal mentoring poses to the son's claim of a spiritual inheritance from the literary father are exacerbated in the case of a daughter, whose relation to the father is more likely to be interpreted by all concerned in terms of personal affection rather than symbolic inheritance. What happens is that writing women are (under some circumstances) admitted into a patrilineal literary tradition, but that their place there is not the spiritualized one Dryden can assume when he implicitly claims to be the metaphorical son of Chaucer and Shakespeare. Rather, their relation to literary tradition is understood more literally in terms of their biographical relations with fathers and father substitutes. In Burney's entry into the literary world, we can see a struggle going on between this biographical understanding of the daughter's role and her attempt to claim a spiritual inheritance from patrilineal tradition.

Burney's first novel, *Evelina* (1778), elicited a response beyond any previously accorded to a woman's novel, and Burney was greeted as a successor to Richardson and Fielding. *Cecilia* (1782) consolidated her dominance of the contemporary fictional field. Response to her later works, though, especially to *The Wanderer* in 1814, largely succeeded in displacing her as an inheritor of a masculine tradition and situated her instead in a devalued woman's realm.[76] Because of the superabundance of material relating to the Burney family, her self-presentation and her reception can be studied in detail. My focus here is on the Burney of 1778 and 1779: the anxious and jubilant author of *Evelina*, painfully emerging from anonymity, becoming an intimate of Hester Thrale and Samuel Johnson at the Thrales' house in Streatham, hearing her novel highly praised, being encouraged by Richard Brinsley Sheridan to write for the stage,

[76] For Burney's reception see Julia Epstein, *The Iron Pen: Frances Burney and the Politics of Women's Writing* (Bristol: Bristol Classical Press, 1989), 197–231.

writing *The Witlings*, and allowing her influential 'daddies', Samuel Crisp and Charles Burney, to suppress this second literary venture. Her responses to the events of this exciting and turbulent time show that in the period between the publication of her first novel and the suppression of her first play, Charles Burney's daughter, struggling to deal with her new identity as an author, turned to Samuel Johnson as a different kind of father figure: one who invited her to join a masculine literary tradition. Johnson's encouragement of Burney rested implicitly on the assumption that a writing woman could take up literary life and literary quarrels on much the same terms as men. Burney gained a sense of herself as a legitimate member of English literary tradition through adopting Johnson as a mixture of paternal friend and literary father. Burney's experience with *The Witlings,* however, showed that a writing woman's position was more complex and difficult than Johnson allowed; while the play itself suggests that her allegiance to a literary father was expressed through repudiating the figure of the female patron.

For Burney, the biographical father–daughter relation was inextricably entwined with the question of literary paternity and daughterhood. Charles Burney was not only the 'author of [her] being', as she addressed him in the famous poem prefaced to her first novel, but the author of the multi-volume *History of Music*, in progress throughout the early part of her career. As Janice Farrar Thaddeus points out, the experience of writing *Evelina* after being employed as her father's amanuensis on the *History* encouraged her to imitate some of his phrases and would have given her a sense of identification with him.[77] At the same time, her felt need to disguise her handwriting when working on the novel, to avoid any recognition by the printers of the connection between the two manuscripts, suggests a painful disjunction between writing as the father's transcribing daughter and taking a place in written tradition herself.[78] Her own

---

[77] Janice Farrar Thaddeus, *Frances Burney: A Literary Life* (Basingstoke: Macmillan, 2000), 40.

[78] Ibid. 23.

hand has to be laboriously disguised before she can write on her own behalf. Charles Burney's later acceptance of his daughter's novel—in a scene Burney repeatedly returned to in her writing—relieved her of the worst of this position, but the tension between Burney the novelist and Burney the daughter of the historian of music remained. She compared her own writing to her father's. In 1800, when—a second time—her father intervened to prevent her staging a comedy, she wrote to him defending her dramatic practice. She insisted on the inferiority of her own writing to his, but simultaneously linked her own work to his example, inviting him to look at her drama and to say to himself, 'After all—'tis but *like Father like Child* ... She took my example in writing—She takes it in ranging.'[79] In writing the late work *Memoirs of Dr Burney*, she suppressed, even destroyed, large swathes of his own memoirs, substituting material from her own journals, and ignored some of his own works while describing the publication of her own novels. The story of his life and career gave way at certain points to the story of her authorship.[80]

Burney's relationship to her own father made it initially difficult for her to stake her claim as an author; and the accounts by Doody and others have shown how her growing confidence entailed her gradually moving away from his authority. What I wish to emphasize is the way that, from the beginning of her writing career, Charles Burney the author-father had a rival: the paternal line of earlier writers who offered Burney a tradition to join. The idea of a literary tradition seems to have been enabling to her, helping her to overcome the sense of unworthiness her father inspired. In *Evelina,* the dedicatory poem expresses the young writer's overwhelming sense of inferiority to the author-father. She confesses herself unable to record his worth and asks only for concealment: 'Obscure be still the unsuccessful Muse, | Who cannot raise, but would not sink, your fame.' However, the novel's preface, dealing with the public instead of the private

---

[79] *Journals and Letters of Fanny Burney (Madame d'Arblay)* ed. Joyce Hemlow et al. (Oxford: Clarendon Press, 1972–84), iv. 395.

[80] See Roger Lonsdale, *Dr Charles Burney: A Literary Biography* (Oxford: Clarendon Press, 1965), 432–55; Thaddeus, *Frances Burney*, 180–202.

realm, shows much greater confidence. Here, Burney looks quite calmly to a patrilineal tradition of writers, attempting to rescue the respectability of novel-writing by reference to illustrious male practitioners:

> Yet, while in the annals of those few of our predecessors, to whom this species of writing is indebted for being saved from contempt, and rescued from depravity, we can trace such names as Rousseau, Johnson, Marivaux, Fielding, Richardson, and Smollet, no man need blush at starting from the same post, though many, nay, most men, may sigh at finding themselves distanced.[81]

The original anonymity of the preface and the reference to 'men' make this appear as a typical claim by a putative literary son to join his chosen fathers. This is later modified by a strong denial of literary imitation:

> however zealous ... my veneration of the great writers I have mentioned, however I may feel myself enlightened by the knowledge of Johnson, charmed with the eloquence of Rousseau, softened by the pathetic powers of Richardson, and exhilarated by the wit of Fielding, and humour of Smollet; I yet presume not to attempt pursuing the same ground which they have tracked: whence, though they may have cleared the weeds, they have also culled the flowers, and though they have rendered the path plain, they have left it barren. (*Evelina*, 9)

Rather the writer claims inspiration only from 'nature', defining the novel's aim as 'to draw characters from nature ... and to mark the manners of the times', and its heroine as 'the offspring of Nature, and of Nature in her simplest attire' (*Evelina*, 7, 8). Certainly there seems to be here a coded reference to the anonymous author's female difference, rejecting a literary inheritance in favour of one from (feminine) nature. But the denial of literary imitation should not be taken at face value. The writer of *Evelina* is claiming originality

---

[81] Frances Burney, *Evelina: or the History of a Young Lady's Entrance into the World*, ed. Edward A. and Lilian D. Bloom (Oxford: World's Classics, 1982), 7.

of subject—moving to fresh ground—while simultaneously leading the reader to expect some of the characteristics—knowledge, eloquence, pathetic powers, wit, humour—that 'he' identifies in 'his' predecessors. This is to place oneself within a literary tradition, promising to be like one's precursors yet with something new to offer. Moreover, the rather Johnsonian ring to this critical discussion of the novel indicates the author's choice of literary father.[82]

Of course, what is suppressed in this passage is the relation to literary mothers: the novel is presented as the legacy of literary fathers, or at best a collaboration between paternal tradition and maternal nature without reference to human female agency The repression of the novel's link with Behn, Manley, and other 'scandalous' early women writers was general at this time;[83] more specifically ignored in the preface to *Evelina* might be its debts to the Eliza Haywood of *Betsy Thoughtless* and, perhaps, to the epistolary exploration of feminine sensibility in writers like Frances Brooke and Elizabeth Griffith.[84]

As an attempt to claim a place in a masculine and elevated tradition of fictional writing, *Evelina* enjoyed early success. The first reviews—William Kenrick's brief notice in the *London Review* for February 1778, and a rather longer one in the *Monthly Review* for April—agree in finding it above the common run of modern novels. The *Critical Review,* in September, went further, describing the novel's combination of the comic and sentimental and its appeal to old and young, male and female, and declaring that the work 'would

[82] C. B. Tinker noted many years ago that Burney's 'formal' style was adopted early in her career. He used this to absolve Johnson of any blame for it, since he apparently considered Burney could not have been influenced by his style before her friendship with him—an instance of the way women's relation to tradition is understood in terms of biography and bodily proximity. In my reading, Burney is adopting a Johnsonian style to develop an authoritative critical voice in her earliest published work. See Burney, *Dr Johnson and Fanny Burney: Being the Johnsonian Passages from the Works of Mme d'Arblay,* ed. C. B. Tinker (London: Andrew Melrose, 1912), pp. xix–xx.

[83] See Ros Ballaster, *Seductive Forms: Women's Amatory Fiction from 1684 to 1740* (Oxford: Clarendon Press, 1992), 198–207; William Warner, *Licensing Entertainment: The Elevation of Novel Reading in Britain, 1684–1750* (Berkeley and Los Angeles: University of California Press, 1998), 41–4.

[84] For the connections between *Evelina* and *Betsy Thoughtless* see J. P. Erickson, '*Evelina* and *Betsy Thoughtless*', *Texas Studies in Literature and Language,* 6 (1964), 86–103.

have disgraced neither the head nor the heart of Richardson'.[85] Comparisons to great male precursors were also forthcoming from Burney's family and from their many friends in the literary world—a reception minutely documented by the author herself. She began her journal for 1778 with a mock declaration of the 'grand & most important Event' that opened the year, the publication of *Evelina*.[86] As the year continued she described family's and friends' reactions to the novel. At first she could observe these from the safety of her anonymity, and she clearly enjoyed the assumption that the novel was 'the Work of a *man*!', and the comparisons made to male writers: cousin Richard considered that he had 'read nothing like it, since Fielding's Novels', and when he got wind that the author was known to the Burney family he thought it must be by Frances's father (*EJL* iii. 6, 10, 11). Even more gratifyingly, her father himself, once the secret of her authorship had been divulged, pronounced it 'the best Novel I know excepting Fieldings,—&, in some respects, *better* than his!' (ibid. 28). He thought it better than Smolletts', too; and he also linked her to Samuel Johnson, another of the men invoked in her preface, praising above all the voice of the novel's (over)-protective father figure, Mr Villars, by declaring that 'Johnson could not have expressed himself better' (ibid. 53).

During the year Burney charted the gradual loss of the 'snugship' (anonymity) under cover of which she had ventured into the literary world. As each new family member was let into the secret, she made them promise not to tell anyone else; but once her father knew, she did not feel it appropriate to extract a promise of secrecy from him. Once it was clear that *Evelina* was a success, Charles Burney lost no time in making its authorship known to the circle of polite and literary London to which he had access. He told Hester Thrale, the fashionable intellectual hostess whose house was a second home to the renowned Dr Johnson; and she told her friends.

[85] *Critical Review*, 46 (1778), 202.
[86] *The Early Journals and Letters of Fanny Burney, iii. The Streatham Years, Part I, 1778–1779*, ed. Lars E. Troide and Stewart J. Cooke (Oxford: Clarendon Press, 1994), 1 (further refs. to this edn. will be in the form *EJL* iii).

As Burney's fame spread, she heard the flattering comparisons to male writers repeated in a wider circle. As Richardson and Fielding were by this time acknowledged as the two greatest writers of the novel, and the guarantors that fiction could be a dignified literary form, to be seen as comparable to them was implicitly to be included within the patrilineal tradition. It was when Samuel Johnson stamped his authority on this placing of her work, that it rapidly became an established view. In July 1778 Burney reported to Samuel Crisp that Mrs Thrale and Dr Johnson had praised *Evelina*, not knowing the author; later in the same month Hester Thrale reported to Charles Burney that Johnson had said that 'there were passages in it which might do honour to Richardson' (*EJL* iii. 60). When Frances Burney heard of this, it sent her dancing a jig in delight (ibid. 61). Soon afterwards she was to meet Johnson at Hester Thrale's house in Streatham, and hear his praises of her portrait of Mr Smith: 'Harry Fielding *never* drew so good a Character!' (ibid. 90). Hester Thrale reported that Johnson recommended the book to Mr Lort in glowing terms: 'there were things & Characters in it *more* than worthy of Fielding!' (ibid. 115). By early 1779, this was a view being expressed by the dramatist Richard Brinsley Sheridan. Sir Joshua Reynolds told her that Sheridan said he held *Evelina* superior to Fielding; and that it must be true, because he said it 'publicly at our Club' (ibid. 233). To be so praised at Samuel Johnson's and Sir Joshua Reynolds's well-known Literary Club meant more, Reynolds implied, than the drawing-room compliments Burney had been hearing; the Club is a public place, a place of truth. It is also, of course, an all-male place; there was no question of Burney herself joining the Club that had accorded her so high a literary position; the 'true', 'public' praise was the one she must hear second-hand, in private. This encapsulates the poignancy of the good literary daughter's position: highly praised but never sure how truly; almost included on equal terms, but not quite.

In Burney's relationship with Johnson, we can see the advantages and difficulties, the complexity and ambiguity, of the literary daughter's place with the literary father. As we have seen, she was already looking to him as a literary father in the preface to *Evelina*. As their friendship developed, he took on a more personal significance. Her relation with him became a mixture of the quasi-paternal one of the patron or mentor, offering praise, encouragement, advice, and instruction; and the more distant one of the metaphorical literary father, her precursor in a tradition of serious fiction, and a model for her writing. Quite early in their acquaintance, in September 1778, there is a discussion of literary and artistic patronage, beginning with Cumberland's patronage of Romney. Johnson remarks that he himself has had no 'Hero', or protégé, for years: 'Dr Goldsmith was my last: But I have had none since his Time.—till my little Burney came!' Mrs Thrale adds, 'Miss Burney is the Heroine now' (*EJL* iii. 168). Being adopted as Goldsmith's replacement must have been all the more delightful because a month earlier, Johnson had said that *The Vicar of Wakefield* was not a good novel: implicitly, the daughter had outdone the son she was replacing (ibid. 95). At the same time the daughter, unlike the son, is treated like an infant: straight after the remark on Goldsmith's novel, Burney reports that Johnson 'then seated himself upon a sopha, & calling to me, said 'Come,—*Evelina*,—come & sit by me',—I obeyed;—& he took me almost in his arms,—that is, *one* of his arms, for *one* would go 3 times round me,—&, half laughing, half serious, he charged me *to be a good Girl!*' (ibid.). This babying seems to have been welcome to the 26-year-old devotee of father and father figures; it was somewhat reminiscent of her relationship with 'Daddy' Crisp, and indeed the following March she was to write that 'Dr. Johnson is another Daddy Crisp to me' (ibid. 255).

Johnson's literary encouragement, however, was a world away from Daddy Crisp's. Crisp, perhaps still affected by the long-ago failure of his tragedy *Virginia*, and certainly extremely sensitive in all matters of feminine propriety, offered at best contradictory advice: wanting her to write more, and to profit financially, he encouraged her to write a comedy, but hedged his approval with so much advice about avoiding indelicacies that the effect must have been inhibiting. He invoked the image of Burney in girlish abandonment—one of the most vivid glimpses we have of her wild side—only to turn her away from it: 'Do You remember about a Dozen Years ago, how You Used to dance Nancy Dawson on the Grass plot, with Your Cap on the ground, & your long hair streaming down your Back, one shoe off, & throwing about your head like a mad thing?—now you are to dance Nancy Dawson with Fetters on—there is the difference' (*EJL* iii. 238–9). Johnson did not prescribe fetters. On the contrary, he invited her to be a wit like himself, and specifically to follow him by taking up an aggressive stance in the series of rivalries that, for him, made up the literary world. Comparing her work to Fielding's and Richardson's, he made it clear that he saw her as competing within a masculine tradition. He would have liked her to be their contemporary, so that he could have witnessed the battle of wits between them:

> he said he wished Richardson had been alive. 'And then, he added, you should have been Introduced to him,—though, I don't know, neither;—Richardson would have been afraid of her!'
>
> 'O yes!—that's a likely matter!' quoth I.
>
> 'It's very true, continued he; Richardson would have been really *afraid* of her; there is merit in Evelina which he could not have borne.—No, it would not have done!—unless, indeed, she would have flattered him prodigiously.—Harry Fielding, too, would have been afraid of her,—there is nothing so delicately finished in *all* Harry Fielding's Works, as in Evelina … (*EJL* iii.109–10)

Burney, as her interruption here shows, was somewhat uncomfortable with Johnson's depiction of her as an aggressor, but also delighted.

At the time that Burney met Johnson, he was nearly 70, with a long-established reputation as the author of the *Rambler*, the *Dictionary of the English Language*, and the editor of Shakespeare. He had recently accepted a commission to write the series of biographical prefaces that became the *Lives of the Poets*, and was at work on these when they met. While he ranked Burney highly as a novelist, she was of course not a contender in the more prestigious tradition of poetry. Indeed, no women were included in Johnson's *Lives*. The

poets were chosen by the booksellers who planned the edition, and
they seem simply to have assumed that female poets did not count,
or were best treated in separate specialized anthologies. Johnson
did not challenge this, confining his own additions to a few extra
men (Blackmore, Watts, Pomfret, and Thomas Yalden). Burney's
welcome into a masculine fictional tradition, then, has to be seen
against the background of the implied exclusion of women from the
poetic tradition.

Burney did not comment on this: for her, it was enough of an entry
into male tradition simply to be engaging with Johnson's critical
work. Ever fearful of being stigmatized as a bookish woman, she tried
not to be seen reading at Streatham, with the result that Johnson
commented on her apparent lack of interest in books—whereupon
she proudly drew out his *Life of Waller* from under her gloves (*EJL*
iii.172). His praise of her works was an honour, but she was not
sure she had the right openly to read his, much less comment on
them. Yet she also recorded, without comment, remarks indicating
that some people assumed she and Johnson were working together:
Mr Lort speculated that Johnson 'might keep her to help him
in his Lives of the Poets' (ibid. 119). Clearly she took pride in
the association between herself and Johnson's work, but needed
constant reassurance that it was permissible. This insecurity was
shown very strongly in her dread of becoming a flatterer. She had
been very struck by the story of how Johnson had rebuked another
woman writer, Hannah More, for too fulsome praise. She described
the incident, related to her by Hester Thrale, in her journal in
August 1778:

> [Hannah More] began singing [Johnson's] praises in the
> warmest manner: & talking of the pleasure & the instruc-
> tion she had received from his writings, with the highest
> encomiums. For some Time, he heard her with that quietness
> which a long use of praise has given him ... till, at length, he
> turned suddenly to her, with a stern & angry Countenance, &
> said 'Madam, before you flatter a man so grossly to his Face,

you should consider whether or not your flattery is worth his having'! (*EJL* iii. 120)[87]

Burney was determined not to disgust in the same way, with the result that Johnson had to angle for her praise: later he asked whether she had read his *Life of Cowley*, and what she thought of it. Her refusal to flatter led to an interesting reversal, as Hester Thrale noted: 'Miss Burney never flatters [Johnson], though she is such a favourite with him;—but the Tables are turned,—for *he* sits and flatters her!' (*EJL* iii. 119).

In these incidents concerning Johnson's latest works, Burney reveals two salient characteristics: a retiring modesty excessive even by eighteenth-century feminine standards, and an underlying pride. Together they inhibited her from developing a closer relationship with Johnson. When he hinted to Mrs Thrale that Burney might write to him, she responded with an uncommunicative little flurry of words added to a letter from Mrs Thrale's eldest daughter, Hester ('Queeney'). This thoroughly annoyed him; when she explained that it was her fear of his censure that held her back he softened, but she never took him into her confidence by writing the witty and personal things to him that she did to her sister Susanna or to Daddy Crisp.[88] She was comfortable with affection, recording his kiss with delight and wanting to hear that he loved her; and she was happy with the more distant relationship of literary imitator. What she was nervous of was direct intellectual interaction with him as mentor.

What did the relationship mean to Johnson? Burney was only the most recent of a number of women whose writing careers he had supported and encouraged, notably Hannah More and Charlotte Lennox. That she was younger than they, the daughter of his friend Charles Burney, and living more or less as a member of the family

---

[87] This story was told differently by More's sister Sally, who represents the exchange between More and Johnson as a good-humoured competition in flattery: see Clarke, *Johnson's Women*, 169.

[88] See *EJL* iii. 411–12, 436–7.

with the Thrales, put her more emphatically into the role of substitute daughter. At the time they met he was 'far advanced' in the writing of his *Life of Dryden*, and planning to write Milton's soon.[89] The *Life of Milton*, as Kevin Pask argues, was a particular challenge to Johnson: an engagement with the key sublime figure in the English poetic tradition, by a critic who opposed him politically.[90] Johnson linked Milton's republicanism with his objectionable treatment of women:

> It has been observed that they who most loudly clamour for liberty do not most liberally grant it. What we know of Milton's character in domestick relations is, that he was severe and arbitrary. His family consisted of women; and there appears in his books something like a Turkish contempt of females, as subordinate and inferior beings.[91]

This 'contempt of females' was most vividly illustrated by the story told by Milton's first biographer, Edward Philips, that Milton in his old age and blindness made his daughters read aloud to him from a number of languages, 'the Hebrew (and I think the Syriac), the Greek, the Latin, the Italian, Spanish and French. All which sorts of books to be confined to read, without understanding one word, must needs be a trial of patience almost beyond endurance.'[92] Pask argues that Johnson's condemnation of Milton's treatment of his daughters is a question of the eighteenth-century 'elevation of the domestic or the private to matters of public concern', introducing a distinction between Milton as 'a *literary* classic' to be admired, and 'the *social* Milton' whose domestic tyranny is to be deplored.[93] In the light of this, Johnson's relationship to Burney, at the time he was considering Milton's relation to his daughters, can be seen

---

[89] Samuel Johnson, 27 July 1778, to John Nichols; quoted by the editor in *Johnson's Lives of the Poets: A Selection*, ed. J. P. Hardy (Oxford: Clarendon Press, 1971), p. viii.
[90] Kevin Pask, *The Emergence of the English Author: Scripting the Life of the Poet in Early Modern England* (Cambridge: CUP, 1996), 161–6.
[91] *Lives of the English Poets*, ed. Waugh, i. 109.
[92] Edward Philips, quoted in ibid. 102.
[93] Pask, *Emergence of the English Author*, 163.

as his conscious attempt to unite literary merit with the social and domestic merit his precursor did not display. Johnson wished to be a better 'father' to Burney than Milton was to his daughters. Where Milton, according to Phillips, made his daughters serve male literature without understanding it, Johnson invited his 'daughter' to share and belong to a masculine literary tradition. One significant gesture towards this was his offer to teach her Latin, alongside 'Queeney' Thrale. Lessons began in May 1779 and were mentioned as continuing in July and being resumed in December of the same year. This venture allowed Johnson to replace the picture of the tyrannical poet surrounded by ignorant and unhappy daughters with a modern, happier one of himself as teacher sharing his knowledge. His *Life of Milton* suggests that Milton's method harmed himself as well as his daughters:

> In the scene of misery which this mode of intellectual labour sets before our eyes, it is hard to determine whether the daughters or the father are most to be lamented. A language not understood can never be so read as to give pleasure, and very seldom so as to convey meaning.[94]

For Johnson women, like men, need fully to inhabit the language they speak; in denying this to his daughters, Milton denies himself pleasure and communication. Johnson himself claims the pleasure due to a benevolent father who will share his intellectual inheritance with his daughters.

Burney must have been something of a disappointment as a Latin scholar: whatever ability she may have shown, her attitude eventually undermined her study. Though delighted 'that this great & good man should think me worthy his instructions' (*EJL* iii. 268), she was characteristically worried about being found out in masculine pursuits, and seems to have given up when her father disapproved of the lessons (Queeney continued). In other ways, however, she adopted Johnson very thoroughly as her mentor; and throughout

---

[94] *Lives of the English Poets*, ed. Waugh, i. 102.

the progress through the never-performed play *The Witlings* to the second novel *Cecilia*, there are marks of his influence.

The Witlings

During the period that she was writing *The Witlings*, Burney was surrounded by encouragement and offers of help. Not only were Mrs Thrale and Johnson recommending that she should write a comedy; Richard Brinsley Sheridan, who had just taken over the Drury Lane theatre, and the dramatist Arthur Murphy also wanted her to write a play, Sheridan going so far as to say he would accept it unseen. *The Witlings* was the first of Burney's works written after the fame of *Evelina*, and thus in anxious anticipation of public reaction to her as a known author; and it was written at Streatham during the early warmth of her admiration for Mrs Thrale and her delight in being noticed and encouraged by Johnson. It expresses her ambivalent feelings towards Streatham patronage; her mistrust of a female intellectual inheritance; and her allegiance to Johnson as a fatherly mentor in implicit competition with her two 'Daddies', Charles Burney and Samuel Crisp.

The plot of *The Witlings* concerns a young engaged couple who are almost parted by cold-hearted Lady Smatter, the hero's aunt, when it appears that the heroine has lost her fortune. They are reunited through the actions of Mr Censor, a harsh critic of Lady Smatter and her crowd of witlings, who blackmails the aunt by threatening to expose her meanness to the world in lampoons. The satire on Lady Smatter, a superficial, vain, would-be intellectual, derives from a well-known and popular misogynist dramatic tradition mocking the learned woman, of which Molière's *Les Femmes savantes* is the prototype. The play asks its audience to enjoy the insistent correction of the female witling's errors by the male critic. When Lady Smatter speaks of Cecilia's 'unhappy situation', Censor pounces on her attempt at literary allusion.

LADY SMATTER. . . . poor Thing, great allowance ought to be made for her unhappy situation, for, as the Poet has it, misfortune renders every body unamiable.

CENSOR. What Poet?

LADY SMATTER. Bless me, don't you know? Well, I shall now grow proud indeed if I can boast of making a Quotation that is new to the learned Mr. Censor. My present Author, Sir, is Swift.

CENSOR. Swift?—you have, then, some private Edition of his Works?

LADY SMATTER. Well, well, I won't be possitive as to Swift,—perhaps it was Pope. 'Tis impracticable for any body that reads so much as I do to be always exact as to an Author. Why now, how many Volumes do you think I can run through in one year's reading?

CENSOR. More than would require seven years to digest.

LADY SMATTER. Pho, pho, but I study besides, and when I am preparing a Criticism, I sometimes give a whole day to poring over only one Line. However, let us, for the present, quit these abstruse points, and, as Parnell says, 'e'en talk a little like folks of this world.'

CENSOR. Parnell?—you have, then, made a discovery with which you should oblige the public, for that Line passes for Prior's.

LADY SMATTER. Prior? O, very true, so it is. Bless me, into what errors does extensive reading lead us![95]

Lady Smatter, for all her vanity, backs down instantly in the face of Censor's authoritative sarcasm: the exchange suggests his undisputed knowledge of and property in the English poetic tradition, and the illegitimacy of her attempt to own it. The climactic scene, in which Lady Smatter is bombarded with lampoons written by Censor, graphically illustrates his mastery of language as a weapon, and her helplessness before it. She tries in vain to intervene as his poem equates female ageing, loss of beauty, and female ignorance (*Complete Plays*, i. 95). Other lampoons mock her treatment of her nephew and her attempt to rule a literary club. Finally she is threatened that these lampoons will be printed, and Censor warns her: 'If you any longer oppose the union of your Nephew with Miss Stanley, I will destroy the whole peace of your Life' (ibid. 98). The humour is ambivalent here. The humiliation of Lady Smatter certainly expresses Burney's own fears about public exposure as a

[95] *The Witlings*, Act I, in *The Complete Plays of Frances Burney*, i. *Comedies*, ed. Peter Sabor (London: William Pickering, 1995), 39.

female writer; it recalls her own experience of being mentioned (fairly innocuously) in *Warley*, an ephemeral satiric poem, and her horrified reaction. In the play, however, Burney makes the cruelty to the female wit emphatically well deserved. Lady Smatter's dictatorial treatment of her nephew, and her mercenary unkindness towards Cecilia, are emphasized. Censor, by contrast, is an example of rough but true goodness: his harsh tongue is not enough to conceal his warm-heartedness and generosity. In a play suspicious of patronage, in which 'self-dependance' is held up as an ideal, it is notable that Censor is allowed to remain a financial patron, even when his money becomes superfluous. At the denouement, Cecilia shows Censor an order for £ 5,000 he has sent her, which he refuses to take back. This allows hero and heroine to praise the rough man of feeling:

CECILIA. Dwells Benevolence in so rugged a Garb?—Oh Mr. Censor—!
BEAUFORT. Noble, generous Censor! You penetrate my Heart,—yet I cannot consent—
CENSOR. Pho, pho, never praise a man for only gratifying his own humour. (*Complete Plays*, i. 100)

Clearly Censor, rough-spoken but soft-hearted, is a stock sentimental figure. He is also, I think, Burney's attempt to convey something of the Dr Johnson she experienced—sometimes severe and even rude, so that she was frightened of offending him, but really, and certainly to her, generous and kind. It would be a distortion to see the comic characters of Lady Smatter and Censor as intended as representations of Montagu and Johnson; but they do express the feelings roused in Burney by the rivalry of female critic and man of letters. The female intellectual, whether as public role-model or as social patron, arouses in her intense anxiety, and she distances herself from this figure through hostile comedy. The man of letters, frightening in his authority and power to hurt, is seen as ultimately benevolent to the properly gentle and unpretentious woman. In this way, Censor is the product of Burney's fond image of a paternal Johnson.

For Burney's circle, there was also an obvious contemporary model for the learned woman: the well-known, socially powerful critic and 'bluestocking' Elizabeth Montagu. The connection between Montagu and Lady Smatter was all the more likely to be made because Elizabeth Montagu was herself a rich widow who, like Lady Smatter, had adopted her nephew as her heir. Charles Burney's and Samuel Crisp's now-famous suppression of a play whose early scenes had delighted them, and whose success on the stage was very likely, seems to have been mainly motivated by their fear that the play would be taken as a satire on Montagu, and earn Burney (and perhaps her father) a powerful enemy. The satire, they felt, was dreadfully misjudged; and until recently commentators on the play have agreed. Burney's attack on a leading model for a public role for the intellectual woman has been seen as 'singularly perverse', and even 'self-destructive'.[96] However, *The Witlings* has received some long-overdue reassessment from critics willing to challenge the verdict of Burney's 'daddies'. Margaret Doody, in her ground-breaking discussion of the play, points out that there is far more to it than the portrait of Lady Smatter, seeing in its innovative treatment of a bored and inactive society a precursor to theatre of the absurd.[97] She points out the general nature of the satire on the learned woman, and remarks that Lady Smatter's particular foibles—her regular misattribution of quotations, for example—were not characteristic of Montagu. She suggests that Charles Burney's objections might have been rooted rather in suspicion that Lady Smatter bore some resemblance to his wife Elizabeth Burney, much disliked by her stepdaughter, and even that the flatterer and would-be poet Dabler may contain references to Charles Burney himself.[98] Barbara Darby and Peter Sabor have also expanded discussion of the play, moving the focus away from the question of satire on Montagu. Darby sees the threatened exposure of Lady Smatter as a more general comment by Burney on the vulnerability of women in the public

[96] Katharine M. Rogers, *Frances Burney: The World of 'Female Difficulties'* (New York: Harvester, 1990), 19.

[97] M. A. Doody, *Frances Burney: The Life in the Works* (New Brunswick, NJ: Rutgers University Press, 1988), 91.

[98] Ibid. 93, 96.

eye.[99] Peter Sabor points out that the witlings are a mixed-sex group (Lady Smatter, Mrs Sapient, Dabler, and Codger), and that the attack is not on female learning as such but on vanity, superficiality, and cold-heartedness in both sexes.[100] These are good points: but it is still true that the satire on Lady Smatter is particularly sharp and central, and that she is the main antagonist of the critical Censor; and that there remain likely references to Montagu, especially in the matter of the inheriting nephew. Charles Burney and Samuel Crisp were probably right that Montagu would have taken offence if the play had been performed. I think there was an additional objection, felt particularly by Samuel Crisp, which was to do with a sense that the attack on Montagu was influenced by Johnson.

Johnson had strongly encouraged Burney to write a comedy. In response to her request that he read and comment on the draft for her, he offered to hear her read it, and promised all the help he could give. It is not clear whether he did in fact get to know the play—Burney was frightened of reading it to him—but he offered general goodwill and encouragement, and at one point he suggested a title indicating that he thought of it as a satirical treatment of the literary society around her: 'Streatham: a farce'. There had even been suggestions that the two should collaborate like Beaumont and Fletcher.[101] Remarks like this made her feel that they were allies; and his notions of the role of the author and of literary life are a strong influence on the play. This satire on self-styled wits by 'a sister of the order' can be read as a response to Johnson's view of the competitive nature of literary life, and specifically, his injunction to Burney that, as a rising young wit, she should attack the reigning Mrs Montagu.

[99] Barbara Darby, *Frances Burney, Dramatist: Gender, Performance, and the Late-Eighteenth-Century Stage* (Lexington, Ky.: University Press of Kentucky, 1997), 37–8.
[100] Peter Sabor, 'General Introduction' to Burney, *Complete Plays*, vol. i. p. xx.
[101] In Feb. 1779 Burney reported Murphy's attempts to persuade her to write a comedy, during which Johnson, laughing, remarked, 'Suppose Burney & I begin [a comedy] together?' Murphy replied, 'Ah, I wish to God you would!—I wish you would Beaumont and Fletcher us!' *EJL* iii. 245.

In September 1778, when people at Streatham were discussing Elizabeth Montagu's impending visit:

> 'Dr Johnson began to see-saw, with a Countenance strongly expressive of *inward fun*,—&, after enjoying it some Time in silence, he suddenly, & with great animation, turned to me, & cried '*Down* with her, Burney!—*down* with her!—spare her not! Attack her, fight her, & *down* with her at once!—*You* are a *rising* Wit,—*she* is at the *Top*,—& when *I* was beginning the World, & was nothing & nobody, the Joy of my Life was to fire at all the established Wits! (*EJL* iii. 151)

Here Johnson was recommending to Burney his own view of literary life as competitive and aggressive, whatever the sex of the writer.[102] Burney, with her unusually strong investment in ideas of female modesty, was not likely to take up such a challenge—at least, not in Mrs Thrale's drawing room. Shortly after this remark, Johnson repeated the injunction to attack Montagu. This time he seems to have been goaded by her reluctance to enter the literary arena, even to the extent of commenting on his own work. Burney reports:

> Wednesday [16 Sept.]—at Breakfast, Dr. Johnson asked me if I had been reading his Life of Cowley?—'O yes!' cried I. 'And what do you think of it?'
>
> 'I am delighted with it,' cried I; & if I was *somebody*, instead of *Nobody*, I should not have read it without telling you sooner how highly I think of it.' 'Miss Burney, cried Mr. Thrale, you must get up your Courage for this encounter! [with Montagu] I think you should *begin* with Miss Gregory [Montagu's companion]; & *down* with *her* first.

---

[102] On Burney's adoption of Johnson's professional model of authorship, see Betty A. Schellenberg, 'From Propensity to Profession: Female Authorship and the Early Career of Frances Burney', *Eighteenth-Century Fiction*, 14 (2002), 345–70. Schellenberg sees Johnson's rivalry with Montagu as 'the attack of a rising professional system on an earlier hierarchical structure, one built primarily upon the leisured cultivation of conversational skills embodied in the literary salon rather than the disembodied authorial production measured by widespread approbation' (355).

> Dr. J. No, no,—fly at the *Eagle*!—*down* with Mrs. Montagu
> herself!—I hope she will come *full* of Evelina! (*EJL* iii. 153)

Evidently Johnson's remark about a rising wit being 'nothing &
nobody' had rankled with Burney, and rather than seeing the parallel
between herself and the young Johnson, she had thought of her own
journal meditations on 'Nobody' as a female. For her, an attack on
the eagle was nowhere near as simple a matter as it appeared to him.

For Johnson, the joke about setting Burney on Montagu expressed
his own sense of rivalry. Elizabeth Montagu, as a woman of high
social standing, a respected critic, and an acknowledged leader
of the 'bluestocking' circle of literary and intellectual men and
women, was a rival to both Hester Thrale and Samuel Johnson.
Her drawing room and the Thrales' at Streatham were rival centres
of literary discussion. Her *Essay on the Writings and Genius of
Shakespeare* (1769) responded to Johnson's preface to his edition
of Shakespeare four years earlier, offering the dramatic analysis
which she thought he had unaccountably failed to give.[103] For his
part, he had made disparaging comments on her *Essay*. Burney's
journal entries describing the discussion of Montagu's visit are full
of mockery directed at Montagu by Thrale and Johnson, tempered
with careful expressions of respect for her as 'the first woman, for
Literary knowledge, in England' (*EJL* iii.152).

It is not surprising that Burney, introduced to Elizabeth Montagu
by mentors who were her rivals, was disposed to criticize her. We can
see the portrait of Lady Smatter as Burney's way of 'flying at the eagle'.
In doing this Burney is adopting Johnson's view of the aggressive
rivalry of a writer's life: a far cry from the specifically feminine,

---

[103] For a discussion of Montagu's criticism of Johnson's work on Shakespeare see
Elizabeth Eger's introd. to *Bluestocking Feminism: Writers of the Bluestocking Circle,
1738–1785, i. Elizabeth Montagu* (London: Pickering and Chatto, 1999), p. lxiii.
Montagu wrote to Carter in Oct. 1766: 'It has been lucky for my amusement, but
unfortunate for the publick, that [Johnson] did not consider his author in a more
extensive view. . . . if I am glad he left the task [of defending Shakespeare] to my unable
hand, I dare hardly own it to myself. . . . It is strange that Mr Johnson should so
superficially examine the merits and faults of his authors plays: he should have said more
or have said nothing' (*Bluestocking Feminism*, i. 172).

sheltered sort of literary existence that Daddy Crisp advocated. Samuel Crisp, indeed, seems to have perceived Johnson as a rival. When Burney wrote to him that Johnson was a second Daddy Crisp to her, he wrote a complaining letter to his friend Mrs Gast, expressing his fears that Fanny would forget her old friends now that she was spending so much time with grand people in Streatham.[104] When he explained to her his objections to *The Witlings*, one of them was to the character of Mr Censor. His express objection was to the fortune Censor gives Cecilia at the end of the play, presumably because of a sense that a heroine accepting a man's money has compromised herself. Another motive may have been a sense of connection between the character of Censor and Dr Johnson—a sense that Cecilia's affectionate gratitude towards Censor mirrored Burney's own feelings for her new mentor. The vehemence of Charles Burney's, and particularly Samuel Crisp's, response to *The Witlings*, then, expresses their struggle for the writer-daughter's allegiance. They are the familial fathers who wish to shelter the feminine daughter; and they are worried about the influence of potential public patrons like Johnson and Sheridan, who are encouraging the writing daughter to enter a mixed-sex world.

Burney was beginning to move away from the protection of the paternal family into a public domain ruled by the literary father. She adopted the public, masculine mode of the life of a wit as warfare upon earth through the attack on Lady Smatter, who was likely to be interpreted as representative of the woman of wit. In her allegiance to Johnson as literary father, did Burney reject and attack her literary mothers? This is a complicated question, not just because literary motherhood, unlike literary fatherhood, was not a metaphor much used in her time, but because the exemplars of (would-be) female

---

[104] He wrote that Burney 'now in a manner lives at Streatham . . . she is so taken up with these fine Folks, I imagine we shall see but little of her now'. He hoped Burney would write to him after an Easter visit with the Thrales and Johnson to Mrs Montagu, but 'possibly I may flatter myself in vain, considering the Changes occasion'd by Change of Circumstance and Station; but Hetty told me she intended writing soon'. Samual Crisp to Mrs Gast, 28 Mar. 1779; *EJL* iii. 261.

wit mocked in the play do not stand in maternal relation to her writing. Novelists and playwrights like Eliza Haywood and Elizabeth Griffith, carefully not mentioned in the preface to *Evelina*, have a better claim to the title of Burney's neglected mothers than do the bluestockings. Burney, the uneducated late reader and 'dunce' of her family, did not feel herself to be in possession of an inheritance from intellectual women. Yet, as the protégée of the older Hester Thrale, she had to deal with the intellectual woman as patron, and it is well known that her love and admiration for Mrs Thrale coexisted with an anxiety about being treated as a dependant, which her hostess found awkward and at times ungrateful.[105] In a different way, as a young woman entering the literary world she was conscious of a special significance in her meeting with Elizabeth Montagu, 'our Sex's Glory' (*EJL* iii. 144), who herself declared (before reading *Evelina*) that its reputed merit pleased her because it was the work of a woman.[106] Burney, feeling her way in a literary world partly ruled by powerful older women, of higher birth and much richer than her own family, expressed her more resentful feelings about female patronage in *The Witlings*. Mrs Thrale evidently felt that the portrait of Lady Smatter touched on female intellectuals generally, including herself: she wrote that 'none of the scribbling Ladies have a Right to admire its general Tendency',[107] and she was pleased when the play was abandoned. In her *Thraliana* she recorded discussions

[105] In Aug. 1779 she reported, 'Fanny Burney has been a long time from me, I was glad to see her again; yet She makes me miserable too in many Respects—so restlessly and apparently anxious lest I should give myself Airs of Patronage, or load her with the Shackles of Dependance—I live with her always in a Degree of Pain that precludes Friendship—dare not ask her to buy me a Ribbon, dare not desire her to touch the Bell, lest She should think herself injured—lest she should forsooth appear in the Character of Miss Neville & I in that of the Widow Bromley.' *Thraliana: The Diary of Mrs Hester Lynch Thrale (Later Mrs Piozzi) 1776–1809*, ed. Katharine C. Balderston (2nd edn., Oxford: Clarendon Press, 1951), i. 400.

[106] When Montagu and Burney met, Montagu had not read Evelina, but said she was '*proud* that a work *so* commended should be a *woman's*': *EJL* iii. 159. She did not, in the event, like the book, as Hester Thrale told Samuel Johnson. Whether they told Burney of this is not known; but Burney would have noticed the absence of the praise she had received from so many others. See *EJL* iii.162.

[107] Thrale, *Thraliana*, i. 381.

of Elizabeth Montagu's relations with her nephew (post-dating the composition of the play), in which Burney strongly criticized what she saw as Montagu's high-handed treatment of her dependant:

> We were speaking of Mrs Montagu—I believe says Mr Seward She tyrannizes over her Heir pretty much;—why so? why you told me last Year that when he knock'd too hard at the door She sent him a reproving Message by the Servt & bid him Stay til he had a door of his own to knock at so: and if She did quoth I!—If She *did* says Fanny Burney—why with *me* such a Speech would cancel all Obligations: & for my part cries Seward I'd list for a Soldier sooner than lie under such Oppression I swear. Lord have Mercy! What a World is this! Where more ill will is gained by a light Ebullition of Humour, than good will by the Gift of a magnificent Education & ten thousand Pounds a Year.[108]

Here Thrale, at other times disposed to criticize Montagu herself, evidently sides with her fellow patron. The incident both strengthens the idea that there is some reference to Montagu in Lady Smatter, and suggests that the character may also reveal a tension between Thrale the patron and Burney the protegée.

In contrast to these wealthy women, Samuel Johnson had no social and financial patronage to bestow; but he offered prestige, and the vision of a literary world in which the effect of differences in social rank could be diminished. If he petted his 'little Burney' with diminutives he also placed her on an implicit equality with himself, comparing her position to his own in his youth, when he was a social 'nobody' forcing his way in the world through literary competition. For Burney, then, allegiance to the literary father rather than the female patron allowed her to express her resentment of the eighteenth-century culture of social patronage and dependence. This helps to explain the misogyny in *The Witlings*. It was through her relation to a literary father, and not in her relation to a female tradition, that Burney felt that she was offered expressive freedom and a public role.

---

[108] Ibid. (1 Dec 1779), 412.

Burney, as we know, bowed to the wishes of her father and Crisp and gave up all thoughts of staging *The Witlings*. The familial 'daddies' had apparently won, and they now encouraged her to redouble her efforts in what seemed a safer, more feminine form, the novel. However, as Burney continued to write, it was Johnson's influence as mentor that was most important. After giving up *The Witlings*, she wrote *Cecilia*, her most Johnsonian novel.

At first, Burney's association with Johnson was entirely favourable to her. The *Monthly*'s review of *Cecilia* emphatically placed her in a masculine tradition, comparing her to Richardson and Fielding, and remarking that, unlike other women novelists, she did not 'plead any privilege of her sex', but could withstand 'impartial criticism'. This ability to stand with the men was linked to her likeness to Johnson. Her 'peculiarly nervous and perspicuous' style ('nervous' at this time implying strength) was said 'to have been formed on the best model of Dr. Johnson's'.[109] However, Burney carried on writing and publishing in the Romantic era, when Johnson's name was no longer a password to literary esteem, and the elaborate, over-formal style of her later work was interpreted as failed imitation of an outmoded model. Reviews of Burney's later work demoted her from the position of daughter of the paternal line of novelists. William Hazlitt's influential review of her final novel, *The Wanderer*, in 1814 strenuously undid the link between Burney and her male precursors which Johnson had emphasized. Hazlitt used his review of the novel as the occasion for a general assessment of the English novel tradition (later revised and published separately as a general essay on the novel). Burney's novel is broached only at the end of the review, after discussions of Fielding, Richardson, Sterne, and more recent novelists like Godwin and Radcliffe. Rather than being seen as the heir to Richardson and Fielding, Burney is considered a special, and limited, female case. She is

> a very woman. It is this ... which forms the peculiarity of
> her writings, and distinguishes them from those masterpieces

[109] *Monthly Review*, 67 (Dec. 1782), 456–7, 453.

which we have before mentioned. She is unquestionably a quick, lively, and accurate observer of persons and things; but she always looks at them with a consciousness of her sex . . . We thus get a kind of supplement and gloss to our original text, which we could not otherwise have obtained.[110]

This idea of the woman's novel as 'supplement and gloss' to the real, male genre is in complete contrast to Johnson's easy assumption that the novel belongs to both sexes, and reflects the masculinization of the genre which accompanied its early nineteenth-century rise in status. Later in the century the division between male and female novelists was established, and the idea of strict gender division structured the critical response to Burney's *Diary and Letters*, published after her death. Thomas Babington Macaulay, reviewing the *Diary and Letters* in the *Edinburgh* in 1843, had high praise for what he saw as Burney's introduction of moral delicacy into the novel. He thought she had 'vindicated the right of her sex to an equal share in a fair and noble province of letters'; but he saw in her only feminine virtue, and considered her to belong only to a female tradition. In Macaulay's narrative of separate literary spheres, Burney's admiration and imitation of Johnson—made newly visible to nineteenth-century readers through the publication of her diary detailing their friendship—could only appear as a source of error. The moral of Macaulay's article is that Burney, badly served by her real father (who should have educated and guided her more carefully), and happily fostered by Samuel Crisp, who looked after her well and suppressed her misguided play, made the terrible mistake of attempting to take her place as Johnson's disciple, which meant discarding her native, feminine simplicity for a doomed attempt to write like him. Where Burney did succeed in writing well in the Johnsonian manner—in parts of *Cecilia*—the explanation, for Macaulay, was simple: Johnson must have revised and retouched those passages. For the most part, however, Burney, as one of Johnson's 'most submissive worshippers', imitated him in all the wrong ways:

[110] *Edinburgh Review*, 24 (Feb. 1815), 336.

In an evil hour the author of Evelina took the Rambler for her
model. This would not have been wise even if she could have
imitated her pattern as well as Hawkesworth did. But such
imitation was beyond her power. She had her own style. It was
a tolerably good one . . . She determined to throw it away, and
to adopt a style in which she could attain excellence only by
achieving an almost miraculous victory over nature and habit.
She could cease to be Fanny Burney; it was not so easy to
become Samuel Johnson.[111]

With its echoes of Milton's Adam on the Fall of our first mother,
this passage reprimands the woman writer for claiming the privileges
of men.[112] Literary sons had for many years been praised for taking
on the father's mantle, for in effect becoming the dead father. The
literary daughter, Macaulay insists, cannot become the father. If she
tries to do so, she will only succeed in losing the virtues of her distinct
feminine identity.

[111] *Edinburgh Review*, 76 (Jan. 1843), 564.
[112] 'O Eve, in evil hour thou didst give ear | To that false worm', *Paradise Lost*,
ix. 1067–8, in Milton, *Poetical Works*, ed. Douglas Bush (London: OUP 1969), 395.

2

The Mighty Mother

While literary traditions were being built on the paternal metaphor through the construction of historical lineages in which fathers begot sons without mothers, the maternal and the literary were connected very differently. Literary paternity was understood historically; literary maternity was imagined in mythical terms. Ideas of poetry as a form of male motherhood, or conversely of the poet as the son of a maternal Muse, were much stronger than any sense of a matrilineal line of poets. Myths which focus on the poet as a mother's son may treat the relationship positively; but the most memorable treatment of the mothering of poetry in the eighteenth century is the resoundingly hostile treatment of the monstrous 'Mighty Mother' Dulness in *The Dunciad*. This chapter examines various ways of thinking about poetic motherhood, considering Pope's maternal monster and moving on to look at lives and writings in which literal and literary motherhood coincide. Richard Brinsley Sheridan is an example of the writer as son of a writing mother, Frances Sheridan, while Jane and Charlotte Brereton, and Mary Wollstonecraft and Mary Shelley, are writing mothers and daughters; and in the responses of sons and daughters to writing mothers, the myths of poetic maternity are variously invoked, contested, and altered.

Maternity and poetic creativity have long been figuratively linked, with both male and female poets imagining writing in terms of pregnancy and childbirth. The speaker of Sidney's sonnets, 'great with childe to speake, and helpless in my throwes', provides one of many examples of the poet as labouring mother, producing the poem as child.[1] If literary father–son relations gain in value as they become further removed from the literal, further spiritualized, then this form of literary maternity may carry the danger, for the poet, of too close association with the female and with the understanding of the female as (mere) body. Such danger can be avoided through the reader's consciousness that the male poet is not literally a mother. The male use of the childbirth metaphor, Susan Stanford Friedman argues, actually reinforces mind–body dualism, drawing attention to the difference between women's bodily acts of procreation and men's acts of mental creation.[2] Nevertheless, the celebration of male poets' creativity through analogy with childbirth did create positive associations for the maternal body, which could be exploited during the seventeenth century to praise the female poet. In the commendatory ode printed with her works, Abraham Cowley celebrated Katherine Philips as a fecund mother of many poems:

> Thou bring'st not forth with pain,
> It neither Travel is, nor *Labour* of thy Brain.
> So easily they from thee come,
>   And there is so much room
> In the unexhausted and unfathom'd womb;
> That like the *Holland* Countess, thou might'st bear
> A Child for ev'ry day of all the fertile year.[3]

Though the terms of his praise single her out as a dazzling exception rather than a typical mother—like the Virgin Mary, she feels no pain in childbirth—there is a much happier sense here of the writing as the product of a womb than is generally found in the following generations. Eighteenth-century reviewers referred sarcastically to the fruitfulness of the female muse, seeing women's writing as evidence 'that this beautiful sex are resolved to be, one way or other, the joyful

---

[1] *Astrophil and Stella*, Sonnet 1; *The Poems of Sir Philip Sidney*, ed. William A. Ringler, Jr. (Oxford: Clarendon Press, 1962), 165.

[2] Susan Stanford Friedman, 'Creativity and the Childbirth Metaphor: Gender Difference in Literary Discourse', *Feminist Studies*, 13/1 (Spring 1987), 51–6.

[3] 'Upon Mrs. K. *Philips* her Poems', in *Poems by the Most Deservedly Admired Mrs. Katherine Philips* (London: H. Herringman, 1667), sig. B2ᵛ–C1ʳ.

mothers of children', likened women writers to mothers 'in the straw, after having, not very favourably, been delivered of the burthen of a nine-months conception', and described their productions as 'literary bantlings'.[4] Terry Castle contrasts the positive use of the childbirth trope in the Renaissance to the satirical use of it in Dryden and Pope. From the point of view of neoclassical aesthetics, she argues, it is a dangerous trope because 'artistic activity should not be linked, even metaphorically, to physiological process: to do so is to abdicate from responsibility, from reason, from creative independence'. For Pope, for whom the poet should be a 'conscious craftsman' in control of his material, the link between bodily procreation and writing is a monstrous one.[5] In the later eighteenth century and the Romantic period, along with celebration of nature and organic theories of poetic composition and genius, there was a renewed sense of delight in the analogy between writing and giving birth.[6]

This did not translate into a renewed celebration of the maternal creativity of women writers. It was a different aspect of motherhood that did most to authorize female writing: motherhood as social role rather than bodily capacity. From the medieval to early modern periods, women had claimed the right to speak or write in their role as mothers, charged with the duty of teaching their children.[7] During the time from the Restoration to the early nineteenth century, cultural emphasis on the importance of maternal care intensified. At the same time as Pope was developing his satiric picture of the

---

[4] Review of *Jemima and Louisa, By a Lady, Critical Review*, 8 (1759), 165; review of *The History of Miss Harriot Watson*, by Mrs Woodfin, *Monthly Review*, 28 (1763), 162.

[5] Terry Castle, 'Lab'ring Bards: Birth *Topoi* and English Poetics 1660–1820', *Journal of English and Germanic Philology*, 78/2 (1979), 201.

[6] Ibid. 203.

[7] For an interesting example of maternal religious authority in the medieval period see Karen A. Winstead, 'The Conversion of Margery Kempe's Son', *English Language Notes*, 32/2 (Dec. 1994), 9–12. For the maternal authority of women writers in the early modern period see Lloyd Davis, 'Redemptive Advice: Dorothy Leigh's *The Mother's Blessing*', in Jo Wallwork and Paul Salzman (eds.), *Women Writing 1550–1750; Meridian*, 18/1 (2001), 59–72, and Kristen Poole, ' "The fittest closet for all goodness": Authorial Strategies of Jacobean Mothers' Manuals', *Studies in English Literature 1500–1900*, 35 (1995), 69–88.

monstrous mother, eighteenth-century culture was placing increasing importance on the ideal of the good, domestic mother. Toni Bowers has convincingly argued that the sentimentalization of motherhood, sometimes seen as a late eighteenth-century development, was a feature of early eighteenth-century life too; and though it has been argued that this sentimentalization accompanied a decline in mothers' social and legal powers, it did provide the rationale for an increasingly visible public role for the maternal authority of the writer.[8] By the end of the eighteenth century, motherly duty could be fairly widely accepted as the basis for women's involvement in the moral care of the nation.[9]

Mothers could be writers, then, and writing could be maternal, but throughout the period there was very little sense of a matrilineal literary tradition. Because motherhood was not, like fatherhood, understood as generative, and because mothers were not understood as the owners of a heritage to be passed on, people did not generally think of women writers as the founders of tradition or as the metaphorical mothers of poetic heirs, especially not of sons. Writers in the late seventeenth century began to delineate a female tradition of writing, but its matrilineal nature was submerged or at most implicit, in contrast to the explicit celebration of a patrilineal tradition. While Dryden was defining an English literary tradition through the naming of fathers and sons, women writers, and men writing in praise of them, looked back to Sappho as a female ancient who demonstrated women's right to poetry; but Sappho was not called mother, nor were later women writers called her daughters. Dryden himself, in his Ode to Anne Killigrew, described her as a reincarnation of Sappho: her soul, he wrote, had travelled through many great writers and then returned to its origin: 'And was that *Sappho* last, which once it was before'.[10] Abraham Cowley, praising the poetry of Katherine

[8] See Toni Bowers, *The Politics of Motherhood: British Writing and Culture 1680–1760* (Cambridge: CUP, 1996).

[9] See Anne Mellor, *Mothers of the Nation: Women's Political Writing in England, 1780–1830* (Bloomington, Ind.: Indiana University Press, 2002).

[10] *The Poems and Fables of John Dryden*, ed. James Kinsley (Oxford: OUP, 1970), 345.

Philips, 'Orinda', saw her as surpassing Sappho, whose reputation is clouded:

> They talk of *Sappho*, but alas! the shame
> Ill Manners soil the lustre of her fame.
> *Orinda*'s inward vertue is so bright,
> That like a Lantern's fair enclosed light;
> It through the Paper shines where she doth write.[11]

Twenty years later, Aphra Behn was celebrated as the successor to Sappho and Orinda, two predecessors who (in the gallant formula of male encomia on women writers) proved women's special aptitude for poetry, and foreshadowed the greater glory of the later writer:

> 'Twas vain for Man the laurels to persue,
> (E'en from the God of Wit bright *Daphne f*lew)
> Man, Whose course compound damps the Muses fire,
> It does but touch our Earth and soon expire;
> While in the softer kind th'Aetherial flame,
> Spreads and rejoices as from heaven it came:
> This *Greece* in *Sappho*, in *Orinda* knew
> Our Isle; though they were but low types to you . . .[12]

Later women writers added Behn herself to the list of predecessors, forming a female line to which they could compare each other. In one encomium poem Mary Pix called Delarivier Manley

> *Like* Sappho *Charming, like* Afra *Eloquent,*
> *Like Chast* Orinda, *sweetly Innocent* . . .[13]

This female line, however, always held dangers for the women writers who both wanted to belong to it and needed to dissociate themselves from earlier women's reputations. Cowley's praise of Katherine Philips for being *unlike* her predecessor, for not sharing her soiled

---

[11] K. Philips, *Poems*, sig. C1ʳ.

[12] J. Adams, '*To the excellent madam* Behn, *on her Poems*', in Aphra Behn, *Poems Upon Several Occasions* (London: R. and J. Tonson, 1684), sig. A7ᵛ.

[13] 'To Mrs *Manley*', in Delarivier Manley, *The Royal Mischief* (London: R. Bentley, F. Saunders, J. Knapton, and R. Wellington, 1696), sig. A3ᵛ.

reputation, is typical of this period's invocation of Sappho. Even as she is praised for the lyric beauty of her writing on love, she is castigated for being unable to control her passions.[14] Some references to Sappho are entirely hostile. In the eighteenth century, Pope uses her to name Lady Mary Wortley Montagu in an attack which becomes a slight on the idea of women's writing. The mismatch of 'Sappho's diamonds with her dirty smock' epitomizes the disparity between women's poetic pretensions and their bodily reality.[15] Significantly, when maternal imagery is used in connection with Sappho, it is pejorative. In one early eighteenth-century exchange between feminist and misogynist views, 'Sir Thomas', attacking women, does so by impugning the chastity of women writers: 'And now we are fall'n upon *Poetry*, pray how many *honest Poetesses* can you reckon among ye? From *Granny Sappho*, down to *Mother Behn?*'[16] The maternal line 'from Granny Sappho down to Mother Behn' stands in contrast to the paternal line drawn from Homer, through Shakespeare, to contemporary writers. While literary fatherhood was common, serious, legitimate, to be sought, claimed, and openly celebrated, literary motherhood was obscure, dubious, or a joke.

Joan DeJean has shown how the mythology surrounding Sappho was used in sixteenth- and seventeenth-century France to ward off the anxieties she excited as a maternal poetic origin. The story of her love for Phaon, which led her to throw herself to her death (a story now understood to be fictional), dominated accounts of her life through the seventeenth and eighteenth centuries, making her appear less the centre of a group of female poets than the archetypal abandoned woman, in thrall to hopeless longing for a man. In a society where women were prominent as early novelists, the idea of a female source for a literary tradition was perceived as a threat

---

[14] Martha Rainbolt, 'Their Ancient Claim: Sappho and Seventeenth- and Eighteenth-Century British Women's Poetry', *Seventeenth Century*, 12 (1997), 111–34.

[15] 'Epistle to a Lady', *The Poems of Alexander Pope*, iii/2. *Epistles to Several Persons*, ed. F. W. Bateson (London: Methuen and Co., 1961), 51.

[16] Letter XIX, 'Against a She-Wit', by Sir Thomas____. In *The Challenge ... Or, the Female war* (London: E. Whitlock, 1679), 210–11.

by male writers, and attitudes to Sappho, whether openly hostile or apparently sympathetic, can be interpreted as ways of containing that threat, of denying her power as literary mother.[17] A similar anxiety about maternal literary origins can be discerned in English references to Sappho in the seventeenth and eighteenth centuries. In the previous chapter we saw how both Congreve and Burney, in taking up their filial positions in respect of literary fathers, mocked female figures of intellectual or literary authority. In Congreve's case, as we have seen, the name 'Sapho' figures in this process, belonging to the baby daughter in *The Double Dealer* on whom the dilettante Lady Froth pins her hopes of a literary succession. Congreve also called his dog Sapho. He mentioned her with jesting affection in several letters, claiming that one letter had been delayed by her labour, promising to give his friend one of her puppies, and some time later announcing that 'we are at present in great grief for the death of Sapho' and mentioning that she has left orphans. Congreve's attachment to a dog so named implies, for Jennifer Brady, his 'desire to reach Sapphic perfection in his art', as well as an uneasy identification with his own doting Lady Froth.[18] Affection and allegiance, however, are mingled with derogation: equally striking in Congreve's choice of name is the reduction of Sappho from poetic mother to bitch with pups.

To call a woman writer 'our English Sappho'—as Aphra Behn, for example, was called—at once implied a maternal line and contained it within the narrative of Sappho's compromised reputation. Fear of maternal influence put male poets on their guard against being understood as the poetic sons of historical literary mothers, whether ancient like Sappho or modern like Behn; but at the level of myth, a strong tradition identified the archetypal poet as the son of a mother. Orpheus, the legendary poet of Thrace whose song charmed Pluto and (almost) released Eurydice from the underworld,

---

[17] Joan DeJean, *Fictions of Sappho 1547–1937* (Chicago: University of Chicago Press, 1989).

[18] Jennifer Brady, 'Dryden and Congreve's Collaboration in *The Double Dealer*', in Paul Hammond and David Hopkins (eds.), *John Dryden: Tercentenary Essays*, (Oxford: Clarendon Press, 2000), 136.

was the son of Calliope, the chief of the Muses, and was torn to pieces by Bacchanalian women. His story told by Virgil and Ovid, Orpheus was well known in the English tradition. In Milton's pastoral elegy *Lycidas*, his fate highlights the loss of Lycidas/King, and stands for the death of every poet, who can never be saved by his mother Muse:

> What could the Muse herself that Orpheus bore,
> The Muse herself, for her enchanting son,
> Whom universal nature did lament,
> When by the rout that made the hideous roar
> His gory visage down the stream was sent,
> Down the swift Hebrus to the Lesbian shore?[19]

Milton alludes to Orpheus again in *Paradise Lost*, when he invokes the heavenly Muse Urania at the opening of Book VII. The 'Thracian Bard' was destroyed by the Bacchanalian revellers, 'nor could the Muse defend | Her son'; the heavenly Muse, by contrast, has the power to protect Milton.[20] The idea of the dead poet as the son of a mourning mother continues in Shelley's *Adonais*, which, in homage to Milton, identifies the 'melancholy Mother' as the Muse Urania. Once she wept for Milton himself, the poetic 'Sire of an immortal strain'; now she must weep again for her 'youngest, dearest one', Adonais/Keats. In this way Shelley's elegy is part of a tradition building up a line of male poets—Milton, Keats, Shelley himself—united as the sons of a mythical mother.

Pope, *The Dunciad*, and the Mother

The story of Orpheus also figures in *The Dunciad*, which in its 1743 version had as epigraph lines from Ovid's *Metamorphoses*, describing how Phoebus, god of poetry, rescues the remains of the dead Orpheus from a serpent about to eat them. Within the poem this implied identification of Orpheus with Pope is continued.

---

[19] John Milton, *Lycidas*, in *Poetical Works*, ed. Douglas Bush (London: OUP 1969), 144.
[20] *Paradise Lost*, vii. 37–8; in *Poetical Works*, 341.

Orpheus, understood as a force for order and harmony in opposition
to the disorder of the worshippers of Bacchus who destroy him, is an
apt figure for the poet of the *Dunciad*, striving to uphold civilization
against modern barbarism.[21]

The comparison between Pope and Orpheus had been mooted
in a very different context years before. Lines in *The Rape of the
Lock*, ascribing female wit and poetry to the influence of spleen,
had annoyed the poet Anne Finch; she presumably remonstrated
with him about it, citing the examples of women poets of the past
in defence of female poetry, because he wrote her a reply in verse,
praising her own work at the expense of the poetry of all other
women, outshone by her: 'To write their Praise you but in vain
essay; | Ev'n while you write, you take that Praise away.'[22] Finch
responded with a poem of her own, professing herself 'Disarm'd
with so genteel an air' and ready to give up the contest, but warning
Pope to 'shock the sex no more'. Comparing him, in jesting flattery,
to Orpheus, who would have written like Pope if he had had the
benefit of London polish, she advises him to avoid Orpheus' fate,
which in this reading was a punishment from insulted women: he
wrote 'scoffing rhimes' against the women of his time, and so they
tore him to pieces.[23] Rereading the Thracian women as 'Resenting
Heroines' defending their sex against insult, Finch, like other women
writers of her time, subjects influential classical myths to feminist
interpretation. In Pope's work, however, the Orphean myth is given
a more traditional reading. That Orpheus is killed by furious females
makes him a fitting representative of the poet in the *Dunciad*, a work

[21] John V. Regan, 'Orpheus and the *Dunciad*'s Narrator', *Eighteenth-Century Studies*,
9 (1975), 87–101.
[22] 'To the Right Hon:ble Ann Countess of Winchilsea', *The Anne Finch Wellesley
Manuscript Poems*, ed. Barbara McGovern and Charles H. Hinnant (Athens, Ga.:
University of Georgia Press, 1998), 68. The offending lines are those addressing Spleen
as 'Parent of Vapours and of Female Wit, | Who give th'*Hysteric* or *Poetic* Fit, | On
various Tempers act by various ways, | Make some take Physick, others scribble Plays'.
The Poems of Alexander Pope, ii. *The Rape of the Lock*, ed. Geoffrey Tillotson (London:
Methuen and Co., 1950), 185–6.
[23] 'To Mr Pope', *Anne Finch Wellesley Manuscript Poems*, 69.

in which the feminized forces of modern print culture are destroying all proper literary life.[24]

The use of Orphean myth in the *Dunciad* implicitly makes the poet the son of the Muse; but this positive maternal figure is not, of course, prominent in the poem. The Muse is invoked towards the end of Book IV, but invoked 'In vain, in vain,—the all-composing Hour | Resistless falls: the Muse obeys the Pow'r'.[25] She is defeated by the power of a rival maternal figure, the goddess Dulness, in a poetic action that could be described as the triumph of the bad mother. In the four-book *Dunciad* of 1743, the revised opening emphasizes the centrality of Dulness as mother:

> The Mighty Mother, and her Son who brings
> The Smithfield Muses to the ear of Kings,
> I sing. Say you, her instruments the Great!
> Call'd to this work by Dulness, Jove, and Fate;
> You by whose care, in vain decry'd and curst,
> Still Dunce the second reigns like Dunce the first;
> Say how the Goddess bade Britannia sleep,
> And pour'd her Spirit o'er the land and deep.
>
> (i. 1–8; *Poems*, v. 267–9)

This replaces the androcentric focus of the earlier lines, 'Books and the Man I sing, the first who brings | The Smithfield Muses to the Ear of Kings',[26] with a concentration on the mother–son pair of the Goddess Dulness and her Laureate, Cibber; and Warburton's note intensifies the matrifocality, warning the reader 'that the *Mother*, and not the *Son*, is the principal Agent of this Poem . . . the main action of the Poem being by no means the Coronation of the Laureate . . . but the Restoration of the Empire of Dulness in Britain' (*Poems*, v. 269). The line 'Still Dunce the second reigns like Dunce the first' contrives,

---

[24] See Catherine Ingrassia, 'Women Writing/Writing Women: Pope, Dulness, and "Feminization" in the *Dunciad*', *Eighteenth-Century Life*, 14 (1990), 40–58.

[25] *The Dunciad* (B), iv. 627–8; in *The Poems of Alexander Pope*, v. *The Dunciad*, ed. James Sutherland (London: Methuen and Co. Ltd, 1943), 407. Subsequent references to *The Dunciad* are to this edition and are to the 1743 (B) text unless otherwise stated.

[26] *The Dunciad Variorum* (1729) (*Dunciad* A), i. 1–2; *Poems*, v. 59.

through a network of allusions, to suggest that the true political and poetic succession of father and son has been perverted. Echoing Dryden's 'Tom the second reigns like Tom the first', a reference to the succession of poor poet laureates, it implies that the current Laureate, Cibber, is another in a debased lineage, while at the same time making a mocking reference to the succession of George II. In Hanoverian England, Pope suggests, patrilineal succession has been debased through being subordinated to matriarchal authority, as the mighty mother's instruments have brought Dunce the second into power. Yet the allusion to Dryden, implicitly claiming him as Pope's poetic father, counters such cultural decay through the power of true poetry, based on true patrilineage. The opening lines, then, perform a movement that will be repeated throughout the poem: the creation of an apocalyptic vision of cultural ruin, countered by the attempt to express it in ordered poetry. The poetic order is patrilineal; the threatened ruin comes about through maternal rule, as the Goddess pours her spirit over Britain in a parody of biblical accounts of the movement of the spirit of God.

The 'Mighty Mother' Dulness is identified in a note as Magna Mater, the maternal deity once worshipped in Rome,[27] and in his classic study of the *Dunciad*, Aubrey Williams explains her relevance to the action. In the mock-epic's parody of the *Aeneid*, the movement of Aeneas from sacked Troy to Italy, where he founds Rome, is changed to the procession of Dulness from the City of London to Westminster, where she sets up her imperial seat. Dulness's role is analogous to that of Venus, mother of Aeneas, herself historically confused with Magna Mater, whose statue was taken from Troy to Italy, and who became the centre of a Roman cult. Thus Pope's satire on Dulness and her noisy crowd of hack writers parallels Roman satires on the priests of Magna Mater; and descriptions of Magna Mater as mother of all creation are used in the *Dunciad* to establish Dulness as a figure of cosmic significance, an inversion of the Christian God who creates

[27] The 'Great Mother', in *Dunciad* (A), i. 32, is glossed as '*Magna Mater*, here applied to *Dulness*.' *Poems*, v. 64.

darkness and destruction in place of light and life.[28] Later scholars have elaborated on Pope's use of Magna Mater, showing how he drew on seventeenth- and eighteenth-century mythographic works as well as classical sources to create a composite goddess, with elements from Cybele, Nox (Night), Hecate, and others.[29] Confusion between the various mother goddesses occurred historically when cults adopted foreign deities, and in the Renaissance mythographers added to this by identifying one goddess with another. Pope 'not only took advantage of this situation but superimposed other goddesses as well', thus adding to the sense of chaos associated with Magna Mater.[30] This confusion and mingling of identities strengthens Pope's point that the reign of Dulness leads back to primeval Chaos.

At times, Dulness as bad mother goddess is seen as an inversion of more positive maternal figures. In Book III, for instance, she is a parodic version of Berecynthia, mother of the gods: where Berecynthia has 'An hundred sons, and ev'ry son a God', Dulness will 'Behold an hundred sons, and each a Dunce' (iii. 134, 138; *Poems*, v. 326). It has been argued that the creation of Dulness as a parody of ideal goddess figures, and as the 'black opposite' of Queen Anne, whom Pope had celebrated in *Windsor Forest* as a version of the goddesses Ceres, Astrea, and Cynthia, indicates Pope's deep commitment to positive maternal figures.[31] While it is certainly true that Dulness is a parodic figure, and more broadly that all images of the bad mother work by virtue of their implicit opposition to ideals of good motherhood, the overwhelming emphasis in the *Dunciad* is on the negative aspect of the mother. While Dulness may be, for example, a debasement of Berecynthia, Berecynthia herself is not

---

[28] See Aubrey Williams, *Pope's Dunciad: A Study of its Meaning* (London: Methuen, 1955), 19–152.

[29] Thomas C. Faulkner and Rhonda L. Blair, 'The Classical and Mythographic Sources of Pope's Dulness', *Huntington Library Quarterly*, 43 (1980), 213–46.

[30] Ibid. 216–17.

[31] Douglas Brooke-Davies, *Pope's Dunciad and the Queen of Night: A Study in Emotional Jacobitism* (Manchester: MUP, 1985), p. vii. Brooke-Davies, seeing Jacobite sentiment as the core of the *Dunciad*, links this to Pope's 'dedication to the maternal model', found in a feminized Catholicism associated with his mother and home (ibid.).

simply a positive figure. She is herself sometimes identified with Cybele and Magna Mater, whose cult was infamous for obscene and licentious rites, and whose priests were castrated—elements on which Pope draws throughout for his depiction of a set of lewd but ultimately impotent Dunces. Drawing on writers such as Martial and Juvenal, who had ridiculed the cult of Magna Mater,[32] Pope aligns himself with his literary fathers against the castrating power of the mother goddess.

In so doing, he joins a tradition that Marilyn Francus describes as the representation of the 'monstrous mother', including Errour in *The Faerie Queene*, Sin in *Paradise Lost*, and Criticism in Swift's *Battle of the Books*.[33] The monstrous mother's animal nature is stressed; she is enormously fecund, and a bad nurturer of her many offspring; and her maternal attributes are given allegorical significance. Francus finds an intensification of 'maternal misogyny' in the work of Swift and Pope, which she sees as an expression of their reaction against the reduction of literary culture to mass reproduction in the new marketplace.[34] Their fear of the potentially anarchic force of a prolific creative imagination associated with femininity means that they 'validate a male form of creation and production, based on reason and order, to supplant the female imaginative model'. The neoclassical aesthetic, with its valuation of clarity, balance, and order, is thus developed in contrast to a notion of chaotic creativity associated with the uncontrolled mother.[35]

It is against this background that English attempts to build up a national literary tradition should be seen. Dryden, as we have seen, defined this tradition as a legitimate succession of fathers and sons. In the *Dunciad*, the monstrous mother Dulness represents the threat to that succession. The point is not so much to ridicule and exclude women writers, though they come in for their share of mockery,

---

[32] Williams, *Pope's* Dunciad, 28.

[33] 'The Monstrous Mother: Reproductive Anxiety in Swift and Pope', *ELH* 61 (1994), 829–51.

[34] Ibid. 830; see also Ingrassia, 'Women Writing/Writing Women', 44.

[35] Francus, 'Monstrous Mother', 840; see also Castle, 'Lab'ring Bards', 196–7.

and, significantly, are seen as monstrous mothers themselves. Eliza Haywood, with 'Two babes of love close clinging to her waist', is a 'Juno of majestic size, | With cow-like udders, and with ox-like eyes' (ii. 158, 163–4; *Poems*, v. 303). The description of her has been linked to representations of the goddess Nox holding two boys, Sleep and Death.[36] Critical discussions as to whether the babes of love are an accusation that Haywood had illegitimate children, or, alternatively, refer to the 'bastard' literary productions mentioned in the footnote, serve to underline how the figure of the woman writer is used to create confusion between literal and literary progeny, thus contaminating the purity of literature as the production of the mind.[37] The main attack, though, is on writers who are sons of the mother, rather than the father. Book III opens with the vision of the Laureate Cibber, reclining on the lap of his mother:

> But in her Temples last recess inclos'd,
> On Dulness' lap th'Anointed head repos'd.
>
> (iii. 1–2; *Poems*, v. 320)

He is still there, completely inert, at the beginning of Book IV: 'Soft on her lap her Laureate son reclines' (iv. 20; *Poems*, v. 341) and there he stays, representing literature returned to inaction and infancy. On this view of literary tradition, inheritance from the mother means a return to the womb; only inheritance from the father results in new efforts and renewed generation.[38] Though there are versions of patrilineal inheritance in the poem—Cibber's inheritance of the Laureateship from Eusden, for example—the line has been corrupted. It has been rendered illegitimate by being traced back to a female source, just as Pope can ridicule his contemporaries as 'sons of sons

[36] Faulkner and Blair, 'Sources', 230.

[37] Ros Ballaster, *Seductive Forms: Women's Amatory Fiction from 1684 to 1740* (Oxford: Clarendon Press, 1992), 160–1.

[38] See Michael Seidel, *Satiric Inheritance, Rabelais to Sterne* (Princeton: PUP, 1979) for a reading of the *Dunciad* as a poem in which no succession is possible because father–son inheritance has been replaced by 'the mindless inheritance' (247), a return to the mother, ultimately seen as the return to 'undifferentiated creation' (249).

of sons of whores' (iv. 332; *Poems*, v. 376). Dulness rejoices in the
'line immortal' of city poets, succeeding each other as father to son:

> She saw, with joy, the line immortal run,
> Each sire imprest and glaring in his son:
> So watchful bruin forms, with plastic care,
> Each growing lump, and brings it to a Bear.
> She saw old Pryn in restless Daniel shine,
> And Eusden eke out Blackmore's endless line;
> She saw slow Philips creep like Tate's poor page,
> And all the mighty Mad in Dennis rage.
> In each she marks her Image full exprest,
> But chief in BAYS's monster-breeding breast . . .
>
> (i. 99–108; *Poems*, v. 276–7)

This parodic lineage has been produced not by spiritual transmission
from father to son but by analogy with a maternal and animal process,
the bear's legendary licking into shape of its infant cubs; the writers
bear the image not of their heavenly Father, but of poetic fathers who
are ultimately created in the image of their mother; and her truest son,
Bays/Cibber, is so like her that he seems a monstrous mother himself.

This monstrous and illegitimate literary tradition, derived from the
mother, is of course marked by its misuse and confusion of language.
One aspect of this is the overvaluation of mere words. Pope's
attack on scholastic traditions in Book IV links the brutality of
public schools to their narrow educational agenda: the schoolmaster,
wearing a garland of bloodstained birch from the beatings he has
given, declares, 'Since Man from beast by Words is known, | Words
are Man's province, Words we teach alone' (iv. 149–50; *Poems*,
v. 356). He uses words perversely to stifle instead of to direct the
schoolboy's developing mind:

> We ply the Memory, we load the brain,
> Bind rebel Wit, and double chain on chain,
> Confine the thought, to exercise the breath;
> And keep them in the pale of Words till death.
>
> (iv. 157–60; *Poems*, v. 357)

His is emphatically a male world, formed by taking young boys too soon away from their mothers (his garland is 'Dropping with Infant's blood, and Mother's tears'), but under the control of men who have remained too long attached to the mythic mother, Dulness (iv. 142; *Poems*, v. 355). The schooling he provides leads to the pedantry attacked throughout the poem and parodied in the notes. Richard Bentley, editor of classical writers and of Milton, is portrayed in Pope's Aristarchus, who boasts:

> 'Tis true, on Words is still our whole debate,
> Disputes of *Me* or *Te*, of *aut* or *at*,
> To sound or sink in *cano*, O or A,
> Or give up Cicero to C or K.
>
> (iv. 219–22; *Poems*, v. 364)

The suggestion here is that the pedant's overemphasis on words breaks them up, reduces them to letters and sounds, and deprives them of meaning. In this way the pedant is closely related to the bad poets mocked elsewhere in the poem, whose words have also been disconnected from proper meaning. In the writing produced under Dulness's influence, prose and verse get mixed up and 'random thoughts now meaning chance to find, | Now leave all memory of sense behind' (i. 275–6; *Poems*, v. 290.).

Throughout the poem, the reign of Dulness produces nonsense: the 'fluent nonsense' which 'trickles from [the] tongue' of Orator Henley (iii. 201), the 'new-born nonsense' encouraged into life by theatres and publishers in a travesty of the Creation described by Milton (i. 60; *Poems*, v. 274).[39] In Book I, the Mighty Mother watches delighted as the bad poets produce a muddle of linguistic figures and literary genres, and, as a result, in their representations, a hopelessly confused reality:

---

[39] The newborn nonsense is part of the creation emerging from Chaos under the influence of 'genial Jacob, or a warm Third day'. Jacob is the publisher Jacob Tonson: for a discussion of his 'geniality' and of the punning connection between playwrights' payments and the third day of creation as described in *Paradise Lost*, see Valerie Rumbold's note in Alexander Pope, *The Dunciad in Four Books* (Essex: Pearson Education Ltd., 1999), 106.

> There motley Images her fancy strike,
> Figures ill pair'd, and Similes unlike.
> She sees a Mob of Metaphors advance,
> Pleas'd with the madness of the mazy dance:
> How Tragedy and Comedy embrace;
> How Farce and Epic get a jumbled race;
> How Time himself stands still at her command,
> Realms shift their place, and Ocean turns to land.
>
> (i. 65–72; *Poems*, v. 275)

In Book II, Pope describes the dunces' competition to make noise, alluding to the noisy processions of Magna Mater's cults and juxtaposing the names of dunces with the sounds they make. The alliterative connections between 'Noise and Norton, Brangling and Breval, | Dennis and Dissonance' deprive the dunces of individuality and suggest a merging of differences (ii. 238–9; *Poems*, v. 307).[40]

As meanings are changed to their opposites, and distinctions confounded, language starts to fail in its task of differentiation. Scholars' and poets' perverse attachment to words leads eventually to the failure of words. In Book II, 'hush 'd with mugs of Mum', a drink whose name connects silence and a word for mother, the snoring audience shows difference reduced to sameness in sleep: 'all tun'd equal, send a gen'ral hum' (ii. 385–6); the clerks reading to the sleepers soon yawn and doze themselves, and the book ends on a vision of sleeping dunces (ii. 385–6, 390; *Poems*, v. 316). This foreshadows the apocalyptic failure of language in Book IV, where Dulness herself is silenced:

> More had she spoke, but yawn'd—All Nature nods:
> What Mortal can resist the Yawn of Gods?
>
> (iv. 605–6; *Poems*, v. 406)

At the end Chaos is restored, his 'uncreating word' acting as a reversal of the Word of God which originally began the Creation

---

[40] Maynard Mack, *Collected in Himself: Essays Critical, Biographical and Bibliographical on Pope and Some of His Contemporaries* (London: Associated University Presses, 1982), 42.

by announcing the distinction between light and darkness: differentiation ends 'And Universal Darkness buries All' (iv. 656;
Poems, v. 409).

That Pope ascribes the replacement of language by noisy nonsense
(and eventually by silence) to the dominion of a mother goddess links
the *Dunciad* to psychoanalytic theories of language that ascribe language acquisition to the child's emergence from a pre-Oedipal period
of mother–infant bonding characterized by prelinguistic babble. For
Julia Kristeva, symbolic language needs to be disrupted for there to
be creative use of language: semiotic discourse, 'asserting as it does
the writer's return to the pleasures of his preverbal identification with
his mother and his refusal to identify with his father and the logic
of paternal discourse', is to be valued.[41] In the *Dunciad*, it is to be
mocked and dreaded. Kristeva sees the semiotic as available only in
the gaps and ruptures of the symbolic, which the speaking or writing
subject must necessarily inhabit: there can be no real return to the pre-
Oedipal. Some theorists go further and describe a feminine language
that refuses definitions and limits. Helene Cixous's ideas of the writing and speech of 'woman' are related to the notion of closeness to the
preverbal bond with the mother: 'her writing can only keep going,
without ever inscribing or discerning contours . . . She alone dares and
wishes to know from within, where she, the outcast, has never ceased
to hear the resonance of fore-language. She lets the other language
speak—the language of 1,000 tongues which knows neither enclos-
ure nor death.'[42] The outpourings of Cixous's unbounded 'woman'
sound very like the uncontrolled noise encouraged by Pope's Goddess Dulness, except of course that they are valued positively instead
of negatively. Pope denounces disorder, Cixous embraces it, but both
trace it back to a powerful mother figure. Naomi Schor has warned
against feminist investment in notions of feminine language, which

[41] Ann Rosalind Jones, 'Writing the Body: Toward an Understanding of *l'écriture
féminine*', in Robin R. Warhol and Diane Price Herndl (eds.), *Feminisms: An Anthology
of Literary Theory and Criticism* (Basingstoke: Macmillan, 1997), 371.
[42] Helene Cixous, 'The Laugh of the Medusa', tr. Keith Cohen and Paula Cohen, in
Warhol and Herndl (eds.), *Feminisms*, 358.

she ascribes to a mistaken belief in 'the myth of a sort of prelapsarian preoedipus'.[43] Pope's Dulness is the misogynist reversal of that myth.

The savage strength of the *Dunciad*'s denunciation of the poets in thrall to the Mighty Mother prompts the question, does this reveal a repressed desire as well as a fear? Pope's attack on Grub Street has always been seen as full of paradox, revelling in the very indecencies it attacks: as Emrys Jones puts it, 'What Pope as a deliberate satirist rejects as dully lifeless his imagination communicates as obscurely energetic.'[44] One critic of the 1728 *Dunciad* complained that '*O[rdur]e* and *U[rin]e*, and such like Figures, are plentifully interspers'd with equal Variety and Absurdity', while one of Pope's victims responded to the 1743 version with the retort that 'Your *whole Piece* is only refining on the low Jests of *Porters* and *Fish-Women, as you live by the Water-side*'.[45] As Peter Stallybrass and Allon White argue, the 'mitigating fact of Pope's superior poetic ability could not save him from being immersed in the very process of grotesque debasement which he scorned in others'.[46] This contradiction is of a piece with what Brean Hammond calls the 'ideological impasse' of Pope's enormous success as 'a consummate professional writer whose major poems stand as an attack on professional and commercial writing'.[47] Is Pope's contradictory position also expressed as a longing for the maternal embrace the poem ostensibly scorns? Emrys Jones remarks that the pissing and tickling contests of Book II show Pope indulging 'feelings of an infantile nature',[48] and Dustin Griffin

[43] 'Eugenie Grandet: Mirrors and Melancholia', in S. N. Garner, Claire Kehane, and Madelon Sprengnether (eds.), *The (M)other Tongue: Essays in Feminist Psychoanalytic Interpretation*, (Ithaca, NY: Cornell University Press, 1985), 223.

[44] 'Pope and Dulness', in J. V. Guerinot (ed.), *Pope: A Collection of Critical Essays* (Englewood Cliffs, NJ: Prentice-Hall, 1972), 142–5.

[45] 'W.A.', letter in *Mist's Weekly Journal* (8 June 1728); John ['Orator'] Henley, *Why How now, Gossip Pope?* (1743), in John Barnard (ed.), *Pope: The Critical Heritage* (London: Routledge and Kegan Paul, 1973), 212, 344.

[46] 'The Grotesque Body and the Smithfield Muse', in Brean Hammond (ed.), *Pope* (London: Longman, 1996), 218.

[47] Brean Hammond, *Professional Imaginative Writing in England, 1670–1740: 'Hackney for Bread'* (Oxford: Clarendon Press, 1997), 294.

[48] Jones, 'Pope and Dulness', 142.

develops this view, suggesting that Pope's personal life of constant pain and illness, characterized by a trembling sensitivity and irritability frequently expressed in his poetry, might well have made him long to surrender to the unconsciousness promised by Dulness. 'So aware of an imperfect body, so conscious of his defects as a sexual being, and so attached well into maturity to his mother—Pope may have longed, or at least imagined longing, to be enveloped by a figure both maternal and sexual, to be swallowed at last, "covered" or "buried" by universal dulness/darkness.'[49]

If this is so, the maternal misogyny of the *Dunciad* carries, underneath the satire, traces of its opposite. That opposite can be found consciously articulated in some of Pope's correspondence, where his deep devotion to his mother, Edith Pope, is evident.[50] Her death, at the age of 91, he described as 'indeed a Grief to mee which I cannot express, and which I should hate my own Heart if it did not feel, & yet wish no Friend I have ever should feel'.[51] A letter written to Swift five years before this, reflects on the effect his close relationship with his mother has had on him:

> My greatest [Tye], both by duty, gratitude, and humanity, Time is shaking every moment, and it now hangs but by a thread! I am many years the older, for living so much with one so old; much the more helpless, for having been so long help'd and tended by her; much the more considerate and tender, for a daily commerce with one who requir'd me justly to be both to her; and consequently the more melancholy and thoughtful; and the less fit for others, who want only in a companion or a friend, to be amused or entertained.[52]

It has many times been noted that Pope's small stature, deformity, and constant weakness made it impossible for him to embody the

---

[49] Dustin H. Griffin, *Alexander Pope: The Poet in the Poems* (Princeton: PUP, 1978), 236.

[50] For Pope's relationship with his mother and with other women see Valerie Rumbold, *Women's Place in Pope's World* (Cambridge: CUP, 1989).

[51] To William Fortescue, 7 June 1733; *Correspondence of Alexander Pope*, ed. George Sherburn (Oxford: Clarendon Press, 1956), iii. 374.

[52] To Swift, 23 Mar. 1727/8; ibid. ii. 480.

ideals of masculinity pertaining in his world and ours. In this letter, he makes clear how his relationship with his mother enabled him to accept an identity culturally coded feminine: to be helpless, considerate, tender, to live a life of sad thought somewhat removed from the social world. The Alexander Pope created in this passage has not undergone what Nancy Chodorow describes as the problematic journey into male gender identity: problematic because it involves a rupture with the 'early, nonverbal, unconscious, almost somatic sense of primary oneness with the mother, and underlying sense of femaleness that continually, usually unnoticeably, but sometimes insistently, challenges and undermines the sense of maleness'. He has not, like other men, responded to the difficulties of developing adequate masculinity by denying the feelings experienced as feminine: 'feelings of dependence, relational needs, emotions generally'.[53]

This feminine Pope is obviously far removed from the manly satirist constructed in Pope's *Epistles,* or the malicious aggressor many readers found in the *Dunciad.* Pope's identities included a personal, tender, family self, the loving son of a good mother, and a more masculine self belonging to the wider 'family' of the English poetic tradition, the son of fathers. This pattern is complicated by the fact that Pope was also very warmly attached to his own father, and indeed has more to say about him in his poetry than about his mother, an emphasis which, as Valerie Rumbold shows, underlines the male-centredness of the traditions on which he draws.[54] The private or family self and affections can be publicly expressed in the poetry, but its conventions favour the father–son tie. It was elsewhere that he celebrated maternal connections. His love for his mother is found in his ambiguously private–public letters—supposedly private, and belonging to a genre culturally coded feminine, but

[53] Nancy Chodorow, 'Gender, Relation and Difference in Psychoanalytic Perspective', in Hester Eisenstein and Alice Jardine (eds.), *The Future of Difference* (New Brunswick, NJ: Rutgers University Press, 1985), 13. For a full exposition of Chodorow's theories see her *The Reproduction of Mothering: Psychoanalysis and the Sociology of Gender* (Berkeley and Los Angeles: University of California Press, 1978).
[54] Rumbold, *Woman's Place,* 17–18.

whose publication Pope secretly arranged. Here, also, he recorded his lasting affection for his nurse, Mary Beach: when she died in 1725 he wrote to Lord Oxford that she had 'lived in constant attendance & care of me, ever since I was an Infant at her Breast', and applied to her a line from his own translation of Homer's *Odyssey*, calling a nurse 'The tender Second to a Mother's cares'.[55] He also made public tribute to her, inscribing a plaque to her at Twickenham from 'Alex. Pope, whom she nursed in his infancy and constantly attended for thirty-eight years'. The satirist who expressed his scorn of Cibber by depicting him as an overgrown infant babied by a monstrous nursing mother had himself spent much of his adult life literally dependent on the care of his nurse; and he had taken the risk of making public acknowledgement of that care. The irony was not lost on his detractors. In November 1744 the *Gentleman's Magazine* published, alongside epitaphs on Pope himself, a verse on Mary Beach, parodying his own commemoration of her and ascribing his 'genius' to her nursing:

> Here lies *Mary Beech*, exempt from all care,
> Who nurs'd *Alex. Pope* full thirty eight year:
> No wonder his genius was so stout and so strong,
> When he lugg'd, and he tugg'd at her bubby so long.[56]

Pope's unusually early and single-minded dedication to a poetic vocation suggests that the literary life compensated for his inability to take other masculine roles within his society. The split from the

---

[55] *Correspondence*, ii. 336.

[56] *Gentleman's Magazine*, 14 (Nov. 1744), 611. The further irony suggested by Maynard Mack (*Alexander Pope: A Life* (New Haven: Yale University Press, 1985), 153), that Pope's crippling tuberculosis of the bone was (unknown to Pope and his contemporaries), contracted from Mary Beach's breast milk, is not warranted: the disease is transmitted through cows' milk. The fullest discussion of Pope's disease is found in Marjorie Nicolson and G. S. Rousseau, *This Long Disease, My Life: Alexander Pope and the Sciences* (Princeton: PUP, 1968), 7–86. For the association between bovine infection and tuberculosis of the bone see *Encyclopedia Britannica*, 'Tuberculosis'. For a discussion of bovine tuberculosis see F. B. Smith, *The Retreat of Tuberculosis 1850–1950* (London: Croom Helm, 1988), 175–94. I am grateful to George Rousseau for discussing this point with me.

mother that was not fully made in his personal life was enacted in the poetry; and in the *Dunciad,* the loving son of a mother created his place in satiric tradition by attacking a mythical Mighty Mother and her sons. However, the likely psychological reasons for the strong split between Pope's personal feeling for his mother and his poetic representation of motherhood do not mean that the *Dunciad's* maternal misogyny should simply be ascribed to an individual pathology. The cultural resonance of its misogynist imagery comes, as we have seen, from widespread myths of the powerful mother, themselves arising from feelings that Dorothy Dinnerstein argues are universal to cultures in which mothers are responsible for infant care: an original association of power with the female, and a fear of female power that arises from our 'terror of sinking back wholly into the helplessness of infancy'.[57]

However widespread such feelings are, historical forces change the way and the degree to which they are expressed at different times. The monstrous mother of the *Dunciad* has been linked to the reaction, from the position of neoclassical aesthetics, against a feminized mass literary culture. Putting together Dryden's articulation of a patrilineal literary tradition, discussed in the previous chapter, and Pope's insertion of himself into that tradition through joining his literary fathers and rejecting the mythic mother, we can begin to discern the way in which allegiance to fathers and repudiation of motherly influence were driving forces in the Augustan development of a sense of national literary tradition. The fathers provided the elite inheritance; the mythic mother was blamed for the development of a mass culture that seemed to threaten that inheritance.

Nature's Darlings

Not all eighteenth-century representations of the powerful mother figure made her monstrous. Shortly after the publication of the

[57] Dorothy Dinnerstein, *The Rocking of the Cradle, and the Ruling of the World* (London: Souvenir Press, 1978), 161. (1st pub. 1976 as *The Mermaid and the Minotaur*).

Dunciad, celebratory images of the maternal Muse appeared in the work of Gray, Collins, Akenside, and Joseph Warton. John E. Sitter links their 'positive mother-figures' to a changed conception of poetry that unequivocally delights in fancy and the 'wild creation' decried by Pope. The mid-century lyric poets represented the poet as an isolated, privileged figure, protected by a maternal figure to whom he is son and lover.[58] One example of this revaluation of the mother is found in Gray's *The Progress of Poesy* (1757). Here is the positive view of poetic progress of which Dulness's procession in the *Dunciad* offers a parody. Poesy moves from Greece, to Rome, and eventually to Britain. As in Dryden and Pope, the national literary tradition is seen as inherited between men: the form, a Pindaric ode, announces Gray's allegiance to an ancient Greek lyricist, while the last three stanzas delineate an English succession running through Shakespeare, Milton, and Dryden to the speaker himself, the 'daring spirit' who would attempt the lyre after these predecessors. This patrilineal succession, like Pope's line of dunces, comes under the protective power of a maternal figure, but her influence here is positively valued. The 'heavenly Muse' and 'goddess' is a mother figure who 'deigns to hear the savage youth' of primitive nations sing their 'wildly sweet songs'.[59] The nine muses, being dedicated to liberty, leave Greece and then Rome when these nations become tyrannies, and move to freedom-loving Albion (England). Addressing Albion, the poet continues:

> Far from the sun and summer-gale,
> In thy green lap was Nature's darling laid,
> What time, where lucid Avon strayed,
> To him the mighty Mother did unveil
> Her awful face: the dauntless child
> Stretched forth his little arms and smiled.
>
> (*Poems*, 172)

[58] John E. Sitter, 'Mother, Memory, Muse and Poetry after Pope', *ELH* 44 (1977), 312–36.

[59] *The Poems of Gray, Collins and Goldsmith*, ed. Roger Lonsdale (London: Longman, 1969), 176, 167, 170, 169.

In these lines, Shakespeare, who for Dryden is one of the great poetic fathers, is represented as the little child of three mothers: the land herself, Albion, in whose lap he lies rather as Pope's Cibber lies in the lap of Dulness; Nature, whose darling he is; and the Muse, who is here the 'mighty Mother'. Gilbert Wakefield, commenting on these lines in 1786, noted that 'Wicked memory brings into mind the *Queen* of the *Dunces*'.[60] Given this celebration of the poet as mother's son, the final stanza, with its depiction of the poet as a child gazing at forms lit up for him by the Muse, develops an alternative view of poetic inheritance that complicates its traditional patrilineal narrative:

> Oh! lyre divine, what daring spirit
> Wakes thee now? Though he inherit
> Nor the pride nor ample pinion,
> That the Theban Eagle bear
> Sailing with supreme dominion
> Through the azure deep of air:
> Yet oft before his infant eyes would run
> Such forms as glitter in the Muse's ray
> With orient hues, unborrowed of the sun.
>
> (*Poems*, 176–7)

The poet expresses anxiety that he may not inherit the wings of Pindar, whom he imitates; but his comparison of himself to a passive child with visions running before his eyes links him to Shakespeare. Both are the privileged sons of a mighty mother who shows them sights withheld from other men.

The celebratory image of the poet as son of a mythic mother is repeated in the Romantic period. In Shelley's *Adonais,* the heavenly Muse Urania is an entirely positive 'mighty Mother', mourning for the loss of her poet son:

> Where wert thou, mighty Mother, when he lay,
> When thy Son lay, pierced by the shaft which flies

---

[60] Quoted in Sitter, 'Mother, Memory', 313.

> In darkness? where was lorn Urania
> When Adonais died?[61]

Shelley's use of the pastoral elegy for the dead poet looks back to
Milton's *Lycidas* and beyond to the elegies of Bion on the death of
Adonis, and of Moschus on the death of Bion, fragments of which
he translated. Venus, the lover of Adonis who begs the dying youth
to stay awhile, 'That I may kiss thee now for the last time— | But
for as long as one short kiss may live', is transformed to Urania,
mother goddess whose presence almost revives Adonais and who also
begs him, 'Kiss me, so long but as a kiss may live' (*Poetical Works*,
722, 437). *Adonais* depicts the mourning of all nature for the dead
poet just as Moschus, in Shelley's translation, has woods, waves,
streams, and flowers lament because 'Bion the [sweetest singer] is no
more'. The glance back to Moschus salutes a poet who had elegized
a previous poet, while the transformation of Venus to Urania makes
the mother goddess central to the elegy. As in Gray's *Progress of Poesy*,
then, the poem links together a patrilineal tradition of poetry under
the overall protection of a maternal figure. The pattern is repeated
for the modern poetic line: Urania's mourning for Adonais/Keats is
a renewal of her earlier lament for Milton, who is 'the third among
the sons of light' (the first two being Homer and Shakespeare) and
also 'the Sire of an immortal strain'. Adonais/Keats, as Urania's
'youngest, dearest one', the 'nursling of thy widowhood', is both
mother's son and the last in a line of poetic fathers and sons. Shelley
himself, usually understood to figure in the poem as the 'frail Form'
who joins the mourners and faces Urania's question 'Who art thou?',
seeks in the writing of *Adonais* to join the line of her sons (*Poetical
Works*, 722, 432, 433, 439).

Barbara Gelpi links Shelley's interest in the mother goddess to
his early closeness to his own mother, Elizabeth Shelley, and sees
that relationship in turn as affected by the image of the perfect
mother created in educational literature and hymns for children.

---

[61] *Adonais*, in Shelley, *Poetical Works*, ed. Thomas Hutchinson, corr. G. M. Matthews
(London: OUP, 1970), 432.

This burgeoning tradition, she suggests, made a 'close association . . . between providential and maternal care' and at times elevated the maternal to the divine. For Shelley, his mother 'was the avatar of the goddess who emanated from the prolific literature on motherhood throughout his formative years'.[62] His work exemplifies the deepening veneration both for nature and the maternal developing in the early nineteenth century, which placed new cultural emphasis on the long-standing symbolic equation of the two. Nature is Mother and is divine, and is the source of the poet's genius. This set of equivalencies could act, as numerous critics have pointed out, to ground male poetic identity on a takeover or expulsion of the maternal. Alan Richardson suggests that 'in moving from an "Age of Reason" to an "Age of Feeling", male writers drew on memories and fantasies of identification with the mother in order to colonize the conventionally feminine domain of sensibility'.[63]

The Romantic cult of the mother, then, carried for women some of the same dangers as the maternal monster. Whether the mythic mother is a teeming monster or a divine teacher, she makes things awkward for the historical woman. The mother goddess may preside over a line of poetic sons, but can women join that line as mothers and daughters? The good mother may write, her authority bolstered by a strong cultural investment in the idea of mother as teacher, but can the historical woman be recognized as a maternal source? These questions come into focus when we consider examples of women who wrote and whose own sons or daughters wrote.

Mother and Son: Frances and Richard Brinsley Sheridan

Frances Sheridan (1724–66) and her son Richard Brinsley Sheridan (1751–1816) were unique in their time as a mother–son pair who

---

[62] Barbara Gelpi, *Shelley's Goddess: Maternity, Language, Subjectivity* (New York: OUP, 1992), 72, 80.

[63] Alan Richardson, 'Romanticism and the Colonization of the Feminine', in Anne Mellor (ed.), *Romanticism and Feminism* (Bloomington, Ind.: Indiana University Press, 1988), 13.

both achieved literary fame; and that he used elements of her work in his own raises the question of maternal literary inheritance. There was a certain amount of embarrassment for Richard Brinsley in his mother's literary legacy, but this was contained by his being able to respond to her not at all as the 'Mighty Mother' of myth, but as the family woman whose writing identity was bound up in the family enterprise to which it contributed.

The Sheridans were a literary family. Frances Sheridan was the first to gain celebrity, for her novel *Memoirs of Miss Sidney Bidulph* (1761) and her first comedy *The Discovery* (1763). Her husband, Thomas Sheridan, an actor and theatre manager, also had literary ambitions of a different sort: he wrote and delivered lectures on elocution, wrote an English grammar, a grammar in English and French, and over many years a dictionary that was finally published in the 1780s. Their playwright son was their most famous child, but their daughter Alicia also wrote, and turned her mother's novel *Eugenia and Adelaide* into a comic drama for the Dublin stage.[64] Her grandson, Joseph Sheridan Le Fanu, was to become a best-selling mystery writer in the Victorian period. Thomas and Frances's second daughter, Betsy, kept a journal and wrote a novel; and her daughter, Alicia Le Fanu, wrote novels and a biography, *Memoirs of the Life and Writings of Mrs Frances Sheridan* (1824), from which much of what is known of Frances's life derives. This family tradition of literary work, or what Thomas Moore called 'the sort of *gavel-kind* of genius allotted to the whole race of Sheridan', complicates the question of the mother–son literary legacy.[65] For one thing, there are other family lines that might be explored. Richard Brinsley's use of his mother's work is also connected to his father's linguistic

---

[64] Alicia Le Fanu, *Memoirs of the Life and Writings of Mrs. Frances Sheridan* (London: G. and W. B. Whittaker, 1824), 8.

[65] Thomas Moore, *Memoirs of the Life of the Right Honourable Richard Brinsley Sheridan* (London: Longman, Hurst, Rees, Orme, Brown, and Green, 1825), 493. *Gavelkind* is a legal term referring to the equal distribution of property between sons: Moore, using this phrase to refer to the talents of Alicia Le Fanu, is giving an egalitarian twist to the literary inheritance metaphor, and silently assuming the inclusion of inheriting daughters.

interests, and Frances clearly left a literary legacy to daughters and granddaughter. For another, the biographies of mother and son have both been strongly marked by family legend, which itself is embedded in the glorification of maternal influence typical of the early nineteenth century.

The literary relationship between Frances and Richard Brinsley Sheridan, then, needs to be seen in the context of family legend as well as drama criticism. While Richard Brinsley's editors and critics have been meticulous in detailing the son's borrowings from his mother, these have usually been understood as merely material acquisitions, in contrast to the more spiritual legacy he gains from male dramatists, so that the mother's work is sidelined from the English dramatic line. Family legend, as it informs Le Fanu's 1824 *Memoirs* of her grandmother, Thomas Moore's 1825 *Memoirs of the Right Honourable Richard Brinsley Sheridan*, and the biographical tradition derived from these, concerns itself less with the matter of literary borrowing and more with the question of Frances Sheridan's maternal character and influence. Because of their desire to counteract charges that the younger Sheridan was a derivative writer, family sources were sometimes grudging in acknowledging the son's use of his mother's works, but, far more than critics and editors, they were generally inclined to see the mother as an important source of the son's talent. They also, as we will see, idealized her in ways that have obscured one aspect of her literary relationship to her son, the propensity they shared to challenge the conventions of theatrical acceptability.

Frances Sheridan's literary career was a varied one, driven always by the need to boost the erratic family income. Thomas Sheridan's career as actor and manager had very mixed success, and he left Smock Alley after disastrous riots.[66] His plans for a school came to nothing; his writing and lecturing were more fruitful but not always lucrative. The Sheridans were constantly in debt, and moved

---

[66] For a discussion of his Dublin career see Esther K. Sheldon, *Thomas Sheridan of Smock Alley* (Princeton: PUP, 1967).

between Dublin, London, and France in search of livelihood. When Frances was writing *Sidney Bidulph*, she hid the manuscript from her husband, not from any shame attached to it but because she did not want to raise his hopes of profit too soon.[67] The novel explores the predicament of a heroine who follows her mother's advice to reject the man she loves because he has seduced and abandoned another woman. Married to Mr Arnold instead, she puts up with a difficult life, and in widowhood seems to have the chance of reunion with her first love, but her hopes are dashed in a melodramatic denouement. Samuel Johnson admired the novel and told Sheridan, 'I know not, Madam, that you have a right, upon moral principles, to make your readers suffer so much'.[68] It was dedicated to Samuel Richardson, and praised in the reviews as a worthy successor to his work.[69] *The Discovery* also gave a real boost to the family fortunes. With its intricate plot concerning young lovers and blocking parents, its comic picture of the quarrelling Sir Harry and Lady Flutter, and its chastening of the tyrannical Lord Medway, it conformed to popular demand for comedy with clear morality and a harmonious ending. With Garrick provoking laughter in the part of Sir Anthony Branville, and Thomas Sheridan playing Lord Medway, it had a very good run of seventeen nights and was revived several times later in the century. Her second comedy, *The Dupe* (1763), was much less successful, and her third, *A Journey to Bath*, was rejected by Garrick. It was never performed, and not published in her lifetime. Her other late ventures were more successful, though she did not live to witness it: the second part of *Sidney Bidulph* and the oriental tale *Nourjahad* were published after her death from seizures at the age of 42.

Richard Brinsley Sheridan, who was 15 when his mother died, began writing a few years afterwards. By 1774, following a scandalous elopement and two duels, he was married to Elizabeth Linley, and

---

[67] Le Fanu, *Memoirs*, 109.

[68] James Boswell, *Life of Johnson*, ed. R. W. Chapman, corr. J. D. Fleeman (Oxford: OUP, 1970), 276.

[69] *Critical Review*, 11 (1761), 186.

(having refused to allow her to continue with what would have been a highly profitable career as a public singer) in desperate need of money. He wrote *The Rivals* in the space of two months at the request of the Covent Garden manager, and expected to get at least £600 by it.[70] The comedy, with its tyrannical father and its references to elopements and duels, contains allusions to his own recent experiences, turned into farce; the publicity surrounding his life added to the interest roused by the play. The basic pattern of *The Rivals*, with two pairs of young lovers and the conflict between the generations, follows that of many other comedies of the period, its main plot innovation being eligible Captain Absolute's disguise as poor Ensign Beverley in order to win Lydia Languish, who is determined to elope with a forbidden lover. Sheridan was drawing on a common stock of plots and character types, and George Colman's *Polly Honeycombe* (1760), which had recently been revived, is one likely direct source for the heroine given romantic notions by her reading. The young dramatist was also drawing in various ways on the work of his mother.

Some of this took the form of echoes from her well-known work. His Faulkland, the over-refined and suspicious lover of Julia, has the same name as Orlando Faulkland, the rash object of the heroine's unfortunate love in *Memoirs of Miss Sidney Bidulph*. The scene where Faulkland tests Julia's love by pretending that he has to flee the country after a duel recalls one in *Sidney Bidulph* where Orlando Faulkland really does have to flee the country, and tries to persuade Sidney to go with him. The plots are very different. In *Sidney Bidulph* the romantic complications end tragically, with Sidney marrying Faulkland only to discover that the unfaithful first wife he believed he had killed has survived. In *The Rivals* there are no obstacles to the lovers' union beyond Faulkland's temper, and their differences are comically resolved. Still, there is a similarity in the high-flown rhetoric both sets of lovers use, and in both authors'

[70] To Thomas Linley the Elder, 17 Nov. 1774; *The Letters of Richard Brinsley Sheridan*, ed. Cecil Price (Oxford: Clarendon Press, 1966), i. 85.

criticism of their Faulklands for self-dramatization and lack of trust. Frances Sheridan was still a celebrated literary name in the 1770s. One old gentleman in Bath had befriended Richard Brinsley as the son of Frances Sheridan, while Hannah More was inclined to favour his first play because, she reported, 'I love him for the sake of his amiable and ingenious mother'.[71] In later years Richard Brinsley Sheridan, apparently embarrassed to be thought to be in his mother's literary debt, claimed not to have read *Memoirs of Miss Sidney Bidulph*, but in 1775 he could hardly have expected his audience to miss his allusion to her novel.

His more substantial borrowing, though, was from her unpublished work. The manuscript of *A Journey to Bath*—three acts only are extant—had been passed on to him by his father, a literal inheritance from his mother. His sister Alicia, the source for this information, rather played down its significance, writing to her friend Lady Morgan that 'My mother's sketch of a comedy, unfinished, was put into my brother Richard's hands by my father at Bath, when we were resident there; but my father never hinted that he had made any use of it in "The Rivals". Of my own knowledge I can say nothing, for I never read it.'[72] However, a number of similarities between the two plays can be found. Both comedies are set in Bath, though the plots are very different. *A Journey to Bath* concerns the scheme thought up between Lord Stewkly and Lady Filmot, evidently one-time lovers, to gain Edward as her husband, and Lucy as his wife. The similarities are in some characters and phrases. Frances Sheridan's Sir Jeremy boasts of 'a line of ancestry, that wou'd convince you we are not a people of yesterday', and admits that 'the land and the mansion house has slipp'd thro' our fingers boy; but thank heaven the family pictures are still extant', while her son's Sir Lucius O'Trigger exclaims, 'I could shew you a range of ancestry, in the O'Trigger line, that would furnish the

[71] Le Fanu, *Memoirs*, 297–8; *The Dramatic Works of Richard Brinsley Sheridan*, ed. Cecil Price (Oxford: Clarendon Press, 1973), i. 51.

[72] W. Fraser Rae, prefatory note to *Sheridan's Plays ... and ... A Journey to Bath* (London: David Nutt, 1902), p. xxxx.

new room; every one of whom has killed his man!—For though the mansion-house and dirty acres have slipt through my fingers, I thank Heav'n our honour and the family-pictures, are as fresh as ever.'[73]

The Rivals' most important use of *A Journey to Bath* is found in the creation of Mrs Malaprop, who became so famous that she gave her name to the misuse of words. Her character and some of her errors are taken from Frances Sheridan's Mrs Tryfort. Both are that comic stock figure, the older woman acting as guardian to a desirable young girl—in Mrs Tryfort's case, her daughter, in Mrs Malaprop's, her niece. Both are under the impression that they are being courted by a man (Sir Lucius O'Trigger in *The Rivals*, Lord Stewkly in *A Journey to Bath*) who is in fact pursuing the younger woman. Both refer to 'contagious countries', say 'progeny' instead of 'prodigy', and get mixed up about female punctilio.[74] In *A Journey to Bath* the emphasis is on Mrs Tryfort's lack of gentility, and her linguistic errors indicate how far she is out of her social depth, while Mrs Malaprop is more of a satire on intellectual pretension. Mrs Tryfort commits many of her linguistic blunders in the context of her comic obsession with the obviously inaccessible Lord Stewkly. 'Oh in everything ma'am he is a progeny!' she exclaims, her mistake neatly indicating her problem: she is of the wrong generation. Mrs Malaprop is more typically caught in situations where she tries valiantly to defend female education against the misogynist Sir Anthony Absolute. Girls should have some education, she insists, though 'I would not have my daughter be a progeny of learning'.[75] The Larpent manuscript of *The Rivals*, which records the version first played on the stage and instantly withdrawn for alterations, reveals that in revision, Sheridan cut several more borrowings from *A Journey to Bath*, including

[73] *The Rivals*, 3. 4, in Sheridan, *Dramatic Works*, i. 116. The idea of attaching great importance to the family pictures is also used in a famous scene in *The School for Scandal*. The name Surface in the later play may also be taken from *A Journey to Bath*, in which Mrs Surface keeps a lodging house.

[74] *A Journey to Bath*, 3. 3, 2. 2, 3. 13, in *The Plays of Frances Sheridan*, ed. Robert Hogan and Jerry C. Beasley (London: Associated University Presses, 1985), 187, 175, 197; *The Rivals*, 1. 2, 3. 2, *Dramatic Works*, i. 86, 101.

[75] *A Journey to Bath*, 2. 2, *Plays*, 175; *The Rivals*, 1. 2, *Dramatic Works*, i. 86.

Mrs Malaprop's declaration that she would not want Lydia to be 'so inarticulate in her ideas as you mention', an echo of Mrs Tryfort's scolding her daughter with, 'I declare you are so inarticulate in your notions, that I believe you are a changeling'.[76] The interest in language and its misuse demonstrated by both playwrights was a Sheridan family tradition. Thomas Sheridan was working on various linguistic projects, including his dictionary, while Frances Sheridan was writing her comedy, and he was still working on the dictionary when *The Rivals* was written. Family jokes may have contributed to the creation of both.[77] Fintan O'Toole argues that Mrs Malaprop, who, more than Mrs Tryfort, shows a pedantic obsession with the language she mishandles, contains a critique of the writer's estranged father: she is 'both a borrowing from his mother and a satire on his father's obsessions'.[78]

The Sheridans were also drawing on established traditions in their creation of characters with language difficulties. Shakespeare's Dogberry provided one prototype. More recently, novels by Henry Fielding (Mrs Slipslop in *Joseph Andrews*) and Tobias Smollett (Tabitha Bramble in *Humphry Clinker*) had mocked the woman who mixes up her words. In a more general sense, women with intellectual pretensions were a butt of mockery in many plays, and we saw in the previous chapter how both Congreve and Burney used them as part of the strategy for establishing their own identity as playwrights. It is ironic that Richard Brinsley Sheridan's greatest debt to his mother's skill with words was in the creation of a character who comically undermines the authority of the older woman by her linguistic mishaps.

One of Mrs Tryfort's mistakes, as we have seen, is to imply that Lord Stewkly is her son, inadvertently linking this status to his poetic skill. 'Oh in everything ma'am he is a progeny! A perfect progeny,

---

[76] *The Rivals: A Comedy*, ed. from the Larpent MS by Richard Little Purdy (Oxford: Clarendon Press, 1935), p. xxxiii; *A Journey to Bath*, 3. 2, *Plays*, 186.

[77] James Morwood, *The Life and Works of Richard Brinsley Sheridan* (Edinburgh: Scottish Academic Press, 1985), 36.

[78] Fintan O'Toole, *A Traitor's Kiss: The Life of Richard Brinsley Sheridan* (London: Granta Books, 1997), 87.

lady Filmot! In the first place he is a most prodigious wit, and then he speaks all the languages in the world, and is so full of compliments, and such a charming poet!'[79] Richard Brinsley Sheridan borrowed the joke (applying it to a daughter), but there is evidence that he felt some awkwardness attached to a literary debt to his mother that made his own poetic identity that of her progeny. This is suggested by his cuts in the revision of *The Rivals*, and by his later claim not to have read *Sidney Bidulph*. It is indicated too in the preface to the first publication of *The Rivals*, where he goes to great lengths to fend off notions of plagiarism. Readily conceding that the play as first performed was full of errors, he attributed these to his ignorance of the theatre and his determination not to copy others:

> Many other errors there were, which might in part have arisen from my being by no means conversant with plays in general, either in reading or at the theatre.—Yet I own that, in one respect, I did not regret my ignorance: for as my first wish in attempting a Play, was to avoid every appearance of plagiary, I thought I should stand a better chance of effecting this from being in a walk which I had not frequented, and where consequently the progress of invention was less likely to be interrupted by starts of recollection: for on subjects on which the mind has been much informed, invention is slow of exerting itself.—Faded ideas float in the fancy like half-forgotten dreams; and the imagination in its fullest enjoyments becomes suspicious of its offspring, and doubts whether it has created or adopted.[80]

This claim—an odd one from the child of an actor-manager and a playwright—has been attributed to a dislike of his father's profession originating in schoolboy taunting of the 'poor player's son'.[81] However, other factors are at work here, including a clear anxiety about originality. Theatrical critics and historians of the time liked

---

[79] *A Journey to Bath*, 2. 2, *Plays*, 175.

[80] Sheridan, *Dramatic Works*, i. 70.

[81] *The School for Scandal and Other Plays*, ed. Michael Cordner (Oxford: OUP, 1998), 342.

to trace patterns of influence in incident, character, and language, and while it was generally accepted that all playwrights drew on a common stock, there was a growing demand for novelty, and close or extensive borrowing was criticized. Richard Brinsley Sheridan's evocation of the floating, faded ideas he denies having suggests that he protests too much, and that he is worried about whether he has fathered a literary offspring, or only adopted one.

The similarities between *A Journey to Bath* and *The Rivals* are not, in fact, so extensive as to make anyone think he had merely adopted from his mother; but some biographers and editors show a defensiveness on this point which suggests that any debt to the mother is felt as unsettling. Moore, while praising Frances Sheridan's 'considerable talents', attributed the idea that her son had used her work to 'some of those sagacious persons, who love to look for flaws in the titles of fame'.[82] W. Fraser Rae complained of 'ill-informed and ill-intentioned' people who claimed that the son's first play could not have been written without his mother's (*Sheridan's Plays*, p. xxxx). Here, the question of independence from the mother becomes a test for literary authority. If he is seen to depend too much on matter derived from her, his other literary borrowings from a host of earlier dramatists are in danger of becoming tainted. They, too, could be seen as merely the taking of matter, rather than the creative transformation of tradition that defines the son's proper relation to literary fathers. Richard Brinsley Sheridan did suffer some accusations of plagiarism, and these were linked to the idea of his being indebted to women in particular. Most bizarre was the story, circulated after his death, that his most celebrated comedy, *A School for Scandal*, had been stolen in its entirety from a merchant's daughter in Thames Street. She wrote the play, gave him the manuscript, went to Bristol Hot-Wells, and died.[83] The anecdote associates the play with the commercial classes and with

---

[82] Moore, *Memoirs*, 2.

[83] The story, recorded in John Watkins's *Memoirs* of Richard Brinsley Sheridan, was indignantly denied by Alicia Le Fanu; see *Memoirs of Mrs Frances Sheridan*, 404–5.

the feminine; and the merchant's daughter, taking a (fatal) trip to Bristol instead of Bath, calls up the memory of the playwright's dead mother and her manuscript legacy.

To take from the mother, then, may threaten a man's right to authorship. No wonder that many of Richard Brinsley's champions responded to the danger by minimizing his inheritance from Frances, one even going so far as to suggest, with no evidence beyond wishful thinking, that the incomplete manuscript of *A Journey to Bath* represents the son's revision of a lost, and no doubt utterly inferior, work by his mother; that he was originally responsible for the lines which he later echoed in the creation of Mrs Malaprop; and that he was, therefore, 'his own plagiary'.[84] There could hardly be a clearer instance of the fantasy that the son can give birth to himself.

However, if inheritance from the mother calls up exaggerated fears, accusations, and denials, these can be submerged under a calm surface: the acceptance of her literary work as naturally belonging to her male relatives. Frances Sheridan's writing was undertaken to earn money for the family, and after her death her unfinished materials were family property, passed on in the male line and used as needed. For all practical purposes, her son assumed her words were his to use. Others have shared that assumption. One biographer, defending him from charges of plagiarism, remarks, 'the only thefts that can really be brought home to him are from his mother, and thus they assume the character of possessions acquired by inheritance rather than by literary loot'.[85] In literary history, Richard Brinsley Sheridan has been treated as the heir of Wycherley and Congreve. His mother's words have been understood, in line with familiar beliefs, as a material rather than a spiritual inheritance.

Within the Sheridan family tradition, transmission from mother to son was differently conceived. Richard Brinsley's elder sister told the dramatist that he inherited his mother's talents, while many years later his great-grandson wrote that '[p]erhaps . . . it was from his

---

[84] R. C. Rhodes, cited in Sheridan, *Dramatic Works*, i. 37–8.
[85] Lloyd C. Sanders, *Life of Richard Brinsley Sheridan* (London: Walter Scott, n.d.), 30.

mother that Sheridan inherited the subtle attribute which sublimates talent into genius, for the authoress who wrote "Sidney Bidulph" . . . as well as "The Discovery" . . . must have had something of the divine essence.'[86] Genius, so rarely attributed to women in works of literary history and criticism, was easily allowed to Frances Sheridan by her family. In the two important biographies, of mother and son respectively, which appeared close together in 1824 and 1825, close family sources were used to create a picture of Frances Sheridan's literary talent and maternal influence that served a number of purposes.

Le Fanu's biography of her grandmother aims to promote women's literary reputation through the construction of the virtuous female author. Le Fanu got her information from her mother and aunt, and her work reflects family legend, with anecdotes chosen and coloured by the desire to set the writer's career firmly and laudably in a family context. The life features a tyrannical father, who did not even want his daughter to be literate, and supportive brothers, who taught the young Frances Chamberlaine in secret. Her meeting with Thomas Sheridan, her future husband, is connected with her writing: she published a poem taking his side in a current theatrical dispute. When the Sheridans moved to London in 1758, she was encouraged to write *Sidney Bidulph* by Samuel Richardson, who read and liked her early manuscript *Eugenia and Adelaide*; and Le Fanu notes, for the benefit of any readers who may think writing incompatible with women's duties, that this 'authoress of some of the most admired productions of her time, was also acknowledged to excel in every branch of domestic economy'. While 'she could not but have felt pleasure' on finding herself praised by Richardson, she always put the family first, for '[a] mind like Mrs. Sheridan's must have been peculiarly susceptible of maternal claims'.[87] This image of the virtuous maternal writer was deployed to defend her son's reputation. When Richard Brinsley Sheridan died in 1816, his

---

[86] Moore, *Memoirs*, 692; the Marquess of Dufferin and Ava, introd. to Rae, *Sheridan's Plays*, p. ix.
[87] Le Fanu, *Memoirs*, 88, 87, 49.

dramatic triumphs were a long way behind him, his political career was in ruins, and he had spent his last days dodging arrest for debt. To add insult to injury, memoirs began to appear telling stories of his often scandalous private life and impugning his authorship. In Le Fanu's biography, her subject is named on the title page as 'Mother of the late Right Hon. Richard Brinsley Sheridan', and a good deal of space is devoted to correcting mistakes and refuting slurs in John Watkins's recent memoirs of the son. Le Fanu excused her frequent digressions from Frances to Richard Brinsley on the grounds of Frances's own maternal devotion, which would have placed her son's defence above everything (Le Fanu, *Memoirs*, 435).

In his biography of Richard Brinsley Sheridan, Thomas Moore also found the good mother an essential aid to sympathetic treatment of the son. His Frances Sheridan comes from the starry-eyed reminiscences of Richard Brinsley's old schoolteacher. 'I once or twice met his mother,' reported Dr Parr: 'she was quite celestial'.[88] The early loss of his heavenly mother becomes the tragic cause of all the son's later weaknesses. Moore prints a letter to Richard Brinsley from his sister Alicia, lamenting that in youth:

> *You* had lost a mother who would have cherished you, whose talents you inherited, who would have softened the asperity of our father's temper ... As a public man you have been ... 'Sine macula;' ... had you not too early been thrown upon the world, and alienated from your family, you would have been equally good as a private character. (Moore, *Memoirs*, 692)

The family legend of Frances Sheridan as lost guardian angel passed into biographical tradition, so that one life of her son imagines him thinking back to the pure mother:

> How often ... when the stains of the world had soiled that white page of brief companionship, must her figure have recurred to her son Richard ... a tall brunette with a white cap, white hands and white shoulders, simply attired in brown silk,

[88] Moore, *Memoirs*, 8.

> and carrying her snuff-box . . . Her love for her son was surely
> not wasted. She watched over his nurture and that of the 'little
> fairy', his sister, as she watched over their luckless father[89]

Clearly this idealizing strain distorted understanding of both Sheridans, and recent biographies have offered a more complex and convincing account of a mother–son relationship marked by long absences, with the young boy suffering 'a series of expulsions from and re-admittances to the bosom of the family'.[90] My purpose here is not to evaluate the personal tie between son and mother, but to note how the angelic version of Frances has obscured their literary relationship.

Richard Brinsley Sheridan's second prologue to *The Rivals* declared his allegiance to comedy and deplored the influence of 'The Goddess of the woeful countenance– | The sentimental Muse!'[91] Along with Oliver Goldsmith, he has been credited with displacing the maudlin drama of the eighteenth century and restoring laughter to a drooping stage. In this context, his allusion to his mother's famously woeful *Sidney Bidulph* looks like a deliberate attempt to change her tragedy for comedy: her Faulkland comes to a tragic end, his puts on tragic airs but is taken down a peg or two in a comic denouement. Since the 1970s, though, a more nuanced drama criticism has dismantled the simple 'laughing' versus 'sentimental' opposition. It is now clear that Richard Brinsley Sheridan's plays share the flavour of the age of sensibility; and conversely, that his fellow dramatists had never abandoned laughter in the first place. Among those fellow writers whose contribution to eighteenth-century comedy should be reassessed is Frances Sheridan. Overshadowed by Johnson's praise for the suffering Sidney, her comic talent has been overlooked. Alicia Le Fanu, to her credit, recognized this and included some astute literary criticism in her memoirs, pointing out the comic aspects of *Sidney Bidulph*. However, she glossed over some of the more challenging aspects of Frances Sheridan's comic writing.

---

[89] Walter Sichel, *Sheridan from New and Original Material: Including a Manuscript Diary by Georgina Duchess of Devonshire* (London: Constable and Co. Ltd., 1909), i. 251.

[90] O'Toole, *a Traitor's Kiss*, 21.   [91] *Dramatic Works*, i. 75.

Frances Sheridan's second comedy, *The Dupe*, was hissed at Drury Lane in 1763, and even with hasty alterations only survived three nights. Family legend blamed theatrical cabals for the play's failure,[92] but other reasons have been revealed in a study of newspaper reactions to the play.[93] Sheridan's plot and language would have suited the days before stage reform rather than the more refined theatre of the 1760s. Rakish Sir John Woodall does reform, as libertines should, but only when he has been duped and tricked out of money by his mistress Mrs Etherdown. Sharply, who has an affair with the servant Rose, ought to repent and marry her, but he refuses to do so and has the blessing of the other characters on this defiance of stage and moral convention. Words like 'slut', applied to innocent Emily, references to Mrs Etherdown's belonging to the 'sisterhood' (of whores), and such 'low' phrases as 'the spawn of a chimney sweeper' angered the audience. The newspapers castigated the play's 'very low' and 'even very gross' speeches, and its 'highly immoral' attitude to marriage.[94] The *Public Advertiser* printed a letter expressing concern that 'a Lady, a Mother, a Person of fair Character, and good Capacity, such as ought to set her above everything coarse and low' should display 'a conduct so unbecoming, so unfemale'.[95] Nevertheless, the play, with some judicious bowdlerizing, sold well in print. These early reactions show that Frances Sheridan was not quite the fount of maternal morality that later tradition made her; and her son, whose first comedy was also attacked for indecencies (later cut), was following in her footsteps in pushing the boundaries of the theatrically acceptable.

The younger Sheridan was hailed as the writer who had restored Restoration laughter to the Georgian theatre. One poem in the *Bath Chronicle* proclaimed:

> The comic muse Thalia droop'd her head
> Lamenting Wicherly and Congreve dead;
> Lamenting with a sigh her sad disgrace,

---

[92] Frances Sheridan, *Plays*, 24–5.
[93] Samuel P. Chew, Jr., '*The Dupe*: A Study in the "Low" ', *PQ* 18 (1939), 196–203.
[94] Ibid. 200, 201, 198.   [95] Ibid. 199.

> That few alas! Remain'd of all her race:—
> Lo! SHERIDAN a Candidate,—the name
> Reviv'd at once the laughter-loving dame . . .[96]

The risk-taking young comic dramatist, overstepping the bounds of theatrical decorum as he revives the comic muse, has been understood as the son of Wycherley and Congreve, but he is his mother's progeny, too.

Mothers and Daughters: The Breretons, Wollstonecraft, Shelley

As we have seen, the mother–daughter metaphor was submerged or at most implicit in discussions of a female tradition of writing. In cases where real-life mother–daughter pairs wrote, however, the idea of matrilineal literary inheritance was bound to be raised. In the mid-eighteenth century it was explored by the little-known writer Charlotte Brereton, who published poems in memory of her mother, Jane Brereton.

Jane Brereton (1685–1740) is a good example of the respectable, provincial woman poet of the early eighteenth century. Sarah Prescott's discussion of her shows that she represented 'a new model of the relatively obscure middle-class woman poet who lived apart from the capital city most of her life, but did have a literary career and did publish her verse'.[97] Born Jane Hughes near the small town of Mold, in North Wales, she married Thomas Brereton in 1711, and they probably lived in London for the next ten years. Her husband was a writer, and Jane Brereton herself began to publish verse that showed her Hanoverian allegiances and connections (or the desire for connections) with well-known literary figures.[98] Like other women

---

[96] Cited by Rae, *Sheridan's Plays*, p. xxxiv.
[97] Sarah Prescott, *Women, Authorship and Literary Culture, 1690–1740* (London: Palgrave Macmillan, 2003), 36.
[98] Her poems from this period include *The Fifth Ode of the Fourth Book of Horace Imitated, and applied to the King* (1716) and *An Epistle to Sir Richard Steele, On the Death of Mr Addison* (1720).

poets of the time, she was influenced by Pope, and adopted from his poetic epistles a Horatian model of the good-humoured and sociable satirist.[99] On leaving her difficult and violent husband in 1721, she settled with her two daughters in Wrexham, North Wales. Like the younger poet Elizabeth Carter, who was beginning to publish in the 1730s, Brereton found Edward Cave, publisher and editor of the *Gentleman's Magazine*, a helpful route to respectable publication. From 1734 to 1736 she published poems regularly in the *Gentleman's Magazine* under the pseudonym Melissa, and in 1735 Cave published a slim volume of three of her poems, which retrospectively provide the Hanoverian king and queen with British roots by having their glories foretold by Merlin in an ancient prophecy.[100] She died in 1740, and the following year Cave appealed for subscribers for a collection of her poetry, published in 1744 for the benefit of her daughters.[101]

Like other women poets of the period, Brereton was conscious of both a negative and a positive female poetic inheritance: one tainted by Grub Street, the other represented as free from sexual or commercial stain. In one poem she defends good women's writing by attacking the usual suspects—Aphra Behn, Delarivier Manley, and Eliza Haywood—and praising Katherine Philips, Elizabeth Singer Rowe, and Anne Finch, Countess of Winchilsea. Her notion of virtuous women writers as the 'Antidote' to the 'Poison' spread by licentious ones was later used by Samuel Richardson.[102] So strong was this tendency to categorize female writers according to their perceived virtue that it overrode other kinds of division, such as

[99] For women's use of the Horatian model see Claudia N. Thomas, *Alexander Pope and His Eighteenth-Century Women Readers* (Carbondale, Ill.: Southern Illinois University Press, 1994), ch. 5.

[100] *Merlin: A Poem* (London: Edward Cave, 1735).

[101] *Poems on Several Occasions: By Mrs. Jane Brereton* (London: Edward Cave, 1744).

[102] 'Epistle to Mrs. Anne Griffiths. Written from London, in 1718', *Poems on Several Occasions*, 34. The volume may slightly misdate the poem: 1718 is early for an attack on '*Heywood*'s soft seducing Style' (ibid. 35), since *Love in Excess*, the novel that first gained Haywood her reputation, was not published until 1719. For Richardson's use of the poison/antidote image, see *Selected Letters of Samuel Richardson*, ed. John Carroll (Oxford: Clarendon Press, 1964), 173.

political ones, allowing Brereton to celebrate the 'Angelic Wit, and purest Thoughts' both of the Dissenter Singer Rowe and the Jacobite Anne Finch. Both were important reference points for a woman writing poetry in the thirty years of Brereton's literary career. Finch was a complicated one—not just because she was politically very different from Brereton, but also because her well-known poem *The Spleen* expressed doubts, going beyond the trope of female modesty, about her poetic powers. Addressing Spleen, Finch laments:

> O'er me alas! thou dost too much prevail:
> I feel thy Force, while I against thee rail;
> I feel my Verse decay, and my crampt Numbers fail.[103]

Brereton echoes these lines in a rejoinder to Mr Hinchliffe, who had praised her as a 'loyal Fair' for her 1716 ode applied to the king. Her reply begins with the bold intention to 'dare the mighty Theme' of panegyric to her sovereign, but tails off in a declaration of female inferiority:

> I feel the Woman now prevail,
> I feel, I want thy manly Fire!
> I feel my Strings, and Numbers fail,
> I'll cease:—and silently admire.[104]

Spleen, the name given to a set of symptoms close to what would now be called depression, was thought to affect women in particular. The sense of poetic failure which Finch blamed on this disorder is more directly attributed, in Brereton's poem, to being female. Yet the echo of Finch adds an ambiguity. Her inheritance from the most important female poet of the day takes the form of an expression of failure; but her reference to Finch also recalls the modesty of a writer whose numbers were not considered a failure at all. There is a covert sense here of a female tradition that provides an alternative to Mr Hinchliffe's 'manly Fire'.

---

[103] *The Poems of Anne, Countess of Winchilsea*, ed. Myra Reynolds (Chicago: University of Chicago Press, 1903), 250.
[104] *Poems on Several Occasions*, 24.

Jane Brereton was very conscious of the power of poetic imitation and allusion to create literary tradition, and concerned that women's part in this process be recognized. In a letter written late in her life, she notes a similarity between Pope's language and that of Elizabeth Rowe:

> Mrs *Rowe*'s Sentiments are noble, and her Language is beautiful. Had Mr *Pope*'s Essay on Man appeared before her Letters, I doubt not, but many Readers would have imagined that she imitated this Couplet of his—
>
> Warms in the Sun, refreshes in the Breeze,
> Glows in the Stars, and blossoms in the Trees, 1st Ep.l.269.
>
> But long before he published his Essay, she had expressed herself, in the following beautiful Manner.—'He chears me in the Glory of the Sun, refreshes me in the fragrant Breeze, is Beauty in the Flowers of the Field, and Harmony in the Nightingale's Voice.'
>
> But who dares say, that the great Poet copy'd Mrs *Rowe*?[105]

Though she does not use maternal imagery to characterize it, Brereton is evidently interested in poetic inheritance from the female, and sees it as applying to male as well as female writers.

Where the maternal is explicitly invoked in her poetry, it is with reference to her own role as mother, concerned with the education of her daughter in virtue and piety, rather than in poetry. 'Verses from a Mother to her Daughter, with Dr. Carter's Sermons', published in the *Gentleman's Magazine* in 1739, exhorts the daughter to learn from the Doctor's 'Method, Doctrine, Sense, and Style', and 'As these Discourses the best Rules impart, | May'st thou, my Dear! Inscribe them on thy Heart!' Sermons are presented less as a duty than a pleasure for mother and daughter to share: 'I, with Delight, have read; 'tis now my Care, | That you so rational a Pleasure share'.[106] The poem acted as an advertisement for the recently published *Sermons*, and despite Brereton's claim not to know their author personally,

---

[105] Ibid., pp. xxxi–ii. [106] *Gentleman's Magazine* 9 (Mar. 1739).

Edward Cave had introduced her to his daughter, Elizabeth Carter, the previous year.[107] Brereton's daughters, then, brought up in North Wales, were connected through their mother with her influential London publisher and the literary culture surrounding him. The opportunity to inherit her position as a writer was there.

Using the pseudonym Carolina, Charlotte Brereton published two poems on her mother in the *Gentleman's Magazine*. The first, 'To the Memory of a Mother', appeared two months after Jane Brereton's death. It addresses the 'blest shade' of the mother, praises her virtues, mourns her loss, and places her in a female poetic tradition by imagining her wandering 'th'etherial plains' with 'spotless Rowe'. In heroic couplets full of the conventional poetic diction of the time, the poem is generally unremarkable, except for the connection drawn between maternal care and poetic pleasure:

> How did her care, her tenderness engage
> The artless fondess of my infant age?
> And when advancing in the years of youth
> Teach me the ways of wisdom and of truth?
> The happy hours flew unperceiv'd along,
> While native wit flow'd, tuneful, from her tongue:
> Her gentle numbers charm'd the listn'ing ear,
> MELISSA's name was to the Muses dear.[108]

Poems written in response to this daughter's tribute developed the idea of a matrilineal poetic inheritance. One addresses Charlotte as her mother's 'fondest care, her justest pride, | Not less by genius, than by blood ally'd, | Best guardian of thy lov'd *Melissa*'s fame'; hopes that the mother's 'spirit' will 'inspire' the daughter's breast; and prays that heaven will pass on the mother's 'ev'ry gift' to the daughter, so that she can charm the earthly world while her mother sings in heaven.[109] Another praises Charlotte's song by placing her

[107] Prescott, *Women, Authorship and Literary Culture*, 36.
[108] 'To the Memory of a Mother', *Gentleman's Magazine*, 10 (Oct. 1740), 518; repr. in *Poems on Several Occasions*, p. lxii–lxiii.
[109] 'To the memory of Mrs. Brereton. Inscribed to Mrs. Charlotte Brereton', *Gentleman's Magazine*, 10 (Oct. 1740), 518.

in a pastoral world where listening shepherds have mistaken her voice for her mother's, and ends with the consolation that 'MELISSA's better part remains, | MELISSA lives in You.'[110] The following year, adapting a device of Elizabeth Rowe's, who had written a poem on the anniversary of her husband's death, Charlotte Brereton wrote one on the anniversary of her mother's. Where Rowe had complained that 'In vain the cheerful spring returns', and declared that the anniversary day would be 'sacred still to grief', Charlotte Brereton complains 'To me in vain her treasures *Autumn* spreads', and promises that the muse will 'on this day with *grief distinguish'd* mourn'. Jane Brereton's '*writings*' and '*example*' will guide her daughter to heaven.[111]

Charlotte Brereton's poems and the replies they elicited, both given prominence in the collected volume of Jane Brereton's poetry, indicate that the notion of poetic inheritance through the mother was developing. As an extension of her maternal role in giving her daughter love, care, and a virtuous upbringing, the good writing woman might pass on a poetic legacy to her daughter. However, Charlotte Brereton's later life is obscure, and we do not know to what extent she continued to follow her mother's literary example.

A much more extensive and better-known maternal literary legacy is that of Mary Wollstonecraft to her daughter, Mary Shelley. The two form the earliest example of a famous mother–daughter pair of writers. As in the case of the Sheridans, the literary relationship between mother and child was only one of a network of familial writing influences. Shelley was for many years considered mainly in relation to her husband, who, as we have seen, was taking up his own place in the literary patriline. Early work on her 'assumed that

---

[110] [R. Yate], 'To Miss Charlotte Brereton', *Gentleman's Magazine*, 10 (Dec. 1740).

[111] Elizabeth Rowe, 'On the Anniversary of her Husband's death', *Gentleman's Magazine*, 9 (Feb. 1739), 98; Charlotte Brereton, 'Written August 7, being the Anniversary of a Mother's Death', *Gentleman's Magazine*, 11 (Aug. 1741), 438. For Charlotte Brereton's life, poetic career, and the poem 'To Miss A[nn]a M[ari]a Tra[ver]s', see Roger Lonsdale (ed.), *Eighteenth-Century Women Poets: An Oxford Anthology* (Oxford: OUP, 1989), 188–90.

she was in effect the product of Percy Shelley's ideas'.[112] The legacy from her father, William Godwin, was also of crucial importance. Estranged from him for a period after her elopement at the age of 16, she remained emotionally bound to him and determined to be his intellectual heir, and her fiction can be seen as the main continuation after him of the historical and political Godwinian novel.[113] The young Mary Godwin grew up in a family where, as her stepsister Claire Clairmont later remarked, 'if you cannot write an epic poem or novel, that by its originality knocks all other novels on the head, you are a despicable creature, not worth acknowledging'.[114] For her the literary and political aspects of her parents' influence were inextricably linked, and she felt throughout her life a pressure, in many ways unwelcome, to follow their example and contribute to radical political causes in her writing.[115] As she explained to the social reformer Frances Wright, her mother's 'greatness of soul and my father['s] high talents have perpetually reminded me that I ought to degenerate as little as I could from those from whom I derived my being'.[116] Of the two her father, whom in childhood she adored and with whom in adulthood she maintained a troubled relationship, is in some ways a more obvious influence than Wollstonecraft, whom she could not remember. But her father taught her to revere the mother whose portrait, painted during her second and last pregnancy, hung in his study; and she inherited a profound literary legacy from Wollstonecraft, whose name she shared, who died as a result of her birth, who was famous as the author of *A Vindication of the Rights of*

[112] Anne Mellor, *Mary Shelley: Her Life, Her Fiction, Her Monsters* (New York: Routledge, 1989), p. xi.

[113] See Pamela Clemit, *The Godwinian Novel: The Rational Fictions of Godwin, Brockden Brown, Mary Shelley* (Oxford: Clarendon Press, 1993).

[114] Cited ibid. 143.

[115] See the journal entry for 21 Oct. 1838, where she defends herself from accusations of 'lukewarmness in the "Good Cause" . . . the cause of the advancement of freedom & knowledge—of the Rights of Women &c'. *The Journals of Mary Shelley 1814–1844*, ii. *1822–1844*, ed. Paula R. Feldman and Diana Scott-Kilvert (Oxford: Clarendon Press, 1987), 553.

[116] 12 Sept. 1827; *Selected Letters of Mary Wollstonecraft Shelley*, ed. Betty T. Bennett (Baltimore: Johns Hopkins University Press, 1995), 179.

Woman, and whose writings show her own concern with matrilineal inheritance and the fate of daughters.

The education of daughters was traditionally an acceptable arena for female authority, on the understanding that daughters were to be educated in the service of the patriarchal order. In taking a post as governess to Lord and Lady Kingsborough, Wollstonecraft was following a traditional path for a single woman, and in writing *Thoughts on the Education of Daughters* (1787) she was taking an expected course for a woman writer. *Original Stories from Real Life* (1791), a children's book dramatizing scenes of instruction between Mrs Mason and her two female charges, continued Wollstonecraft's early career as educationalist. Even in these early works, conventional in many of their messages, she promoted an independence of thought not usually advocated to daughters. In her later work, maternal advice to daughters is radicalized.

Wollstonecraft was delighted with the birth of her first daughter, Fanny Imlay, in 1794. 'I feel great pleasure at being a mother,' she told her friend Ruth Barlow; and she found happiness in detecting, not the usual feminine charms, but strength, spirit, and intelligence in her baby, who was being imagined as her literary and political heir by the time she was a week old:

> I have got a vigorous little Girl, and you were so out in your calculation respecting the quantity of brains she was to have, and the skull it would require to contain them, that you made almost all the caps so small I cannot use them . . . My little Girl begins to suck so *manfully* that her father reckons saucily on her writing the second part of the R——ts of Woman.[117]

Before long, Imlay's desertion of her encouraged gloomier feelings about bringing up a daughter. In the account of her Scandinavian journey published in 1796, Wollstonecraft expresses her anxieties about Fanny's future in a world of male tyranny. 'You know that as a female I am particularly attached to her—I feel more than a

---

[117] To Ruth Barlow, 20 May 1794; *Collected Letters of Mary Wollstonecraft*, ed. Ralph M. Wardle (Ithaca, NY: Cornell University Press, 1979), 255–6.

mother's fondness and anxiety, when I reflect upon the dependent
and oppressed state of her sex.'[118]

This theme was expanded in her final work, the unfinished,
posthumously published *Maria; or, the Wrongs of Woman* (1798). In
this novel, when Maria's baby daughter is snatched from her breast,
it is a synecdoche for all male oppression of women, while Maria's
journal, addressed to her absent child, is an attempt to counter
that oppression through matrilineal communication. She writes as a
mother who has suffered the misery society inflicts on women, for
'[I]t is, my child, my dearest daughter, only such a mother, who will
dare break through all restraint to provide for your happiness'. The
story Maria writes for her daughter reveals the tyranny of marriage,
and the message she gives, opposing all conduct books of advice to
daughters, is about the need for action and self-determination:

> From my narrative, my dear girl, you may gather the instruc-
> tion, the counsel, which is meant rather to exercise than
> influence your mind. . . . I would then, with fond anxiety, lead
> you very early in life to form your grand principle of action, to
> save you from the vain regret of having, through irresolution,
> let the spring-tide of existence pass away, unimproved, unen-
> joyed. —Gain experience—ah! gain it—while experience is
> worth having, and acquire sufficient fortitude to pursue your
> own happiness; it includes your utility, by a direct path.[119]

In its fragmentary nature, the novel suggests tragic death or heroic
survival as alternative responses to women's wrongs. One note for
an ending indicates 'Pregnancy—Miscarriage—Suicide'; another,
more developed, has Maria taking laudanum, as her creator had
done in 1794, but recovering to be united with her daughter, and
vowing to live for her child (*Mary* and *The Wrongs of Woman*, 202).

---

[118] *Letters written during a Short Residence in Sweden, Norway and Denmark* (*Letters from Norway*), in *The Works of Mary Wollstonecraft*, ed. Janet Todd and Marilyn Butler (London: William Pickering, 1989), vi. 269.

[119] *Mary* and *The Wrongs of Woman*, ed. Gary Kelly (Oxford: World's Classics, 1980), 124.

Wollstonecraft's novel becomes a subversive variant on the traditional text of advice to children, in which a mother or maternal figure offered instruction in a woman's role. Such texts were often predicated on the mother's absence. Some early works of maternal instruction, such as Elizabeth Jocelin's *The Mothers Legacie, To her unborne Child* (1624), were by women anticipating death in childbirth, and wishing to leave a written legacy to their children,[120] while in the more recent *An Unfortunate Mother's Advice to her Absent Daughters* (1761), Lady Sarah Pennington addressed the daughters from whom she had been separated by her estranged husband. Wollstonecraft's heroine is, like Pennington, trying to contact her daughter across the barrier of enforced separation; but Wollstonecraft's own death, in the aftermath of childbirth and before her novel's completion, gave the work—for her daughters—a similar kind of resonance to that found in Elizabeth Jocelin. Separated by death, the mother contacted her children through the text.

Fanny Imlay and Mary Godwin, brought up in Godwin's household, were early introduced to the written word as their mother's legacy, Mary being taught to read with the aid of *Ten Lessons*, a reading book Wollstonecraft had prepared for Fanny. The elder daughter, the only one who had known their mother, was not the one to take up the literary inheritance. She followed her mother more tragically. Wollstonecraft had made two suicide attempts; Fanny Imlay made one, taking laudanum in 1816 as her mother had done in 1794. Unlike her mother, she was successful. Mary Godwin was left to take on the legacy and burden of following the mother in living and writing.

Mary Godwin's elopement with a married man was itself connected to the pursuit of her dead mother. Not only was Shelley attracted to her as the child of 'glorious parents', whose mother's life and fame shone on her;[121] she was clearly drawn to him partly by his reverence

---

[120] Wendy Wall, *The Imprint of Gender* (Ithaca, NY: Cornell University Press, 1993), 283–96.

[121] P. B. Shelley, 'Dedication' to *The Revolt of Islam; Poetical Works*, 39–40.

for her mother's work and his willingness to see Wollstonecraft in her—an attitude she recalled many years later, writing that '[t]he memory of my Mother has always been the pride & delight of my life; & the admiration of others for her, has been the cause of most of the happiness I have enjoyed'.[122] The two went for walks to Wollstonecraft's grave in St Pancras churchyard, the scene of Mary Godwin's visits as a lonely child, suggesting that for her Shelley seemed to offer the maternal care she had missed. She chose this place for her declaration of love for Shelley, indicating her sense of the importance of her dead mother's blessing on the unconventional relationship that (despite his earlier opposition to the institution of marriage) outraged her father.

Mary Godwin knew her mother through her writings. She probably read her works at an early age, and she certainly read them, intensively, during the first year of her relationship with Shelley: *Mary, a Fiction* in August 1814, *Letters from Norway* in August and September, *Maria, or the Wrongs of Woman* in October, *Elements of Morality, for the Use of Children* in October, *An Historical and Moral View of the Origin and Progress of the French Revolution* in December. A mutual desire for Wollstonecraft inflected the relationship between Percy Shelley and Mary Godwin, and coloured the circumstances of her early writing. He expected her to inherit her mother's identity as revolutionary writer, while she looked to him for maternal care as she discovered or rediscovered her mother's writings in his presence. Sometimes he read aloud to her from Wollstonecraft's works. Their journal records them travelling down the Rhine on Wednesday, 31 August. *'Pursue our voyage in the slight canoe that accompanied our boat. Shelley reads aloud from the letters from Norway'*: her mother's words from her lover's mouth.[123]

[122] *Selected Letters of Mary Wollstonecraft Shelley*, 179.
[123] *The Journals of Mary Shelley 1814–1844, i. 1814–1822*, ed. Feldman and Scott-Kilvert, 22, 55. For a discussion of Mary Shelley's reading of her mother's texts see Charles E. Robinson, 'A Mother's Daughter: An Intersection of Mary Shelley's *Frankenstein* and Mary Wollstonecraft's *A Vindication of the Rights of Woman*', in Helen Buss, D. L. Macdonald, and Anne Whirr (eds.), *Mary Wollstonecraft and Mary Shelley: Writing Lives* (Ontario: Wilfred Laurier University Press, 2001), 127–38.

Mary Shelley's writings can be seen as, in part, attempts to com-
municate with and to negotiate the complex question of inheritance
from her dead mother. As Lisa Vargo puts it, 'through writing, Shelley can symbolically speak to her mother and demonstrate that she
has not degenerated from Wollstonecraft's example'.[124] Although she
makes few direct references to Wollstonecraft's works, her response
to Wollstonecraft has been traced in various ways. She was reading *A
Vindication of the Rights of Woman* as she composed the Safie episode
for *Frankenstein* in December 1816, and Safie's story of her education
by her mother can be seen as an allegory of Mary Shelley's education
by her mother's works: 'For Safie, her mother's Christianity—and
for Mary Shelley, her mother's rational religion—could help redeem
daughters (and sons) from an ideology of oppression.'[125] Her much
later novel, *Lodore* (1835), explores the education of daughters in
ways that echo Wollstonecraft's concern with female independence
in several of her works.[126] Jeanne Moskal has analysed the art criticism of Mary Shelley's *Rambles in Germany and Italy* (1844), as
autobiographical reflections that concern themselves with her feelings
about her mother.[127]

The question of a daughter's inheritance from her mother is central
to Mary Shelley's second novel, *Valperga* (1823), where it is treated
in two figures, Euthanasia and Beatrice.[128] This historical novel tells
the story of Castruccio's ambition and rise to power in fourteenth-
century Italy.[129] While he gradually degenerates into corruption and
cruelty, the heroine, Euthanasia, Countess of Valperga, becomes a

[124] 'Further Thoughts on the Education of Daughters: *Lodore* as an Imagined
Conversation with Mary Wollstonecraft', in Buss et al. (eds.), *Mary Wollstonecraft and
Mary Shelley*, 178.
[125] Robinson, 'Mother's Daughter', 134–5.
[126] Vargo, 'Further Thoughts', 177–87.
[127] 'Speaking the Unspeakable: Art Criticism as Life Writing in Mary Shelley's
Rambles in Germany and Italy', in Buss et al. (eds.), *Mary Wollstonecraft and Mary Shelley*,
189–216.
[128] *Valperga*, in *Novels and Selected Works of Mary Shelley*, iii, ed. Nora Crook
(London: William Pickering, 1996).
[129] For a discussion of *Valperga* emphasizing its inheritance from Mary Shelley's
father's writing, see Clemit, *Godwinian Novel*, 175–183.

Florentine leader, trying to bring peace between the warring factions of Guelphs and Ghibelines. Euthanasia is educated by her blind father, but she inherits her title through her mother, a woman who, as she tells Castruccio, was an active politician: 'She was a Guelph, a violent partizan, and, heart and soul, was taken up with treaties of peace, acquisitions in war, the conduct of allies, and the fortune of her enemies: while she talked to you, you would have thought that the whole globe of the earth was merely an appendage to the county of Valperga' (*Novels and Selected Works*, iii. 82). Euthanasia inherits political power from her mother and tries to use it in maternal care of her dependants, considering the question of possible alliances with Florence or Lucca only in the light of whether they will bring peace and happiness to her people (ibid. 100). Loving Castruccio, but opposed to his growing tyranny, Euthanasia eventually takes part in a conspiracy against him, is defeated, and drowns on her voyage to exile in Sicily. Her matrilineal power destroyed, she 'was never heard of more; even her name perished', while Castruccio's reign is remembered in history (ibid. 322).

Beatrice, meanwhile, also has an inheritance from her mother, but not a publicly recognized one. She is the illegitimate daughter, unrecorded by history, of a historical figure, Wilhelmina of Bohemia, who was the founder of a heretical, woman-centred sect. Wilhelmina is described in the novel as believing herself to be 'the Holy Ghost incarnate upon earth for the salvation of the female sex' (*Novels and Selected Works*, iii. 130–1). Orphaned at the age of 2, Beatrice has 'inherited from her mother the most ardent imagination that ever animated a human soul' (ibid. 152): the inheritance of imagination does her even less good than Euthanasia's inheritance of political power does her. She falls in love with Castruccio, is abandoned by him, and dies. It has been suggested that Wilhelmina 'echoes Wollstonecraft',[130] but both pairs of dying mothers and inheriting daughters would seem to suggest some aspect of Mary Shelley's relation to her mother. If the tragedy of the imaginative Beatrice

---

[130] Jeanne Moskal, 'Speaking the Unspeakable', 209.

suggests an anxiety about female creativity, that of the Countess of Valperga shows similar anxieties about female political action, corresponding to those Mary Shelley later expressed when trying to justify herself for not furthering the cause of 'the Rights of Women &c'.[131] *Valperga* follows Wollstonecraft in its analysis of male tyranny at the same time as it encodes a message about the difficulty of inheriting an imaginative or political role from the author of *A Vindication of the Rights of Woman* in the politically reactionary years of the early nineteenth century.[132]

Mary Shelley's most famous work, *Frankenstein*, responds to her mother's legacy in ways that go beyond the rational education of the minor character Safie. The reception of the novel itself raises interesting questions about women's place in the literary canon. Its huge popularity, especially as mediated through stage and later film versions, has made Mary Shelley one of the most culturally influential of English writers. The openness to interpretation of its central image, Frankenstein's creation of a monster that turns on him and destroys his family, has allowed the story to stand as a fable for different anxieties in different ages, whether fears of the revolutionary power of the working classes in the nineteenth century, or of the destructive potential of scientific advance in the twentieth. At the same time, Frankenstein's creator has tended to remain a marginal figure in the canon. Her other works were, until recently, given little attention, and the popularity of her first novel has been attributed more to its transmission in other forms than to her original imaginative powers: a case of a woman giving birth to a tradition but the children getting all the credit.

Since the 1970s there has been a growing body of work interpreting *Frankenstein* as a work dealing with maternity and creativity.[133] The

---

[131] *Journals of Mary Shelley*, ii. 553.

[132] For an interesting reading of *Valperga* as a response to the work of a figurative maternal ancestor, Germaine de Stäel's *Corinne*, see Kari E. Lokke, *Tracing Women's Romanticism: Gender, History and Transcendence* (London: Routledge, 2004), 57–83.

[133] See esp. Ellen Moers, *Literary Women* (London: Women's Press, 1980); Barbara Johnson, 'My Monster/My Self', *Diacritics*, 12 (1982), 2–20; Mellor, *Mary Shelley*.

novel's concern with monstrous birth has been read biographically as a reflection of the author's own complex feelings of guilt and anxiety: guilt at being the cause of her mother's death, anxiety about her own capacity to mother after the death of her first baby. The dream that 'my little baby came to life again—that it had only been cold & that we rubbed it by the fire & it lived' can be seen as the germ for the preoccupation with reanimation in *Frankenstein*.[134] The suicides of Fanny Imlay and Harriet Shelley during the composition of the novel must also have aroused powerful feelings, Fanny's reminding her of the darker side their mother's legacy, Harriet's that her relationship with Percy Shelley, whom she married the month his first wife died, was built on his abandonment of another mother. The novel she later called 'my hideous progeny' had a closer than usual relationship to the common metaphor of book as baby.[135] As Anne Mellor points out, her third child, Clara Everina, was conceived during the time of the book's composition, and the work expresses 'the most powerfully felt anxieties of pregnancy', while the nine months of the book's main narrative can be dated through its calendar entries to the year of its author's birth, its final entry set two days after Wollstonecraft's death. Deaths within and outside the novel 'can all be seen as the consequences of the same creation, the birth of Mary Godwin-the author'.[136]

The narrative of *Frankenstein*, which, as many critics have pointed out, is about a man's attempt to create life without involving a woman, can be read as an indictment of a world built on a masculinist notion of creativity. The loss of mothers throughout the novel, Victor Frankenstein's removal of himself from feminine influences in order to create life by himself, and his failure to care for the creature he brings to life, all suggest that monstrousness is born from the absence of mothering. In this way *Frankenstein* forms a counterpart to the misogynist view of creativity found in the *Dunciad* and other texts dealing with the monstrous mother.

---

[134] *Journals of Mary Shelley*, i. 70.
[135] Introd. to 1831 edn. of *Frankenstein; Novels and Selected Works*, i. 180.
[136] Mellor, *Mary Shelley*, 41, 54.

Most crucial is the initial innocence, goodwill, and rationality of the unnamed Creature, considered a hideous monster by his horrified creator, but never causing harm until rejected by humankind. He is the opposite of an unthinking monster. When he tells his story to Frankenstein, what is noticeable is his attempt to offer a clear analysis of the beginning of consciousness:

> It is with considerable difficulty that I remember the original aera of my being: all the events of the period appear confused and indistinct. A strange multiplicity of sensations seized me, and I saw, felt, heard and smelt, at the same time; and it was, indeed, a long time before I learned to distinguish between the operations of my various senses. By degrees, I remember, a stronger light pressed upon my nerves, so that I was obliged to shut my eyes. (*Novels and Selected Works*, i. 76)

This depiction of a mind beginning to make distinctions, followed by the Creature's quick and pleasurable acquisition of language through listening and imitation, and his self-education through reading, expresses a faith in the natural capacities of reason that is both a Godwinian and a Wollstonecraftian inheritance. Whereas in the *Dunciad*, reason is inherently fragile, always under threat from the undifferentiating dullness of the Mighty Mother, in *Frankenstein* reason is a natural strength leading to progressive understanding. What perverts it, is not the regressive embrace of the dark mother but maternal deprivation. Rejected by his creator and gradually coming to understand his own needs, first for food and shelter, later for companionship and love, the Creature fixes his hopes on the De Lacey family, living near them undetected and imagining that one day 'by my gentle demeanour and conciliating words, I should first win their favour, and afterwards their love' (*Novels and Selected Works*, i. 85–6). Their rejection of him is compounded by the response of the rustic who shoots him after he has rescued a young girl from drowning. His own naturally protective instincts violently punished, he turns against humanity, and it is at this point that his murderous attacks on Frankenstein's family begin.

The *Dunciad* offers a neoclassical vision of creative and uncreative forces in which chaos and monstrousness come from being unable to progress beyond the mother. Civilization is precious, its best values upheld by the paternal line of poets to which Pope joins himself. In *Frankenstein*, product of the radical Enlightenment and of the Romantic revaluation of the maternal, creation is perverted when the mother is left out of account, and a mistaken civilization threatens the natural benevolence and rationality of an innocent being. Mary Shelley does not confidently join a clear line of literary ancestors, but doubtfully takes up a troubled inheritance in which literary and personal influences are mingled. Her haunting and uneven novel is not only a response to her mother, a version of that second volume of *The Rights of Woman* that Wollstonecraft had imagined coming from Fanny Imlay, but through that, an attack on the patrilineal vision of creativity as the province of men without women.

3

Brothers, Sisters, and New Provinces of Writing

Parent–child metaphors allow writers and critics to imagine literature as an estate to be inherited; they organize a writer's attitude to the literary past. Other kinship relations are brought into play when attention is focused on groups of contemporary writers. Brotherhood is invoked to describe relations of fellowship, equality, and rivalry among writers, especially where they belong to the same social circle or work in the same genre. Critics adapting the Bloomian model of influence have argued for the importance of fraternal rivalry in male writers' struggle for poetic identity. For Marlon Ross, the crucial contest for the male Romantic poet is 'the competition that ensues between the poet and his contemporaries, his fellow (compatriot, co-equal, male) poets, who represent as much a threat to his self-creation and self-possession as his progenitors'; this rivalry is more immediate and intense than the struggle with the father, since the brother poets are fighting at the same time for the same territory, and the outcome is unpredictable.[1] If rivalry is one aspect of fraternal literary relations, equally important is the collaborative fellowship involved in the development of new literary movements, a fellowship that can be conceived as the brothers' joint attempt to emerge from their subjection to paternal authority. The long line of studies of the Wordsworth–Coleridge collaboration is one testimony to our fascination with fraternal creativity.

[1] Marlon B. Ross, *The Contours of Masculine Desire: Romanticism and the Rise of Women's Poetry* (New York: OUP, 1989), 92.

Clearly there are links to be made between the political and literary realms here. From the seventeenth century to the nineteenth, kinship metaphors were heavily used to describe political systems and mount political arguments. Dryden's discussions of the importance of legitimate poetic succession from father to son were played out against the background of an attempt to shore up Stuart authority on a theory of absolutism defended in terms of patriarchal rights, most notably by Sir Robert Filmer, whose *Patriarcha* derived all political authority from a father's divinely appointed rights over his children. Filmer's arguments were countered by John Locke, whose *Two Treatises of Government* argued for the limits of paternal power. Political theory over the following hundred years moved from the metaphor of paternal authority to that of fraternal equality. Social contract theory, as developed by Locke and later by Rousseau, challenged patriarchalism with a new idea of civil society, the rules of which were to be set 'by a collective body of men who stand to the law and each other as equals, as a fraternity'.[2] The idea of fraternity was important in the American Revolution, whose participants saw themselves as grown-up children, throwing off the tyrannical authority of the parent country. The French Revolution, with its ideals of liberty, equality, and fraternity, can be seen as the culmination of this move from fatherhood to brotherhood; and Juliet Flower MacCannell sees it as inaugurating a new, post-patriarchal social order in which a band of brothers takes political control.[3] Certainly Edmund Burke, England's early and most influential critic of the Revolution, called the revolutionaries 'those children of their country who are prompt rashly to hack that aged parent in pieces'.[4] Lynn Hunt has described the French Revolution as the historical enactment of what Freud, in *Totem and Taboo*, saw as the primal urge of sons to kill the father and take over his authority; and, through

[2] Carole Pateman, *The Disorder of Woman: Democracy, Feminism and Political Theory* (Cambridge: Polity Press, 1989), 42.

[3] *The Regime of the Brother: After the Patriarchy* (London: Routledge, 1991).

[4] *Reflections on the Revolution in France*, ed. Conor Cruise O'Brien (London: Pelican, 1968), 194.

an analysis of Revolutionary painting and novels, has suggested that the 1790s in France saw a radical and short-lived attempt to imagine political authority in the hands of an equal fraternity who would—unlike the sons in Freud's story—refuse to take on the father's identity themselves.[5]

Hunt argues persuasively for some very specific links between the Revolutionary metaphor of fraternity and Revolutionary art. In more general, broad terms, we can see during the English eighteenth century a movement from the neoclassical location of literary authority in a group of fathers to whom the modern writer must prove his legitimate filial relation, to the emphasis on original genius, which attempts to deny the importance of the father. In 1759, Edward Young remarked that 'an Original author is born of himself, is his own progenitor'. Comparing one original author, Shakespeare, to ancient writers, he insisted that he 'is not their Son, but Brother; their Equal'.[6] Wordsworth saw himself as an original author in Young's terms. In his 1800 *Preface* to the *Lyrical Ballads*, he referred reverently to Shakespeare and Milton, but insisted on his own bold break from paternal tradition. His rejection of poetic diction had 'necessarily cut me off from a large portion of phrases and figures of speech which from father to son have long been regarded as the common inheritance of Poets'.[7] In *The Prelude*, he mentioned earlier English poets in terms of fraternal recognition: reading Spenser, 'I called him brother, Englishman, and friend'.[8] The story of historical shift, however, should not be pushed too far. The idea of a fellowship of literary brothers was already found in the seventeenth century, while literary fathers—one father, Milton, in particular—continued to haunt the Romantics. Where the fraternal

[5] *The Family Romance of the French Revolution* (London: Routledge, 1992).

[6] *Conjectures on Original Composition* (London: A. Millar and R. and J. Dodsley, 1759), 68, 78.

[7] *Lyrical Ballads and Other Poems, 1797–1800*, ed. James Butler and Karen Green (Ithaca, NY: Cornell University Press, 1992), 748.

[8] *The Prelude* (1805), Bk. 2, l. 285; in *The Prelude: 1797, 1805, 1850*, ed. Jonathan Wordsworth, M. H. Abrams, and Stephen Gill (New York: W. W. Norton and Co., 1979), 106. Further references are to this edition and to *1805* unless otherwise stated.

metaphor seems to me to have most significance for literary relations is in the way it is used to establish new literary paradigms.

Two signal literary innovations of the eighteenth century are the mid-century establishment of the novel as a serious genre, and the late-century inauguration of the Romantic revolution. Each is strongly associated with the work of pair of writers whose relationship is in some way fraternal: Richardson and Fielding in the novel, Wordsworth and Coleridge in Romanticism. In each case, the brothers had a sister: literal sister to one of the pair and literary sister to both. The literary relations among Henry and Sarah Fielding and Samuel Richardson, in the middle of the century, and Dorothy and William Wordsworth and Samuel Taylor Coleridge, at the turn of the nineteenth century, can tell us something about the way literary novelty is produced and claimed, and about the different kinds of participation in literature that are allowed to women in their role as men's sisters.

That writing women might be conceived of as a sisterhood was beginning to be recognized by the late eighteenth century. Whether the relationship between brother and sister translated into a literary relation—and if so, of what kind—was and remains a moot point.

The two triangular sets of relationships considered here—Henry–Sarah–Samuel and William–Dorothy–Samuel—were very different both in their personal and their literary aspects. The later trio were intensely bound together. William and Dorothy Wordsworth, separated in childhood after their mother's death, settled together at Racedown in 1795, and lived together for the rest of their lives, in an intimacy altered but not severed by William's 1802 marriage to Mary Hutchinson. Dorothy's *Journals*, especially those of the early years at Grasmere, testify to the extremity of her devotion to the brother she referred to as 'my Beloved'. William's poetry, especially in the years 1797–1802, records her centrality to his life and his identity as a writer. Not just his housekeeper, amanuensis, and inspiration, nor just the diarist whose words he could use in his poems, she enabled him to develop the relationship with Nature that is the foundation of his poetic self. His poetry and their life together have been seen as a collaborative effort, the joint creation of 'Wordsworthianism'.[9] Coleridge turned this twosome for a while into a close-knit trio. He visited the brother and sister at Racedown in 1797, encouraged them to rent a house close to his own home, collaborated with William in the 1798 *Lyrical Ballads*, hailed him as Milton's true successor, and urged him to write a great philosophical poem. The two men's poetic relationship, so close that Thomas McFarland named it a symbiosis, has been closely studied, revealing the way the dialogue between their different understandings of nature, spirituality, and imagination informs their poetry.[10] While Coleridge was initially drawn to William rather than his sister, a strong bond between him and Dorothy developed, and as early as July 1797 he was referring to her as 'My Sister'.[11] Looking back on this period later, Coleridge jokingly compared himself, William, and Dorothy to the Holy Trinity: 'tho we were three persons, it was but one God'.[12]

The relations between the two Fieldings and Richardson are less well documented and very different in flavour. Samuel Richardson and Henry Fielding published their greatest novels, *Clarissa* and *Tom Jones*, in quick succession in 1747–8 and 1749 respectively. Shortly

[9] Elizabeth A. Fay, *Becoming Wordsworthian: A Performative Aesthetics* (Amherst, Mass.: University of Massachusetts Press, 1995).

[10] Thomas McFarland, 'The Symbiosis of Coleridge and Wordsworth', *Studies in Romanticism*, 11 (1972), 263–303; *Romanticism and the Forms of Ruin: Wordsworth, Coleridge and Modalities of Fragmentation* (Princeton: PUP, 1981). See also Lucy Newlyn, *Coleridge, Wordsworth and the Language of Allusion* (1986; 2nd edn., Oxford: OUP, 2001); Paul Magnuson, *Coleridge and Wordsworth: A Lyrical Dialogue* (Princeton: PUP, 1988); Nicholas Roe, *Wordsworth and Coleridge: The Radical Years* (Oxford: Clarendon Press, 1988); Gene W. Ruoff, *Wordsworth and Coleridge: The Making of the Major Lyrics 1802–1804* (New Brunswick, NJ: Rutgers University Press, 1989); Richard E. Matlak, *The Poetry of Relationship: The Wordsworths and Coleridge, 1797–1800* (Basingstoke: Macmillan, 1997). Of these, Matlak's work gives the greatest weight to Dorothy Wordsworth's relationship to the two men.

[11] In an early draft of 'This Lime-Tree Bower My Prison', written while William, Dorothy, and Charles Lamb were out walking, he addresses them twice as 'my Sister & my Friends!' *Letters of Samuel Taylor Coleridge*, ed. E. L. Griggs (Oxford: Clarendon Press, 1956), i. 197. The phrase was later altered to 'my gentle-hearted Charles'. *The Collected Works of Samuel Taylor Coleridge: Poetical Works*, ed. J. C. C. Mays (Princeton: PUP, 2001), i. 353–4.

[12] *Letters of Samuel Taylor Coleridge*, i. 422.

afterwards the two works were praised together as 'two wonderful Performances' by the 'brother Biographers';[13] but in this case the fraternal bond was entirely one of rivalry. Their creative differences did not emerge, like Coleridge's and Wordsworth's, from a base of shared views and aims, but were stark and polar. Henry Fielding's development as a novelist was in part shaped by his opposition to Richardson, whose *Pamela* he parodied in *Shamela* and responded to more subtly in *Joseph Andrews*. Though Fielding later expressed admiration for *Clarissa*, he and Richardson did not share friendship or literary vision. Sarah Fielding's place in this triangle was very different from Dorothy Wordsworth's with William and Coleridge. Like the Wordsworths, the Fieldings were part of a large sibling group, but where Dorothy had only brothers, Sarah Fielding had three sisters, Catharine, Beatrice, and Ursula, and spent much of her life with them until their deaths in close succession in the years 1750–1, when she was entering her forties. She also had fairly close relations with her brother Henry, living with him and looking after his family in the period between his first wife's death in 1744 and his remarriage in 1747. The beginnings of her literary career were very much bound up with his writing, as her first publications took the form of contributions to his fiction. Rather than becoming absorbed, like Dorothy Wordsworth, in sustaining her brother's writing life, Sarah Fielding was interested in developing as an author on her own account. She worked with others besides Henry. Her lifelong friend Jane Collier was a close literary associate, and they probably collaborated on *The Cry* in 1753. Richardson became a friend in the 1740s. She visited his home and was very impressed by the affection of his family circle. He printed a number of her works and offered advice on *The Governess* and *The Cry*; she published *Remarks on Clarissa*, an appreciative criticism of his work, in 1749. Sarah Fielding, her first published work incorporated into a novel by her

---

[13] *Charlotte Summers* (London, 1750), i. 220–1. For a discussion of Richardson's attitude to the comparison between himself and Fielding in this anonymous novel, see T. C. Duncan Eaves and Ben D. Kimpel, *Samuel Richardson: A Biography* (Oxford: Clarendon Press, 1971), 300.

brother which uses mockery of Richardson as its starting point, and her later work influenced by her admiration for her brother's rival, made an uneasy sort of link between two male writers who stood in strong opposition to each other.

Very different as these two sets of relationships are, they have elements in common. In both cases the 'brothers'—Fielding and Richardson working in opposition, Wordsworth and Coleridge in close collaboration—have entered literary history as important founders of a new kind of writing. In both cases, the question of the sister's contribution to that new writing is a contested one that needs to be examined in two ways, for what she enabled the brothers to do, and for what she did herself. Though William Wordsworth and Henry Fielding construed feminine sensibility very differently, each made use of the idea of his sister's feminine otherness in the process of creating his own writing self. For each of them in very different ways, his relation with his sister mediated his relation with his fellow male writer. As we will see, the rivalry between Henry Fielding and Richardson was played out in a struggle for possession of Sarah as sister writer, a struggle in which her writing independence was both necessary and under attack. For William Wordsworth, in contrast, his closeness to Dorothy was what allowed him to differentiate himself from Coleridge and to become the poet of the egotistical sublime.

Brother Novelists and the Sister: Henry Fielding, Samuel Richardson, Sarah Fielding

The novel gained its critical legitimacy in the wake of Henry Fielding's and Samuel Richardson's novels. Novelists, like other writers, might look to a paternal inheritance to legitimize their writing: in *Joseph Andrews*, Henry Fielding looked back to the lost comic work of Homer, the 'Father of this [epic] Species of Poetry', for a mythic origin for his fictional practice. However, writers of prose

[14] Henry Fielding, *Joseph Andrews*, ed. Douglas Brooks (Oxford: OUP, 1971), 3.

fiction had fewer fathers to emulate, less of an established literary tradition to join, than writers of drama or poetry. Their inheritance from the seventeenth-century romance and from recent forms of amatory fiction—both feminized forms, associated with women as writers and readers—can be construed as a maternal legacy, and one that many novelists, certainly both Fielding and Richardson, wished to deny. Both writers made claims for the novelty of their work: in *Tom Jones* Fielding boasted of being 'the Founder of a new Province of Writing', and therefore 'at liberty to make what Laws I please therein'; while Richardson wrote of his hope that *Pamela* would institute a 'new species of writing' which would lead readers away from improbable romance, and 'promote the cause of religion and virtue'.[15] Fiction, to use Fielding's metaphor, was a new province to be established, not inherited, and both 'brother Biographers' staked a claim to it. Through their rivalry and through contemporary critical discussions that polarized the differences between their work, the novel was defined as the work of brothers, and it gained its legitimacy through this process rather than as a result of descent from literary fathers.

To see the 'elevation' of the novel as the work of rival brothers is to raise the question of the place of the sister in this process. Carole Pateman argues that women are not full participants in the 'fraternal social contract', but are assumed to relate to men conjugally—their place is as subordinate wives.[16] Juliet Flower MacCannell describes the Enlightenment replacement of patriarchal with fraternal authority as a further devaluation of women, arguing that in modern social relations, repression and denial of the mother is replaced by repression and denial of the sister.[17] Within the literary field, however—specifically, within the field of prose fiction—it was not possible simply to deny the participation of women. The

---

[15] Henry Fielding, *The History of Tom Jones, a Foundling*, bk. 2, ch. 1, ed. Martin C. Battestin and Fredson Bowers (Oxford: Clarendon Press, 1974), i. 77; Samuel Richardson to Aaron Hill, 1741, in *Selected Letters of Samuel Richardson*, ed. John Carroll (Oxford: Clarendon Press, 1964), 41.

[16] Pateman, *Disorder*, 43.   [17] MacCannell, *Regime*, 12, 16, 18.

fraternal rivalry between Henry Fielding and Samuel Richardson
needs to be understood through their respective relationships to an
important sister author, Sarah Fielding.

Given that a number of their female contemporaries were writing
fiction and that the novel was in many ways a feminized genre,
Samuel Richardson and Henry Fielding were bound to be conscious
of women novelists and to take up some stance in relation to them.
Richardson in particular, whose works are indebted to the amatory
fictions of a previous generation of women writers, was deeply
concerned to differentiate his writing from theirs. I have argued
elsewhere that Aphra Behn, whose *Love Letters between a Nobleman
and his Sister* anticipates some of *Clarissa*'s themes from a very
different standpoint, functioned for Richardson as a literary mother
who needed to be repudiated, and her influence denied, in the process
of staking his claims for his own fiction.[18] For Henry Fielding, secure
in his place in a masculine, classical tradition, the question of literary
mothers was less important, though he too made some disparaging
remarks about Behn. Both men encouraged contemporary female
authors while disparaging earlier ones. Henry Fielding helped launch
his sister Sarah's literary career. Richardson surrounded himself with
female correspondents, usually much younger women whom he
thought of as daughters rather than sisters. Like his rival, he also
helped contemporary women novelists. Both men were supportive
of Charlotte Lennox, Richardson through his help with revision and
publication of *The Female Quixote* and Henry Fielding through his
favourable review of this novel in *The Covent-Garden Journal*.[19]

We can see these relations with writing women as the replacement
of potentially threatening maternal influence with a subordinate
feminine figure who stands as sister or daughter to the male writer.
This is similar to the strategies Ross finds in the Romantic poets,

[18] Jane Spencer, *Aphra Behn's Afterlife* (Oxford: OUP, 2000), 134–41.
[19] For Richardson's help with Lennox's novel, see Duncan Isles's appendix in
Charlotte Lennox, *The Female Quixote*, ed. Margaret Dalziel (Oxford: World's Classics,
1989), 419–28. Fielding's recommendation of *The Female Quixote* is in *The Covent-
Garden Journal*, ed. Bertrand A. Goldgar (Oxford: Clarendon Press, 1988), 158–61.

who wished to escape maternal influence, in their case the influence
of maternal Nature, by 'relying on the "natural" condition of
the feminine as subordinate other', a condition they looked for
in 'sympathetic sister-wives'.[20] It is noteworthy, however, that the
eighteenth-century novelists were generally more disposed than the
Romantic poets to encourage the sister as writer. Henry Fielding
and Samuel Richardson do not accord their sister writers equality,
but nor do they refuse to value them. Henry Fielding offers a nice
illustration of the way rejection of the literary mother is accompanied
by praise of the literary sister. While the narrator of *Tom Jones*
makes ironic reference to 'Mrs. *Behn's* Novels' as the 'improving'
bedtime reading of the young rake Mr Maclachlan, the novel's
heroine seriously endorses a more recent novel, 'the Production of a
young Lady of Fashion, whose good Understanding, I think, doth
Honour to her Sex, and whose good Heart is an honour to Human
Nature'—probably a reference to Sarah Fielding's *The Adventures of
David Simple*.[21]

   Sarah Fielding has too often been seen as most importantly Henry
Fielding's sister, and we need to remember the other relationships
that were central to her life and work. Living much of her time with
her three sisters, forming close relationships with the Collier sisters,
and being supported in her later years by a group of wealthier female
friends, Sarah Fielding offers a strong illustration of the importance
of real and metaphorical sisters to women writers of her time.[22] I
concentrate here on her relations to her brother and to Richardson
because these offer an illuminating example of the position of the
sister between two rival brother novelists. She was, of course, doubly
Henry Fielding's sister writer, being related to him by real as well as
metaphorical kinship ties; while she was connected to Richardson as

[20] Ross, *Contours*, 88, 91.   [21] Henry Fielding, *Tom Jones*, ii. 530; i. 286.
[22] For biographical accounts of Sarah Fielding see Linda Bree, *Sarah Fielding*
(New York: Twayne Publishers, 1996), 1–28; *The Correspondence of Henry and Sarah
Fielding*, ed. Martin C. Battestin and Clive T. Probyn (Oxford: Clarendon Press, 1993),
pp. xviii–xliii; and Peter Sabor, Introd. to *The Adventures of David Simple* and *Volume
the Last* (Lexington, KY.: University Press of Kentucky, 1998), pp. ix–xxxvii.

sister to his rival and friend to himself, and as an admirer and defender of his writing. She occupied 'the awkward position of intermediator'.[23] The rival 'brothers', Henry Fielding and Samuel Richardson, mediated their relationship through her, each of them in different ways trying to claim her allegiance as a writer. Sarah Fielding responded to her position as sister through a discussion of brother–sister relationships in her writing and through critical remarks in her prefaces. For her, the fraternal bond was important as a means of imagining egalitarian social relations, and in her literary sisterhood to her brother and to Richardson she sought a connection to both of them that would not confine her to being the disciple of either.

Henry Fielding's career as a novelist was intimately linked to his rival's from the beginning. *Shamela* was one of a number of anti-*Pamela* attacks that responded to Richardson's best-selling first novel, and in *Joseph Andrews* (1742), his distinctive comic voice as a novelist began to emerge from a further engagement with Richardson's novel. Despite the way the younger novelist's work grew out of an antagonistic exchange with the elder's, there is evidence of friendship between them in the late 1740s when both *Clarissa* and *Tom Jones* were being written.[24] What part Sarah Fielding may have played in this we do not know. Linda Bree suggests that by 1747 her growing intimacy with Richardson annoyed her brother, while Peter Sabor surmises that her influence mediated between the two.[25] What is clear is not only that both brother and sister strongly admired Richardson's new work in progress, but that Henry Fielding was on sufficiently friendly terms with Richardson in 1748 to receive a copy of the fifth volume of *Clarissa* before publication. His appreciative letter to Richardson, signed 'Yrs. Most Affectionately', is the only

[23] Peter Sabor, Introd. to Sarah Fielding, *Remarks on Clarissa Addressed to the Author* (Los Angeles: William Andrews Clark Memorial Library, 1985), p. iii. See also Peter Sabor, 'Richardson, Henry Fielding, and Sarah Fielding', in Thomas Keymer and Jon Mee (eds.), *The Cambridge Companion to English Literature 1740–1830* (Cambridge: CUP, 2004), 139–56.

[24] Eaves and Kimpel, *Samuel Richardson: A Biography*, 292–4.

[25] Bree, *Sarah Fielding*, 13; Sabor, introd. to *David Simple*, p. viii.

surviving remnant of what was presumably a more extensive friendly correspondence between them. The letter details Fielding's response to the volume, a response he characterizes as 'the Overflowings of a Heart which you have filled brimful'.[26] This is indeed 'one of the warmest letters of praise ever written by one author to a rival'.[27] It also alludes very frankly to that rivalry, and reveals some of Fielding's anxieties as he contemplated the chances of his own *Tom Jones*, soon to be published.

After praising Richardson's work, Fielding turns in the final part of the letter to an appraisal of their relationship:

> This last [remark] seems to come from the Head. Here then I will end: for I assure you nothing but my Heart can force me to say Half of what I think of *the* Book. And yet what hinders me? I cannot be suspected of Flattery. I know the value of that too much to throw it away, where I have no Obligation, and where I expect no Reward. And sure the World will not suppose me inclined to flatter one whom they will suppose me to hate if the[y] will be pleased to recollect that we are Rivals for that Coy Mrs. Fame.
>
> Believe me however if your Clarissa had not engaged my Affections more than this Mrs. all your Art and all your Nature had not been able to extract a single Tear: for as to this Mrs. I have ravished her long ago, and live in a settled cohabitation with her in defiance of that Public Voice which is supposed to be her Guardian, and to have alone the Power of giving her away.
>
> To explain this Riddle. It is not that I am less but more addicted to Vanity than others; so much that I can wrap my self up as warmly in my own vanity, as the Ancient could involve himself in his Virtue. If I have any Merit I certainly know it and if the World will not allow it me, I will allow it my self.
>
> I would not have you think (I might say know) me *to be* so dishonest as to assert that I despise Fame; but this I solemnly

[26] *Correspondence of Henry and Sarah Fielding*, 70.
[27] Eaves and Kimpel, *Samuel Richardson*, 294.

aver that I love her as coldly, as most of us do Heaven, so that
I will sacrifice nothing to the Pursuit of her, much less would I
bind my self, as all her Passionate Admirers do, to harbour in
my Bosom that Monster Envy which of all Beings either real
or imaginary I most heartily and sincerely abhor.

You will begin to think I believe, that I want not much
external Commendation. I will conclude then with assuring
you. That I heartily wish you Success. That I sincerely think
you in the highest manner deserve it. And that if you have it
not, it it [sic] would be in me unpardonable Presumption to
hope for Success, and at the same time almost contemptible
Humility to desire it.[28]

The fraternal rivalry between the novelists is defined through a
struggle over the possession of a woman. Even as he praises his
rival, Henry Fielding claims 'Mrs. Fame' as his own, revealing an
underlying fear that the author of *Clarissa* will take her for himself.
Mrs Fame, however, is a sexualized and devalued female: Fielding
has been living with her for years. It is the highest of compliments
to Richardson that it is his heroine, the type of the elevated,
spiritualized woman, who represents the merit that is to be opposed
to mere fame. That Fielding prefers Clarissa to Fame indicates his
own magnanimity, but the cost of the preference is perhaps indicated
by the fact that (as he ruefully admits) he spends so much of this
letter of praise to Richardson praising himself. The high compliment
to Richardson is tempered by a certain tendency to play down
Richardson's creative role. The way she is described here, Clarissa
seems independent of her author: it is she, not his 'Art' and 'Nature'
(the very qualities we might have thought created her) who has
moved Fielding to tears.

In this letter Fielding attempts to transcend the novelists' rivalry
by devaluing the fame for which they both contend and emphasizing that both aspire to a higher goal; and in the face of some
discomfort, he grants that Clarissa, representing that goal, belongs to

[28] *Correspondence of Henry and Sarah Fielding*, 71–2.

Richardson. Elsewhere, Fielding mediated his rivalry with Richardson through a different figure, another elevated female who appealed to the heart: his sister Sarah. Richardson, however, increasingly made his own claim to Sarah Fielding's allegiance. An examination of the literary relations among these three writers between 1742, when Sarah Fielding contributed to *Joseph Andrews*, and the late 1750s, shows first Henry Fielding and then Samuel Richardson using Sarah Fielding as a tool in their rivalry. They struggle for possession of Sarah Fielding as sister author, each using her writing as a way of attacking the other's, and each attempting to enlist her on his side in the clash between their two conceptions of fiction.

From their own time to the present, the differences between Henry Fielding and Samuel Richardson have been interpreted in gendered terms, Richardson's interiority and concentration on nuances of emotion being understood as feminine, Fielding's exteriority, wide social range, and de-emphasis of chastity being seen as masculine. Critics have tended to favour one or the other. In the early- and mid-twentieth century Fielding's reputation was generally the higher, many critics explicitly preferring him on the grounds of greater masculinity.[29] Richardson, meanwhile, was praised by women of his own time, and sometimes by feminist critics of the late twentieth century, as a friend to women.[30] Certainly contrasting attitudes to the feminine, specifically to the place of the feminine voice within fiction, are central to the early clash between the two. In *Pamela* Richardson mimics a feminine voice, or rather develops a voice—naive, ingenuous, introspective, sensitive, moral—which comes to exemplify femininity for his readers. Central to his purposes

[29] In an anecdote that illustrates the macho values associated with Fielding, W. B. Carnochan reports that the support for Richardson in Ian Watt's *The Rise of the Novel* was strange to him when it appeared in 1957. He was more used to praise of Fielding and disparagement of Richardson from a 'rather pugnacious' professor who had been a boxer. Carnochan, ' "A Matter *Discutable*": *The Rise of the Novel*', *Eighteenth-Century Fiction*, 12/2–3, *Reconsidering the Rise of the Novel* (Jan.–Apr. 2000), 178.

[30] Katharine M. Rogers e.g. credits Richardson with 'sensitive feminism': see her *Feminism in Eighteenth-Century England* (Brighton: Harvester Press, 1982).

is the reader's trust in this feminine voice. In *Shamela*, in which all the heroine's sensibilities and concern for her 'vartue' are pretences, Fielding replaces this voice with the voice of woman as sham. In his next response to *Pamela*, he moves beyond this simple mockery of the feminine voice. In *Joseph Andrews*, Fielding can be seen as enacting his fraternal rivalry with Richardson through 'the feminization or emasculation of the rival male'.[31]

This strategy involves an implicit denial of any fraternal bond between the writers and their kinds of writing, expressed through the invocation and rejection of a fraternal relationship between the protagonists of their respective fictions. Jill Campbell persuasively reads *Joseph Andrews*—whose hero is introduced as, but turns out not to be, the brother of Richardson's Pamela Andrews—as a work in which Fielding progressively demotes *Pamela*. First, he feminizes it, for the postulated relationship between Joseph and Pamela suggests that Richardson's novel stands to Fielding's as sister to brother. Later, even this kinship is denied, and '[a]s Joseph is released from a genealogical relation to Richardson's heroine by the revelations of the novel's conclusion, so Fielding's work itself gain[s] a form of autonomy from its predecessor in the course of the novel'.[32] However, Henry Fielding is not simply claiming a masculine territory and repudiating feminine influence. The letter from Leonora to Horatio in Book 2, chapter 4 is introduced as 'written by a young Lady'; and it is likely that it represents Sarah Fielding's first publication.[33] Henry Fielding neither mimics the feminine voice, like Richardson, nor rejects it; rather, he incorporates it into his novel, as a voice different from but framed within the masculine.

In the three-volume *Miscellanies* which Henry Fielding published in the following year, Sarah Fielding's work was probably incorporated again, in the form of Anna Boleyn's narrative in *A Journey from*

[31] Ross, *Contours*, 88.
[32] Jill Campbell, *Natural Masques: Gender and Identity in Fielding's Plays and Novels* (Stanford, Calif.: Stanford University Press, 1995), 61–115, 71.
[33] *Joseph Andrews*, 94.

this World to the Next.[34] Anticipating Sarah Fielding's later *The Lives of Cleopatra and Octavia*, this narrative brings a queen back from the dead to tell her story; and like Sarah Fielding's Cleopatra, Anna Boleyn comes to grief because she acts the seductress and pursues ambition through loveless marriage. Deliberately set off, by the fiction of a gap in the manuscript, from the rest of *A Journey*, Anna Boleyn's story introduces a woman's viewpoint, and is presented as different kind of writing. In a footnote Henry Fielding explains 'that this Chapter is in the Original writ in a Woman's Hand: And tho' the Observations in it are, I think, as excellent as any in the whole Volume, there seems to be a Difference in Style between this and the preceeding Chapters; and as it is the Character of a Woman which is related, I am inclined to fancy it was really written by one of that Sex'.[35] The view expressed here of a woman's writing as complementary to a man's, offering a different style and a specific understanding of female character, is echoed in Henry Fielding's later observations on his sister's writing. In his preface to her *Familiar Letters*, he praises her first novel, *David Simple*, as a work only a woman could have written. A 'Lady of very high Rank', he reports, said that '*so far . . . from doubting David Simple to be the performance of a Woman, I am very well convinced, it could not have been written by a Man*'.[36] A woman only, he explains, could fully understand the mysteries of women's conduct in love, for in this matter they are educated 'in Constraint of, nay, in direct Opposition to, Truth

---

[34] *Miscellanies by Henry Fielding, Esq*, ii, ed. Hugh Amory, introd. Bertrand A. Goldgar (Oxford: Clarendon Press, 1993), 113–28. Goldgar discusses the attribution to Sarah Fielding, first suggested by Aurélion Digeon in 1931, concluding that it should be taken seriously (ibid., pp. xxiv–xxxvi). J. F. Burrows, using controversial stylometric techniques, concludes that Henry Fielding began the work, that Sarah continued it, and that he added the ending or revised hers: see J. F. Burrows and A. J. Hassall, '*Anna Boleyn* and the Authenticity of Fielding's Feminine Narratives', *Eighteenth-Century Studies*, 21 (1988), 444. My own view is that the correspondence of its themes with those later developed in *The History of Cleopatra and Octavia* suggests Sarah Fielding's authorship.

[35] *Miscellanies*, ii. 111.

[36] *Familiar Letters between the Principal Characters in David Simple* (London: A. Millar, 1747), vol. i. pp. xvi–xvii.

and Nature', and are bound to deceive men (*Familiar Letters*, vol. i. p. xvii). There may be a dig here at Richardson, whose work claims access to the secrets of female minds and hearts; at any rate Henry Fielding characterizes such access as a form of male tyranny. Those who disagree with him on woman's superior knowledge of woman are men 'who are not only absolute Masters of some poor Woman's Person, but likewise of her Thoughts' (ibid., pp. xviii–xix). In his comments on his sister's early writing, then, Henry Fielding stresses his respect for a different, specifically feminine viewpoint, which he does not claim to share; and his incorporation of female narrators, sometimes authored by his sister, into his work to represent a female viewpoint has been seen as a tacit admission of the limitations of his ability to present female characters through a masculine narrator.[37]

The feminine viewpoint he praises, however, is not the rendering of feminine subjectivity but an insider's knowledgeable satire on female follies. Women typically exhibit 'such a constant Struggle between Nature and Habit, Truth and Hypocrisy, as introduce often much Humour into their Characters; especially when drawn by sensible Writers of their own Sex, who are on this Subject much more capable, than the ablest of ours' (*Familiar Letters*, vol. i, p. xvii). Accordingly Sarah Fielding has 'exposed some of these nicer Female Foibles, which have escaped most other Writers' (ibid., pp. xix–xx), and indeed may be subject to 'the Resentment of her own lovely Sex . . . for having betrayed the Secrets of the Society' (ibid., p. xix). His sister's distinctive feminine viewpoint is thus seen as a branch of the tradition of satirical writing to which he himself belongs. Elsewhere, Henry Fielding's praise of his sister's writing is calculated to draw her work into the orbit of his. His preface to the second edition of *David Simple* is concerned both to distance the work from his own authorship and to emphasize the writer's relationship to him. Because the novel has been attributed to him he wants to set the record straight: Sarah Fielding wrote it, he did not see most of

[37] Burrows and Hassall, '*Anna Boleyn*', 446, 449.

it before printing, and '*Indeed I believe there are few Books in the World so absolutely the Author's own as this*'. This exonerates him from any blame for the '*Grammatical and other Errors in Style*' in the first edition, which he has now taken care to correct.[38] The changes to the second edition, though usually minor, are indeed extensive, and suggest he took care and time over them. For this he was once praised for improving 'the brave and bungling literary efforts of a loving, trusting sister';[39] more recently, his role has been less favourably interpreted. Janine Barchas reads his revision of Sarah Fielding's punctuation, and especially his deletion of her dashes, as an attempt to expunge the traces of a more 'feminine' sentimental expressiveness typical of Richardson's, and later of Sterne's, work.[40] Henry's description of Sarah's work aligns her novel with his: '*I have attempted in my Preface to* Joseph Andrews *to prove, that every Work of this kind is in its nature a comic Epic Poem, of which* Homer *left us a Precedent, tho' it be unhappily lost*' (*David Simple*, 345). Dividing comic epics into those of single action (Boileau's *Le Lutrin*, Pope's *Dunciad*) and those of serial action (Butler's *Hudibras*, Cervantes's *Don Quixote*), he categorizes *David Simple* as '*of this latter kind*' (ibid. 346). With the authority of Samuel Butler, Alexander Pope, and indeed Homer himself to support her episodic narrative, the author of *David Simple* is drawn firmly into a classical, masculine tradition, and aligned with the work of her brother.

Henry Fielding also took part in his sister's next work of fiction, which capitalized on the success of *David Simple* by presenting a series of letters, many of them supposed to be written by characters from the previous work. As well as writing the preface he contributed five letters. As a series of letters from different characters on miscellaneous subjects, *Familiar Letters* really had little in common with the single viewpoint of *Pamela*; nevertheless, Henry Fielding took the

---

[38] Fielding, *David Simple*, ed. Sabor, 344, 345.
[39] R. S. Hunting, 'Fielding's Revisions of *David Simple*', *Boston University Studies in English*, 3 (1957), 121.
[40] Janine Barchas, 'Sarah Fielding's Dashing Style and Eighteenth-Century Print Culture', *ELH* 63 (1996), 633–56.

opportunity to glance at Richardson in the preface, remarking that 'sure no one will contend, that the epistolary Style is in general the most proper to a Novelist, or that it hath been used by the best Writers of this Kind' (p. ix). Associating Sarah Fielding's work with his own, dissociating it from Richardson's, Henry Fielding laid claim to a sister novelist, who could be added to the classical tradition he was himself constructing for the novel, and whose inclusion incorporated into that tradition the specifically feminine viewpoint which might otherwise be seen as the property of Richardson.

Soon after making this disparaging remark about epistolary method, Henry Fielding was praising the author of *Clarissa* for his 'Penetration into Nature' and 'Power to raise and alarm the Passions', and defending the heroine against readers' contradictory criticisms of her conduct: 'She is too cold; she is too fond. She uses her Father, Mother, Uncles, Brother, Sister, Lover, Friend, too ill, too well.'[41] The letter to Richardson already discussed extended this praise. Sarah Fielding made very similar points in her own *Remarks on Clarissa* (1749), the first sustained critical commentary on the novel. At this point relations among all three writers seem to have been at their friendliest, and it has been suggested that this was due in part to Sarah Fielding's mediation between the two men. Certainly she was personally acquainted with Richardson by this time, and writing to him in warm appreciation of his friendship as well as his novel. Perhaps 'sisterly intervention' kept adverse remarks on Richardson out of the *Jacobite's Journal*; and perhaps Sarah should even be considered, as Aurélion Digeon once described her, as 'confidante and "liaison officer"' between the two men.[42] We do not know enough about the relationships among them to be sure. However, *Remarks on Clarissa* does suggest the close relations of influence among the three writers at this time. Sarah is likely to have been influenced by Henry's critique of *Clarissa*, and both probably formed their views of

---

[41] *Jacobite's Journal*, 2 Jan. 1748; *The Jacobite's Journal and Related Writings*, ed. W. B. Coley (Oxford: Clarendon Press, 1974), 119, 120.

[42] Coley, Introd. to *Jacobite's Journal*, p. lx; Aurélion Digeon, *The Novels of Henry Fielding* (1925; repr. New York: Russell, 1962), 27.

the novel in conversation together. Richardson's influence is clearly present in the manner as well as the matter of *Remarks*. It takes the form of a conversation between characters with different opinions of Richardson's work, echoing his use of multiple points of view, and also recalling the discussions about the novel in Richardson's correspondence. Several of the characters mirror those in the novel, deftly indicating both the bias of their criticisms and the point that the novel itself has anticipated them. One opponent of the heroine is a tyrannical father whose unkindness to his own daughter echoes Mr Harlowe's more extreme treatment of his; a 'sprightly Girl', like Anna Howe, finds Hickman too tame; and Bellario, who gradually becomes an admirer of the heroine, follows a trajectory like Belford's in the novel. While Sarah Fielding provided a Richardsonian defence of Richardson, he reciprocated by using remarks she had given to Miss Gibson and Bellario in later editions of *Clarissa*, so that the pamphlet 'played a significant role in shaping Richardson's revisions and additions to *Clarissa*'.[43]

From around this time, Richardson took a strong interest in Sarah Fielding's work, both as a printer and as a friend. While her first novel was corrected by her brother, it was Richardson who made suggestions for her pioneering schoolchildren's book, *The Governess* (1749). He wanted the work to come out firmly against corporal punishment, a revision Sarah Fielding resisted for fear of antagonizing parents.[44] He continued to encourage her work in the following years and after Henry Fielding's death. However, if Sarah Fielding did indeed attempt to mediate between her brother and his rival, her efforts were not strong enough to overcome Richardson's antagonism. The success of *Tom Jones* seems to have set the seal on his dislike of Henry Fielding, and he kept up his rivalry with his brother novelist. If Henry tried to enlist Sarah on his side early in her career, Richardson's attempts to co-opt her were notable in her later years.

---

[43] Sabor, Introd. to *Remarks on Clarissa*, p. vi.

[44] Jane Collier to Richardson, 4 Oct. 1748, in *The Correspondence of Samuel Richardson*, ed. Anna Laetitia Barbauld (London: Richard Phillips, 1804), ii. 62–4.

Richardson attacked his rival's writing for immorality and addiction to low life, and was scornful of Fielding's forays into what he considered his own territory: Fielding, he thought, could not manage morality—'by several strokes in his Amelia he designed to be good, but knew not how'—or a lady—the heroine of *Tom Jones* was 'the weak, the insipid, the Runaway, the Inn-frequenting Sophia'.[45] He made remarks of this sort to his rival's sister. After reading the first volume of *Amelia* (all he claimed to be able to get through) he reported to Lady Bradshaigh: 'Poor Fielding! I could not help telling his sister, that I was equally surprised at and concerned for his continued lowness.'[46] In a later letter to Sarah Fielding he made a comparison between her and her brother that has become famous:

> What a knowledge of the human heart! Well might a critical judge of writing say, as he did to me, that your late brother's knowledge of it was not (fine writer as he was) comparable to your's. His was but as the knowledge of the outside of a clock-work machine, while your's was that of all the finer springs and movements of the inside.[47]

The 'critical judge of writing' here is generally agreed to be Samuel Johnson, who made a very similar comment on the characteristic difference between Henry Fielding and Samuel Richardson.[48] In a literary world disposed to admire *Tom Jones* and to consider its author, rather than the author of *Clarissa*, the 'founder' of 'a new species of writing',[49] Johnson's strong preference for Richardson's method and morality must have been very welcome. Praising Sarah

[45] *Selected Letters*, 196, 143.
[46] Richardson to Lady Bradshaigh, 23 Feb. 1752, ibid. 198.
[47] Richardson to Sarah Fielding, 7 Dec. 1756, ibid. 330.
[48] According to Boswell, Johnson said 'that there was as great a difference between [Richardson and Fielding] as between a man who knew how a watch was made, and a man who could tell the hour by looking on the dial-plate'. *Life of Johnson*, ed. R. W. Chapman, corr. J. D. Fleeman (Oxford: OUP, 1970), 389.
[49] An anonymous 1751 pamphlet, *An Essay on the New Species of Writing founded by Mr. Fielding*, laid down 'Laws' derived from Fielding's work: Ioan Williams (ed.), *Novel and Romance 1700–1800: A Documentary Record* (London: Routledge and Kegan Paul, 1970), 150–9.

Fielding's knowledge of the human heart, Richardson is effectively praising her for being different from her brother, and for belonging to his own introspective and moral tradition of fiction. Where Henry Fielding claims his sister for the comic epic poem, Richardson claims her for the Richardsonian novel. Each finds it important to have this female novelist on his side, but their respective relations to the sister practitioner differ: where Henry Fielding sees her as different and complementary, Richardson sees her as like. Henry Fielding sees her style as feminine to his masculine: Richardson stages a takeover of the feminine territory so that Sarah Fielding's work appears assimilated to his own. We might see the difference between the two men as the difference between Fielding's use of a literary sister, and Richardson's preference for literary daughters.

Subjected as she was to the rival claims of these brother novelists, Sarah Fielding was in an awkward position. How did she deal with these competing calls for her allegiance, and with the influence of two very different novelists; and to what extent did she gain a writing position independent of them? Sarah Fielding's friend Margaret Collier offers some insight into the frustration of being associated with a famous writing brother. On returning home after travelling to Lisbon with the dying Henry Fielding, she wrote to Richardson:

> I was sadly vexed, at my first coming, by a report which had prevailed here [Ryde], of my being the author of Mr. Fielding's last work, 'The Voyage to Lisbon:' the reason which was given for supposing it mine, was to the last degree mortifying, (viz) that it was so very bad a performance, and fell so far short of his other works, it must be the person *with him* who wrote it. This is the disadvantageous light poor women are held in, by the ill-nature of the world. If they write well, and very ingeniously, and have a brother, then to be sure—'She could not write so well; it was her brother's, no doubt.' If a man falls short of what is expected from his former genius in writing, and publishes a very dull and unentertaining piece, then 'to be sure it was his sister, or some woman friend, who was with him.' Alas! My good Mr Richardson, is not this a hard case?—To

you I appeal, as the only candid man, I believe, with regard to women's understandings; and indeed their only champion, and protector, I may say, in your writings; for you write of angels, instead of women.[50]

When Collier complains about the 'disadvantageous light' women writers are held in, she is clearly thinking not only of herself, in quasi-sisterly relation to Henry Fielding, but also of Sarah Fielding, whose first novel had been attributed to her brother. Collier is also, in this letter, staging a turn from Henry Fielding to Samuel Richardson as, in effect, a better friend and brother—the one who will understand this womanly complaint, the one who appreciates women's minds. It may be tempting to see Sarah Fielding, her early works overseen by Henry and her later ones encouraged by Richardson, as making a similar turn. Certainly her letters to Richardson show that she was drawn to his apparent readiness to see women as intellectually equal. She contrasted his welcome with the superciliousness of a '*hic, haec, hoc*' man, who said, well, I do wonder Mr Richardson will be troubled with such *silly women*'.[51] When Sarah Fielding pursued her own love of Latin (and Greek), her mentors were Arthur Collier and James Harris—not, of course, the relatively unlearned Richardson. Nevertheless it may well be that Richardson was a more encouraging friend for a female classicist than Henry Fielding, who, it has been claimed, fell out with his sister when she learned Latin.[52]

However, Sarah Fielding was not really one of Richardson's circle of 'daughters', though she is sometimes placed among them.[53]

---

[50] Margaret Collier to Richardson, 3 Oct. 1755; in *Correspondence*, ii. 77–8.

[51] Sarah Fielding to Samuel Richardson, 8 Jan. 1749, in *Correspondence of Henry and Sarah Fielding*, 123.

[52] Hester Thrale reported that Arthur Collier had told her that when Henry realized that Sarah could read Virgil, 'farewell to Fondness, the Author's jealousy was become stronger than the Brother's Affection, and he saw her further progress in literature not without pleasure only—but with Pain'. As Collier himself had quarrelled with Henry Fielding, his version may not be reliable. *Thraliana: The Diary of Mrs Hester Lynch Thrale (Later Mrs Piozzi) 1776–1809*, ed. Katharine C. Balderston (2nd edn., Oxford: Clarendon Press, 1951), i. 78.

[53] Battestin and Probyn e.g., describe her as 'inducted by Richardson into the category of honorary daughter'. *Correspondence of Henry and Sarah Fielding*, p. xxxi.

The tone of her correspondence with him is not the intimate and bantering one characteristic of Richardson's relations with the younger women whom he openly called 'daughter', and who often called him 'papa'.[54] She offers him no filial expressions, and her writing maintains an independence from his. While the tragic end of *Clarissa* may have had some bearing on her exploration of tragedy in *Volume the Last* of *David Simple*, she did not follow Richardson in the creation of benign epistolary communities that are so important to his third novel. Her later work maintained a more ironic tone and satiric purpose than his. The struggle between the two men for the sister was won by neither. Throughout her writing career she engaged with both men's work at different points and in various ways, in the pursuit of her independent literary goals.

In her later career she was certainly grateful for Richardson's help financially and with publication. He printed *The History of the Countess of Dellwyn*, and she requested his help in correcting errors for the press.[55] Artistically, however, the novel is not indebted to Richardson. In its basically satiric attitude and its sardonic narrative tone, it is less reminiscent of him than of Henry Fielding, to whose *Tom Jones* the narrator alludes.[56] Most importantly, though, this novel represents one working-out of a theme running through much of Sarah Fielding's work, and original to her: the failure of women's attempts

[54] In correspondence with Hester Mulso, Sophia Westcomb, and Mrs Scudamore Richardson refers to himself as 'father' or 'paternal friend' and to his friends as 'daughter' and 'child'. Sophia Westcomb and Mrs Scudamore both call him 'papa'. M. Klopstock calls herself 'your Hamburg daughter'. See numerous examples in Richardson, *Correspondence*, iii. 157–330. Writing to Sarah Fielding, he refers to Lady Bradshaigh as the 'daughter of my mind', ibid., ii. 101.

[55] See her letter to Richardson, 14 Dec. 1758, in which she refers to his loan of 10 guineas and asks him to 'cast an Eye on the printing' of the *Countess of Dellwyn*. *Correspondence of Henry and Sarah Fielding*, 149.

[56] Discussing the wedding of Miss Lucum with decrepit Lord Dellwyn, the narrator remarks that the wedding ring 'as if it had learned all the Knowledge of the moral Philosopher *Square*, appeared to be so fully acquainted with *the Fitness of Things*, as with great Indignation to decline being placed on the taper Finger of the blooming Virgin, by that withered hand'. *The History of the Countess of Dellwyn* (London: A. Millar, 1759), i. 6.

to gain sexual power over men. She frequently discusses and exposes female 'vanity', by which she usually means a woman's attempt to gain advantage through sexuality. Miss Lucum's tyrannical father is to blame for wanting his daughter to enter a socially grand and physically disgusting alliance with Lord Dellwyn, but she marries the peer to gain power, and 'when she answered *I will*, she never imagined that she had promised more than that she would thenceforward follow implicitly wheresoever Vanity should lead'.[57] It is this vanity, not sexual desire, that later leads Lady Dellwyn into adultery and disaster. She follows a pattern established by Sarah Fielding's Anna Boleyn and Cleopatra: women who attempt sexual conquests are acting not on desire but on the vain hope of gaining social power. They are always disappointed, both because they have ignored their own sexual desires and because the power they have bargained for does not materialize. Sarah Fielding's critique of a female power based on sexual conquest anticipates Wollstonecraft's complaint that

> the regal homage which [women] receive is so intoxicating, that until the manners of the times are changed, and formed on more reasonable principles, it may be impossible to convince them that the illegitimate power which they obtain by degrading themselves is a curse, and that they must return to nature and equality if they wish to secure the placid satisfaction that unsophisticated affections impart.[58]

Sarah Fielding, like Wollstonecraft, envisages a return to nature and equality in male–female relations, but for her this is to be based on an idealized brother–sister bond. It is here that this literary sister most differentiates herself from both her 'brothers', by her attempt to imagine a new basis for the brother–sister relation itself. Recent studies of *David Simple* have shown that the relationships within the novel are notable as relations of equality between brother and sister, and between men and women who relate to each other in

[57] Ibid. 78.
[58] *A Vindication of the Rights of Woman*, ed. M. B. Kramnick (Harmondsworth: Pelican, 1975), 103.

fraternal ways.[59] The novel begins with David's disappointment in his brother Daniel, who tries to defraud him out of his share of their inheritance, and precipitates David's quest to find a substitute for the lost fraternal relationship: 'To travel through the whole World, rather than not meet with a real Friend.'[60] Subsequent friendships and indeed his marriage are attempts to replace the lost brother.

The first of the people he meets to qualify as a 'real friend' is Cynthia, who, despite her gender and her poverty, always appears in the narrative as his equal. While David, with his money and benevolent intentions, clearly has greater social power than Cynthia, the poor gentlewoman living the life of a 'toad-eater' or paid companion, his extreme sensibility is seen as cancelling out that social power. Though he helps her financially this sets up no inequality between them. Meanwhile Cynthia's sharp satirical eye, contrasted to David's habitual naivety, makes her appear the stronger of the two. This relationship is later formalized into a fraternal one by marriage, as each marries one of the brother–sister pair Valentine and Camilla. Valentine and Camilla themselves have enjoyed the happy, equal sibling relationship David had originally wanted with Daniel. As Camilla explains, their love was fostered by an original equality of treatment from their parents: 'We loved each other with a perfect Fondness; there was no Partiality shewn to either of us, nor were we ever told, if we did not do right, the other should be loved best, in order to teach us to *envy*, and consequently to *hate* each other' (*David Simple*, 105). Their wicked stepmother has wilfully misconstrued their relationship as incestuous and they have been driven out of the family. David's benevolent rescue and their subsequent meeting with Cynthia (Camilla's friend and Valentine's

---

[59] See esp. Terri Nickel, ' "Ingenious Torment": Incest, Family, and the Structure of Community in the Work of Sarah Fielding', *Eighteenth Century: Theory and Interpretation*, 36 (1995), 234–47; George E. Haggerty, *Unnatural Affections: Women and Fiction in the Later Eighteenth Century* (Bloomington, Ind.: Indiana University Press, 1998); and Felicity Nussbaum, 'Effeminacy and Femininity: Domestic Prose Satire and *David Simple*', *Eighteenth-Century Fiction*, 11/4 (1999), 421–44.

[60] *David Simple*, 21.

lost love) creates an ideal foursome. As Terri Nickel argues, the characters 'reinvent the family as an alliance of siblings', doing away with paternal power and establishing egalitarian family relations, based on sympathetic identification.[61]

David's new egalitarian family holds its property in common. He is ready to share his fortune so that Valentine and Cynthia can marry:

> [*David*] assured [*Valentine*], if his Fortune could any way conduce to his Happiness, whatever share of it was necessary for him, should be intirely at his Service.
>
> *Valentine* was struck dumb with this Generosity. Tenderness and Gratitude for such uncommon Benevolence, was to be answered no other way, but by flowing Tears. *David* saw his Confusion, and begged him not to fancy he was under any Obligation to him, for that he should think his Life and Fortune well spent in the Service of a Man, whom both Nature and Goodness had so nearly allied to *Camilla*. *Valentine* at last with much difficulty found a vent for his Words, and swore no Passion of his should ever make him a greater Burden than he already was to such a Friend. (*David Simple*, 144)

To avoid the problems of unequal wealth even willingly shared, Fielding provides Valentine and Camilla with their own fortune when their repentant father meets them and makes them both his heirs, ignoring the custom of male primogeniture (*David Simple*, 246). The inset story of Isabelle and her brother also takes up this theme of shared wealth. Isabelle's brother, the Marquis de Staineville, forms a close brotherly relationship with Dumont. When he later meets Dumont penniless, he insists: 'you shall share my Fortune with me; and, from this time forward, the only Favour I beg of you, is to make my House your own' (ibid. 170). Henry Fielding altered this passage for the second edition, omitting the promise, and deleted a later reference to Staineville's plan to share house and estate with his sister and Dumont. Peter Sabor suggests that Henry considered this offer 'implausibly generous' (ibid. 387).

---

[61] Nickel, 'Ingenious Torment', 238.

Certainly it was implausible, but that was Sarah Fielding's point. Her ideal here is at odds with a trend towards greater concentration of inherited wealth during the seventeenth and eighteenth centuries, through the use of strict settlement to keep estates intact for eldest sons.[62] Her representation of equal inheritance among brothers and sisters recalls inheritance customs common in early modern England below the gentry. Here sons and daughters often inherited on an equitable basis, though sons were more likely to inherit land and daughters personal property.[63] Sarah Fielding's sentimental vision of a loving and sharing family is very different from the 'companionate marriage', which Lawrence Stone considered to be the developing form of family relationship in this period.[64] Her version of the affectionate family is rather based on equality of treatment for brothers and sisters; and in her vision a good marriage evolves from and is similar to a brother–sister relationship which she sees as more fundamental.[65]

In her later work Sarah Fielding becomes noticeably more pessimistic about the possibility of a family based on fraternal equality. The sequel to *David Simple, Volume the Last*, details the near-destruction of David's extended family when it loses the wealth that protects its alternative lifestyle, and is left at the mercy of the deadly patronage offered by the Orgueil family. The loving family group,

[62] Ruth Perry, 'Women in Families: the Great Disinheritance', in Vivien Jones (ed.), *Women and Literature in Britain 1700–1800* (Cambridge: CUP, 2000), 111–31.

[63] Amy Louise Erickson, *Women and Property in Early Modern England* (London: Routledge, 1993), 71; Richard Grassby, *Kinship and Capitalism: Marriage, Family, and Business in the English-Speaking World, 1580–1740* (Cambridge: Woodrow Wilson Center Press and CUP, 2001), 356–61.

[64] See Lawrence Stone, *The Family, Sex and Marriage in England 1500–1800* (London: Weidenfeld and Nicholson, 1977). Though his findings have been strongly disputed and cannot be accepted as proving real changes in family relationships, it is clear that 18th-cent. representations of marriage included a new emphasis on companionship and affection as ideals. See Gillian Skinner, 'Women's Status as Legal and Civic Subjects', in Jones (ed.), *Women and Literature*, 92.

[65] On the continuing importance attached in 18th-cent. fiction to the brother–sister tie, often seen as more crucial than the conjugal bond, see Ruth Perry, *Novel Relations: The Transformation of Kinship in English Literature and Culture, 1748–1818* (Cambridge: CUP, 2004), 143–54.

vulnerable within the selfish wider society on which it is economically dependent, is broken by partings, emigration, and the successive deaths of all but Cynthia and her niece Camilla, the daughter of David and Camilla.[66] The darker vision of this sequel was no doubt influenced by Fielding's own experience of the destruction of a family circle, when she lost her three sisters and her nephew within a few months of each other in 1750–1.

Volume the Last also seems to be in dialogue with Richardson's later work. While he had brought his good woman, Clarissa, so starkly into conflict with her social world that her fate had to be tragic, Richardson had a very different idea of the social position of the good man. While composing *Sir Charles Grandison*, he mused on the inherent difficulties of creating such a figure, who could not have the pathetic appeal of a virtuous woman:

> I own that a good woman is my favourite character; and that I
> can do twenty agreeable things for her, none of which would
> appear in a striking light in a man. Softness of heart, gentleness
> of manners, tears, beauty, will allow of pathetic scenes in the
> story of one, which cannot have place in that of the other.
> Philanthropy, humanity, is all that he can properly rise to. And
> glorious indeed are those qualities in a man.[67]

Volume the Last takes issue with the conception of a 'glorious' masculine virtue, inseparable from social power, exemplified by Richardson's final hero, and insists instead on not only the gentleness of manners and softness of heart, but also the social and economic vulnerability, of its good man.

In other later works, she is more pessimistic about the achievement of fellowship and equality in the first place. In *The Cry*, Nicanor's family suffers because the eldest boy has been indulged at the expense

---

[66] For a discussion of *Volume the Last* as an exposure of the impossibility of a self-enclosed, sentimental community see Betty A. Schellenberg, *The Conversational Circle: Re-reading the English Novel, 1740–1775* (Lexington, Ky.: University Press of Kentucky, 1996), 116–30.

[67] Richardson to Lady Bradshaigh, 24 Mar. 1751, in *Selected Letters*, 180.

of the twin brother and sister who follow him. Stories of difficult sibling relations are multiplied. Cordelia dismisses one suitor, for example, on the grounds that he is a bad brother:

> He kept in his house a brother who had fail'd in business as his book-keeper; and fewer privileges did that brother enjoy, than he would have given his father's butler, if he had been qualified for the office. His only sister, whose outward deformity, poor girl, had prevented her ever hoping for any other protection, lived with him as his house-keeper; and how she lived need not be told, since it was with a brother, who worth near a plumb could suffer his sister to remain in that situation.[68]

In *The Lives of Cleopatra and Octavia*, tragedy ensues when principles of harmony and equality between brother and sister are violated. I have argued elsewhere that in this work Fielding explores the difference between the societies of Egypt and Rome through the difference in their brother–sister relations.[69] The Egypt of Cleopatra's youth is a society where brother and sister marry and rule together. Three 'Men of ambitious Spirits', Pothinas, Achillas, and Theodotus, separate Cleopatra from her brothers and start off the chain of events that eventually makes Cleopatra her brother's rival.[70] After the death of her elder brother, she has the younger brother killed in order to avoid sharing the throne with him. However, the power of the Roman world intervenes, and Cleopatra is reduced to seducing and manipulating Caesar. The fraternal, power-sharing marriage gives way to degraded and unequal sexual relations. Meanwhile Octavia accepts her role in the Roman social structure as an object of exchange between powerful men, whose only consolation must be the inner power of the virtuous mind. This is a vision of a fallen world—fallen from an original brother–sister

---

[68] *The Cry: A New Dramatic Fable* (London: R. and J. Dodsley, 1754), i. 272–3.
[69] Jane Spencer, 'Women Writers and the Eighteenth-Century Novel', in John Richetti (ed.), *The Cambridge Companion to the Eighteenth-Century Novel* (Cambridge: CUP. 1996), 212–35.
[70] *The Lives of Cleopatra and Octavia*, ed. Christopher D. Johnson (London: Associated University Presses, 1994), 57.

equality—within which Fielding can offer only limited consolation and no solution.

Richardson, too, had analysed the imbalance of power in brother–sister relationships, allowing Clarissa to point out that her brother James should not wield an authority over her that of right belongs to their father. In *Sir Charles Grandison*, however, his version of a good brother combines loving care for his sisters with a very clear assumption of authority over them. Henry Fielding portrayed sisters variously: in *Amelia*, Booth's rediscovered sister is the focus of strong emotional attachment, while in *Tom Jones* Mrs Western is the source of comic bafflement and irritation to her brother. It was left to Sarah Fielding to analyse the brother–sister relationship as a potential model for sexual equality. At the same time, as her sense of her own relation to literary tradition developed, she became more concerned to assert her independence as a writer from her brother novelists. The preface to the first edition of *David Simple* had very tentatively offered a definition of her practice: she introduced the novel as a *'Moral Romance (or whatever Title the Reader shall please to give it)'* (*David Simple*, 'Advertisement to the Reader'). The second edition, and *Familiar Letters*, both carried prefaces by her brother. By the time of *The Cry*, she had developed a view of her writing purposes far removed from Henry's idea of a comic epic. In their introduction to *The Cry* Fielding and Collier claim to be producing a new allegorical form of fiction that looks back explicitly to Spenser's *Faerie Queene* as its model—that is, it claims to be the daughter of a literary father to whom neither Henry Fielding nor Richardson would be direct heirs. While the aim 'thoroughly to unfold the labyrinths of the human mind', aligns *The Cry* with the 'interior' examination of the human heart which Richardson claimed as his domain, Fielding and Collier look not to him but to 'our master *Spenser*' (and to Ariosto and Milton).[71] Richardson recognized *The Cry*'s independence, writing that 'The Piece is a new Species of Writing, as I may say. The Plan, the Design at least, is new, and I think it deserves, on the whole, a

[71] *Cry*, i. 14, 22.

better reception than it has met with.'[72] The phrase 'new species of writing' echoes the claims Richardson himself made for *Pamela*. If he is seeing Sarah as his literary follower here he recognizes that she is following him by becoming an innovator herself.[73] The *Monthly Review* also recognized the work's novelty, remarking that its plan was 'entirely different from that of any modern novelist'.[74]

In the introduction to *The Lives of Cleopatra and Octavia*, Sarah Fielding again took a confident authorial stance, placing her work in a broad literary tradition by comparing it not only to the work of Henry Fielding and of Richardson, but also to that of Sidney and Cervantes. She praises heroes created by both her 'brothers', but at the same time she makes it clear that she is not following in the footsteps of either:

> Infatuated with a Sort of Knight errantry, we draw these fictitious Characters into a real Existence, and thus, pleasingly deluded, we find ourselves as warmly interested, and deeply affected by the imaginary scenes of *Arcadia*, the wonderful Atchievements [*sic*] of Don *Quixote*, the merry Conceits of *Sancho*, rural Innocence of a *Joseph Andrews*, or the inimitable Virtues of Sir *Charles Grandison*, as if they were real, and those romantic Heroes had experienced the capricious Fortunes attributed to them by the fertile invention of the Writers.
>
> Performances of this Kind have indeed one Advantage; that, as they are the Works of Fancy, the Author, like a Painter, may so colour, decorate, and embellish them, as most agreeably flatter our Humour, and most highly promise to entertain, captivate, and enchant the Mind.
>
> But to balance this, it may be offered in Recommendation of the Lives of Persons who have really made their Appearance

[72] Richardson to Sophia Westcomb, 9 Aug. 1754, cited in Bree, *Sarah Fielding*, 107.

[73] Richardson was, however, lukewarm in his praise of *The Cry*, the ending of which he found unsatisfactory. What he most objected to was the way that Portia's lover, Ferdinand, is left clearly her moral inferior, and he suggested that she revise the work for a new edition, changing the ending 'to make Ferdinand as worthy of his mistress at last, as he was at first' (*Correspondence*, ii. 108–9).

[74] *Monthly Review*, 10 (Apr. 1754), 280.

> on the Stage of the World, that their Actions are better suited
> to inform, and give us juster Notions of ourselves . . . The one,
> like false Coin, is rather calculated to deceive, than profit us;
> while the other, like current Gold, is of intrinsic Value. . .

All four male writers are creators of 'romantic Heroes', delightful but deceitful. Inverting the usual gendered literary judgement
that placed *women's* writing as romantic, entertaining, captivating,
enchanting—but not to be taken seriously—she attributes these
'feminine' qualities to her literary brothers and claims instead for
herself the supposedly 'masculine' realm of sober truth.

Sarah Fielding's most confident literary manifestos, then, show
that she did not think of herself as literary disciple to either Henry
Fielding or Richardson, though she was warm in her praise of both.
In the face of their rivalry, expressed through their rival claims to her,
she maintained a distance from them. Their own attempts to enlist
her to their respective fictional traditions were influential during that
late eighteenth-century and early nineteenth-century period when a
canon for the novel was being established. As Richardson's critical
defender, Sarah Fielding was sometimes placed in his tradition. After
reading her *Remarks on Clarissa*, Edward Young wrote to Richardson: 'I have read Miss Fielding with great pleasure. Your Clarissa
is, I find, the Virgin-mother of several pieces; which, like beautiful
suckers, rise from her immortal root'. More often, though, she was
considered in her relation to Henry. In her history of fiction Clara
Reeve concluded that Sarah Fielding's works were 'not unworthy
next to be mentioned after her brother's, if they do not equal them
in wit and learning, they excell in some other material merits, that
are more beneficial to their readers',[77] adding her own characteristic
slant to Henry's own account of his sister's feminine difference from
him by implying Sarah's moral superiority. Sometimes, as the eighteenth century progressed, her identity was confused with his, and her

[75] *Lives of Cleopatra and Octavia*, 54–5.
[76] Edward Young to Richardson, 5 Nov. 1749, in *Correspondence*, ii. 27.
[77] Clara Reeve, *The Progress of Romance* (Colchester: W. Keymer, 1785), i. 142.

works attributed to him.[78] Later in the nineteenth century and for much of the twentieth she was the object of critical condescension as a 'pale reflection' of her brilliant brother.[79] As Henry Fielding and Samuel Richardson became established as the two rival 'fathers' of the novel, Sarah Fielding's independent and original work fell from critical view, and it is only in more recent times that she has again been recognized as far more than 'Sister to the Novelist'.[80]

'She . . . preserved me still | A Poet': William Wordsworth, Dorothy Wordsworth, and Samuel Taylor Coleridge

Dorothy Wordsworth, in contrast to Sarah Fielding, did not seek an independent position in the literary tradition. Although, especially later in life, she wrote poetry, some of it published in editions of her brother's works, though she published the *Narrative of George and Sarah Green*, and though she wrote the extensive journals on which her now growing critical reputation is mainly based, she not only saw her writing as secondary to her brother's, but viewed much of it as existing for the service of his work. For Sarah Fielding, collaboration with her brother was only one aspect of a life that revolved around sisterhood and sisterly collaboration. Sisterly relationships were important to Dorothy Wordsworth, too, especially her long friendship with Mary Hutchinson, who married her brother. Dorothy and the Hutchinson sisters, Mary and Sara, formed a close-knit group.[81] For Dorothy, though, these sisterly relationships were not literary ones. Her writing life was bound

---

[78] Bree, *Sarah Fielding*, 146.

[79] Stewart J. Cooke discusses the recurring image of 'pale reflection' in comparisons between brother and sister in ' "Good Heads and Good Hearts": Sarah Fielding's Moral Romance', *English Studies in Canada*, 21 (1995), 269–70.

[80] She was so identified by one early reader: in the Bodleian copy of *Cry* (270.g.392) an 18th-cent. hand has written in ink on the title page 'by Miss Fielding', and in pencil on the facing page: 'Sister to the Novelist'.

[81] See Robert Gittings and Jo Manton, *Dorothy Wordsworth* (Oxford: Clarendon Press, 1985); Kathleen Jones, *A Passionate Sisterhood: The Sisters, Wives and Daughters of the Lake Poets* (London: Virago, 1998).

up with her brother's. Coleridge remarked in 1833 that she was 'a Woman of Genius, as well as manifold acquirements; and but for the absorption of her whole Soul in her Brother's fame and writings would, perhaps, in a different style have been as great a Poet as Himself'.[82] This tendency to absorption meant that Dorothy Wordsworth played a very different part in the triangle of herself, William, and Coleridge from the part Sarah Fielding played between her brother and Richardson.

The early relationship between Coleridge and Wordsworth has been intensively studied as the genesis of their best creative work: a time of mutual influence which issued in Coleridge's 'Wordswor thian' Conversation poems, and in Wordsworth's writing the 'poem to Coleridge' that later became *The Prelude*. For all their closeness, it was the working out of their differences that was crucial. Central tenets of the Romantic movement—Coleridge's theory of the Imagination, Wordsworth's understanding of the interaction between man and nature and its importance for the 'growth of the poet's mind'—were rooted in the dialogue between them. Their writing during these years has been read as a series of exchanges in which their different philosophical positions are worked out in poetic form: where Wordsworth finds in Nature an outside source for the imaginative power within himself, Coleridge's subjectivist views oppose the idea of harmonious connection between inner and outer worlds. Gene Ruoff, examining various versions of the poem that became Wordsworth's 'Immortality Ode' and of the verse letter to Sara Hutchinson that became Coleridge's 'Dejection: An Ode', shows how the two poets echoed and responded to each other. Coleridge's emphatic lines, 'Oh Sara! we receive but what we give, | And in *our* Life alone does Nature live', repudiate the faith of Wordsworth's Ode in the child's access, through natural forms, to the 'visionary gleam' of a pre-existing state.[83] In Coleridge's poem 'Wordsworth's celestial

---

[82] *Letters of Samuel Taylor Coleridge*, vi. 959.

[83] 'Letter to Sara Hutchinson', *The Collected Works of Samuel Taylor Coleridge, Poetical Works*, ed. J. C. C. Mays (London: Routledge), ii. 873.

light is shown to come from the self alone',[84] but the self is a continually failing source. Coleridge is the poet of the failure to feel at one
with nature, lamenting that he 'may not hope from outward Forms
to win | The Passion & the Life, whose Fountains are within'.[85]

The two poets' different relations to nature can be understood
in psychobiographical terms as issuing from their different relations
to the mother. In *The Prelude*, Wordsworth celebrated an initial
close mother–infant bond which was transformed, after his mother's
death, into a bond with maternal Nature. Mary Moorman, com-
menting on *The Prelude's* celebration of the 'filial bond | Of nature'
that connects the infant to the world, remarks that

> He could not have written thus if there had not remained
> with him a profound conviction of the beneficence of his
> own mother's care. She it was who first introduced him to
> 'Nature'—and when her own presence was withdrawn, he
> stood safely, though a little solemnly, in that universe which
> she had trusted and in which she had felt so perfectly at home.
> Soon he learnt to transfer to Nature the affection, the faith, the
> 'religious love' which he had felt for his mother.[86]

Coleridge, on the other hand, had a troubled relationship with his
mother and would seem never to have formed a sense of close
belonging to his family. The youngest of a large family of brothers
(and one sister, Nancy, who died when he was 18), he had to compete
for parental affection and felt himself to be a disappointment to his
mother. The sense of not having been properly mothered stayed
with him in later life.[87] For Wordsworth, the identity of the poet
as favoured son of the mother, of nature of the muse, was relatively
easily won, and Coleridge's contrasting lack of poetic self-confidence
was an important factor in their relationship. What McFarland calls

---

[84] Ruoff, *Wordsworth and Coleridge*, 98.

[85] 'Dejection: An Ode', *Poetical Works*, ii. 889.

[86] Mary Moorman, *William Wordsworth, A Biography: The Early Years, 1770–1803*
(Oxford: Clarendon Press, 1957), 3.

[87] Richard Holmes, *Coleridge: Early Visions* (London: Penguin, 1990), 9.

Coleridge's 'deep masochism' led him to subordinate his poetic style to Wordsworth's.[88] It has often been noticed that at the time of their first meeting it was Coleridge, already a rising published poet and intellectually a dominant figure, who might be expected to be the leader in their partnership; yet, concluding that Wordsworth was destined for poetic greatness, he wrote of him as his own superior.[89] 'Wordsworth is a very great man—the only man, to whom at all times and in all modes of excellence I feel myself inferior', he wrote to Southey in 1797.[90] Later remarks make it clear how far Coleridge linked Wordsworth's felt superiority to greater masculinity: Wordsworth is 'greater, better, manlier, more dear, by nature, to Woman, than I—I—miserable I'.[91]

Wordsworth's more privileged position in relation to nature and the maternal was exemplified in his closeness to his sister, who represented for him a link with the natural world that allowed him to become the poet of nature—with special access to the natural, yet differentiated from it. In 'Tintern Abbey', she appears as the representative of the poet's own younger self, for whom 'nature . . . was all in all'. While he has for ever lost the time when the forms of rock, mountain, and wood were to him

> An appetite: a feeling and a love,
> That had no need of a remoter charm,
> By thought supplied, or any interest
> Unborrowed from the eye . . .

Dorothy allows him a vicarious glimpse into a precious past:

> in thy voice I catch
> The language of my former heart, and read
> My former pleasures in the shooting lights
> Of thy wild eyes. Oh! Yet a little while

[88] McFarland, 'Symbiosis', 266. [89] Newlyn, *Language of Allusion*, 16.
[90] *Letters of Samuel Taylor Coleridge*, i. 334.
[91] *The Notebooks of Samuel Taylor Coleridge*, ed. Kathleen Coburn (London: Routledge and Kegan Paul, 1957), ii. 3148.

> May I behold in thee what I was once,
> My dear, dear Sister!
>
> (*Lyrical Ballads*, 118)

By the same token, she herself cannot share the 'sense sublime' of the oneness of all life, that 'motion and a spirit, that impels all thinking things', which is the poet's compensation for lost joys. She represents both the link to a lost relationship with nature and that which he needed to outgrow to become the poet of nature: as Margaret Homans puts it, 'what replaces the lost gleam of childhood is the poetic imagination or the ability to write poetry'.[92]

William's relationship with Dorothy exerted a profound influence on the relationship with Coleridge. McFarland has shown how Coleridge, who, as De Quincey remarked, repeatedly 'levied the services of sisters, brothers, daughters, sons, from the hands of strangers',[93] was attracted to couples who he hoped might provide a combination of the fraternal fellowship and feminine nurture he craved. He expected this from his friendship with Southey and his marriage to Sara Fricker (whose sister Southey married). Later in life his friendship with James and Anne Gillman proved a more lasting source of satisfaction.[94] 'Wordsworth and his exquisite Sister' were one such couple. He admired Dorothy as a sensitive observer, both of the natural world and of poetry: 'her information various—her eye watchful in minutest observation of nature—and her taste a perfect electrometer—it bends, protrudes, and draws in, at subtlest beauties and most recondite faults'. For her part Dorothy saw Coleridge as the epitome of poetic sensibility, whose eye 'speaks every emotion of his animated mind; it has more of the "poet's eye in a fine frenzy rolling" than I ever witnessed'.[95] During the time at Alfoxden, shared phrases

[92] Margaret Homans, *Women Writers and Poetic Identity: Dorothy Wordsworth, Emily Brontë, and Emily Dickinson* (Princeton: PUP, 1980), 54.

[93] *Recollections of the Lakes and the Lake Poets* (Harmondsworth: Penguin, 1978), 97.

[94] McFarland, *Romanticism*, 122.

[95] *Letters of Samuel Taylor Coleridge*, i. 330, 330–1; *The Letters of William and Dorothy Wordsworth*, ed. Ernest de Selincourt, rev. C. L. Shaver (Oxford: Clarendon Press, 1967), i. 189.

in William's poetry, Dorothy's journal, and Coleridge's poetry sometimes indicate such closeness of ideas that it is impossible to sort out a single origin. Richard Matlak suggests that William's writing during the first half of 1798 was partly fed by an unconscious need to struggle with Coleridge for Dorothy's allegiance.[96]

In the dialogue between Wordsworth and Coleridge on nature and philosophy, Wordsworth implicitly used his sister's example to help him create his position. Two Alfoxden poems from the spring of 1798, 'Expostulation and Reply' and 'The Tables Turned', reject books in favour of Nature's teachings. Their immediate occasion may have been a conversation with William Hazlitt, who has been identified with the 'friend ... somewhat unreasonably attached to modern books of moral philosophy' mentioned in the Advertisement to the *Lyrical Ballads*; but in a more general sense they fit into the larger dialogue with Coleridge.[97] In 'Expostulation and Reply' Wordsworth states his ideas of the importance of passively absorbing sense impressions from the natural world:

> The eye, it cannot chuse but see,
> We cannot bid the ear be still;
> Our bodies feel, where'er they be,
> Against, or with our will.
>
> Nor less I deem that there are powers
> Which of themselves our minds impress,
> That we can feed this mind of ours,
> In a wise passiveness.

(*Lyrical Ballads*, 108)

A similar message had been addressed to Dorothy in the lines 'To My Sister', written two months earlier. Calling on her to leave her household tasks and bring no book, the poet famously avers that 'One moment now may give us more | Than fifty years of reason' (*Lyrical Ballads*, 64). Though Dorothy here figures as the domestic

---

[96] Matlak, *Poetry of Relationship*, 105–8.
[97] Moorman, *William Wordsworth*, 379; McFarland, 'Symbiosis', 288.

woman who needs to be recalled to Nature, in a more profound sense she represented for William an example of the attitude he praised. The poems in *Lyrical Ballads* articulate the theory of 'wise passiveness'; Dorothy's journal-writing from this period shows what wise passiveness looks like in practice.

What is extant of the Alfoxden journals—a sixteen-page fragment covering January to May 1798—records, often in note form, walks taken, visitors, trips to the farm to get eggs, Dorothy hanging out the linen, William gathering sticks. These short entries are interspersed with longer passages of natural description, in which Dorothy gives a detailed account of sights and sounds with the minimum of response or interpretation, as if the natural world could simply be transcribed:

> *January 25th*. Went to Poole's after tea. The sky spread over with one continuous cloud, whitened by the light of the moon, which, though her dim shape was seen, did not throw forth so strong a light as to chequer the earth with shadows. At once the clouds seemed to cleave asunder, and left her in the centre of a black-blue vault. She sailed along, followed by multitudes of stars, small, bright, and sharp. Their brightness seemed concentrated (half-moon).
>
> *January 26th*. Walked upon the hill-tops; followed the sheep tracks till we overlooked the larger coombe. Sat in the sunshine. The distant sheep-bells, the sound of the stream; the woodman winding along the half-marked road with his laden pony; locks of wool still spangled with dewdrops; the blue-grey sea, shaded with immense masses of cloud, not streaked; the sheep glittering in the sunshine. Returned through the wood. The trees skirting the wood, being exposed more directly to the action of the sea breeze, stripped of the net-work of their upper boughs, which are stiff and erect, like black skeletons; the ground strewed with red berries of the holly. Set forward before two o'clock. Returned a little after four.[98]

Dorothy writes sentences without main verbs and often suppresses personal pronouns. At other times in the journal she mentions that

---

[98] *Journals of Dorothy Wordsworth*, ed. E. de Selincourt (London: Macmillan, 1952), i. 4.

she walked with William, or with Coleridge, but here no one is named, and the moon has more personal presence than the human observers. She writes as if natural phenonema are the powers 'which of themselves our minds impress', and that the impressions can be transmitted simply, without commentary. This naked immediacy is not maintained throughout the journal, but it is the dominant impression her writing creates, and it corresponds to a crucial strand in the definition of good poetry her brother was later to offer. Here if anywhere is writing which shows that 'the eye of the poet had been steadily fixed upon [her] object'.[99] Matthew Arnold's praise of Wordsworth's 'natural' writing in 'Michael'—'it might seem that Nature not only gave him the matter for his poem but wrote the poem for him. He has no style'[100]—might equally be applied to Dorothy's journals.

However, the difference between Dorothy and William's writing comes into focus in his use of her journal entries for his poetry. The description of the moon quoted above informs a passage in his 'A Night Piece', written in 1798:

> At last a pleasant instantaneous light
> Startles the musing man whose eyes are bent
> To earth. He looks around, the clouds are split
> Asunder, and above his head he views
> The clear moon & the glory of the heavens.
> There in a black-blue vault she sails along
> Followed by multitude of stars, that small,
> And bright, & sharp along the gloomy vault
> Drive as she drives.

The emphasis is on the observer, drawn from earth to a view of the skies, and the poems moves on to reflect:

> At length the vision closes, and the mind
> Not undisturbed by the deep joy it feels,

---

[99] *Essay, Supplementary to the Preface* (1815), in *William Wordsworth*, ed. Stephen Gill (Oxford: OUP, 1984), 651.

[100] Quoted in McFarland, *Romanticism*, 253.

Which slowly settles into peaceful calm,
Is left to muse upon the solemn scene.[101]

Matlak calls this a process of description being transformed into vision, and sees the poem as part of William's dialogue with Dorothy: his
advocacy of transcendence, her refusal of it. Unlike her brother, she
writes 'without betraying interest in speculation', and her allegiance
is to 'the visual supremacy of earthly reality'.[102]

Earthbound, seeming to offer immediate connection to nature
itself—Dorothy's writing fits ancient definitions of the feminine
that were revalued in the Romantic period. Where Henry Fielding
saw his sister's femininity as offering an alternative form of human
understanding, a limited but crucial ability to comprehend a distinct female character, William Wordsworth understood Dorothy's
femininity as more central to his writing and less independent
of him. Her journals represented a feminine matter on which a
masculine poetic mind could work to produce poetry. However
sincerely he valued wise passiveness, he saw it not as that which
made a poet but as what allowed for the perception that could be
actively transformed into poetry. Even more clearly than Richard
Brinsley Sheridan making use of his mother's manuscripts, William
Wordsworth using Dorothy's journals was taking what appeared,
as the work of a close female relative, to be his by right. Her way
of writing deepened this feeling. Entries recording shared experiences, and probably including the recollection of shared discussions,
were not felt by either of them to belong to Dorothy alone. Her
almost complete effacement of herself from the record naturalized
her brother's appropriation of her words, as if her perceptions existed
only to be channelled into his. To an extent Coleridge shared in
this brotherly privilege of appropriation, seen for example in the
way *Christabel* incorporates elements of Dorothy's descriptions of
moonlight.[103] For a short period, Dorothy stood in this sisterly

---

[101] *William Wordsworth*, ed. Gill, 44–5.   [102] Matlak, *Poetry of Relationship*, 101.
[103] e.g. Dorothy's 'When we left home the moon immensely large, the sky scattered
over with clouds. These soon closed in, contracting the dimensions of the moon without

relation to both poets; and at times her words allowed them to write as if their eyes were on the object, when in fact they were making use of her observations of it.

William, at this time, was caught between his sister and Coleridge. Both were strong influences on his work. If she provided the conduit to nature, Coleridge encouraged him to write a philosophical poem. This drive for philosophy is linked to Coleridge's encouragement of Wordsworth's 'masculine' side. Because Coleridge exalted what he saw as Wordsworth's great masculinity, he has been seen as taking up a feminine position in relation to him;[104] but it is important to recognize that Wordsworth's manliness was not something Coleridge simply observed but that he repeatedly demanded of his friend. In 1798 he complained to Hazlitt of 'something corporeal, a *matter-of-factness*, a clinging to the palpable' in Wordsworth's poetry.[105] The corporeal, of course, has long been understood as feminine, and Coleridge's description could as easily describe Dorothy's journal style as her brother's poems. In clinging to the palpable, Wordsworth was clinging to the feminine and to his sister. What Coleridge wanted was for him to turn to a philosophical project that would transcend the body and the influence of the feminine.

It was under Coleridge's influence that Wordsworth planned to incorporate the blank verse he was writing in early 1798 into a long work to be entitled *The Recluse; or Views of Nature, Man and Society.*[106] It was to be his poem about everything. The portion already written, he explained in March 1798, conveyed 'most of the knowledge of which I am possessed', and he added, 'Indeed I know

concealing her', influenced lines in *Christabel*: 'The thin gray cloud is spread on high, | It covers but not hides the sky. | The moon is behind, and at the full; | And yet she looks both small and dull.' See *Journals of Dorothy Wordsworth*, i. 5.

[104] McFarland, citing Coleridge's comment that 'Of all the men I ever knew, Wordsworth has the least femineity in his mind. He is *all* man', comments that his 'relationship to Wordsworth . . . is as a feminine principle to its masculine counterpart'. *Romanticism*, 65.

[105] Quoted in Matlak, *Poetry of Relationship*, 119.

[106] The longest part of these lines formed *The Ruined Cottage*, later incorporated into *The Excursion*. Moorman, *William Wordsworth*, 359–63.

not any thing which will not come within the scope of my plan'.[107]
This epic work—a masculine counterbalance to feminine wise
passiveness—was meant to fulfil his destiny as Milton's successor.
For Coleridge, it seems to have meant that Wordsworth, on his
behalf, would become the great manly poet he felt unable to be
himself. In fact, Coleridge had intended to write a great work,
The Brook, which sounds very like Wordsworth's later plan for
The Recluse: it would 'give equal freedom for description, incident
and impassioned reflections on men, nature and society'.[108] Now
Wordsworth was to write the great poem instead. In October 1799
Coleridge wrote to him: 'I long to see what you have been doing.
O let it be the tail-piece of "The Recluse!" for of nothing but "The
Recluse" can I hear patiently. ... To be addressed, as a beloved
man, by a thinker, at the close of such a poem as "The Recluse"
... is the only event, I believe, capable of inciting in me an hour's
vanity.'[109]

Wordsworth worked on the poem, at intervals, over the next
thirty years, but it was never completed beyond the first book. It
was a work that depended on Coleridge. In 1804, worried about
Coleridge's health, Wordsworth wrote to him: 'I am very anxious
to have your Notes for The Recluse', making it clear that he was
afraid his friend would die without providing them. The following
year, Dorothy reported that her brother was 'very anxious to get
forward with The Recluse ... but I do not think he will be able to do
much more till we have heard of Coleridge'.[110] Wordsworth 'could
do virtually nothing at all on this vast project without Coleridge's
help', and when the two poets became estranged, 'the non-existence
of "The Recluse" was assured'.[111]

For much of his life, then, Wordsworth was busy not writing his
great epic. While he felt this as a failure, biographers and critics have

---

[107] *Letters of William and Dorothy Wordsworth*, i. 212.
[108] Quoted in Moorman, *William Wordsworth*, 363.
[109] *Letters of Samuel Taylor Coleridge*, i. 538.
[110] *Letters of William and Dorothy Wordsworth*, i. 452, 664.
[111] McFarland, *Romanticism*, 222.

seen it as his successful escape from an unsuitable task.[112] Newlyn
suggests that even in 1798 Wordsworth was beginning to assert his
independence from Coleridge, and that this meant, eventually, not
writing *The Recluse* but writing his autobiographical poem instead:
'Wordsworth's triumph in *The Prelude* rests not just on his inability to
write *The Recluse*, but on his refusal to do so'.[113] Gill emphasizes that
Wordsworth's resistance to Coleridge was not just a matter of writing
a different sort of long poem; it was also his development as a lyricist,
making his name with the short poems Coleridge mistrusted.[114]

Wordsworth's relation with Dorothy is a key to his refusal to
become the poet Coleridge wanted him to be. After the Alfoxden
period, the ties between the Wordsworths and Coleridge began to
lose their first intensity. During their German trip in 1799 William
and Dorothy lived in Goslar, apart from Coleridge, and during this
time William wrote the 'Lucy' poems, which Coleridge considered
to be inspired by his relationship with Dorothy. They evoke a lost
female figure, a Dorothy who has been assimilated into nature in
death, 'Rolled round in earth's diurnal course | with rocks and stones
and trees' (*Lyrical Ballads*, 164).[115] The 'Lucy' poems have been read
as central examples of the Romantic poet's founding of masculine
poetic identity on the loss of the loved female. 'Though Lucy leaves
the speaker bereft, her legacy to him is synonymous with the natural
world of which she herself has become a part', and 'she becomes
the ground or background for Wordsworthian figuration'.[116] Her
assimilation into nature silences her; in her absence, he is able to

---

[112] Stephen Gill, *William Wordsworth: A Life* (Oxford: Clarendon Press, 1989), 145.
See ibid. 367–8 for Wordsworth's family's anxieties about his inability to proceed with
the poem in the 1820s, and his continued plans to work on it in 1831.

[113] Newlyn, *Language of Allusion*, 166.   [114] Gill, *William Wordsworth*, 201–2.

[115] Coleridge was the first to link this poem to Dorothy, suggesting that Wordsworth
wrote it because 'in some gloomier moment he had fancied the moment in which
his Sister might die' (*Letters of Samuel Taylor Coleridge*, i. 479). F. W. Bateson argued
that Wordsworth dealt with dangerous intensity of his feelings for his sister by 'killing
her off symbolically' in the Lucy poems: see *Wordsworth: A Reinterpretation* (London:
Longmans, Green and Co., 1954), 153.

[116] Homans, *Women Writers*, 22; Mary Jacobus, *Romanticism, Writing and Sexual
Difference: Essays on The Prelude* (Oxford: Clarendon Press, 1989), 251.

speak. While this is a persuasive reading of these haunting poems, it does not tell the whole story of Wordsworth's access to poetic voice in this period. After Goslar, he and Dorothy set up home together at Grasmere, and there they developed an intense poetic partnership in which his writing was nourished not by absence but by her presence, her audience, and her own words.

Though Coleridge and his family later followed the Wordsworths to the Lake District, the tight threesome was lost. Jonathan Wordsworth has described the early life at Grasmere as William's re-enactment of paradise with himself and Dorothy as Adam and Eve.[117] In 'Home at Grasmere', written in 1800, the union with Dorothy (here called 'Emma'), offers a joy even beyond Eden, a paradise regained:

> The boon is absolute: surpassing grace
> To me hath been vouchsafed. Among the bowers
> Of blissful Eden this was neither given,
> Nor could be given—possession of the good
> Which had been sighed for, antient thought fulfilled,
> And dear imaginations realized
> Up to their highest measure, yea, and more.

'Home at Grasmere' became the first—and only—book of *The Recluse*. Instead of writing a public, philosophical poem, Wordsworth wrote a celebration of his retreat from public life with his sister. In fact, within this poem it is not in philosophy, but in the poet's happiness with his sister, that humanity can find the message it needs. The vision that the poet and 'Emma' have at Hart-Leap Well is 'A promise and an earnest that we twain, | A pair seceding from the common world', will gain at Grasmere:

> A portion of the blessedness which love
> And knowledge will, we trust, hereafter give
> To all the vales of earth and all mankind.[118]

---

[117] Jonathan Wordsworth, *William Wordsworth: The Borders of Vision* (Oxford: Clarendon Press, 1982), 98–148.
[118] 'Home at Grasmere', ibid. 393, 396.

The years 1800–2 at Grasmere, before William's marriage to Mary Hutchinson in October 1802, were the time of greatest collaboration between sister and brother. Dorothy's journal for this period is her fullest. The naturalistic observation characteristic of the Alfoxden journal is mingled with greater concern for social life, recording Dorothy's encounters with neighbours, travellers, and beggars; and with a focus on herself, her feelings, and her relation with William. Dorothy's discussion of the writing of two short poems in March 1802, shows how much her life and journal revolve around William's poetry, and how closely dependent his writing is on her memory, conversation, and writing. Dorothy writes:

> [*March 13th,*] *Saturday Morning.* . . . William finished *Alice Fell*, and then he wrote the poem of *The Beggar Woman*, taken from a woman whom I had seen in May (now nearly two years ago) when John and he were at Gallow Hill. I sate with him at intervals all the morning, took down his stanzas, etc. After dinner we walked to Rydale for letters . . . After tea I read to William that account of the little boy belonging to the tall woman, and an unlucky thing it was, for he could not escape from those very words, and so he could not write the poem. He left it unfinished, and went tired to bed. In our walk from Rydale he had got warmed with the subject, and had half cast the poem.
>
> [*March 14th,*] *Sunday Morning.* William had slept badly— he got up at nine o'clock, but before he rose he had finished *The Beggar Boys*, and while we ate breakfast that is (for I had breakfasted) he, with his basin of broth before him untouched, and a little plate of bread and butter he wrote the Poem to a Butterfly! . . . The thought first came upon him as we were talking about the pleasure we both always feel at the sight of a butterfly. I told them that I used to chase them a little, but that I was afraid of brushing the dust off their wings, and did not catch them. He told me how they used to kill all the white ones when they went to school because they were Frenchmen.
> (*Journals*, i. 122–3)

The poem of 'The Beggar Woman' (eventually entitled 'Beggars') takes its origin from an experience of Dorothy's while William was absent: in the poem the poet's 'I' takes over from hers. She provides the original sense data, emotions to be recollected in tranquillity, the work of an amanuensis, companionship, and audience. So close is she to all aspects of the composition that the effect of her words is sometimes the opposite from their intention: when she reads him her old journal entry her words prevent him forming his own.[119] The effect is temporary; the poem is completed the following day. The journal entry Dorothy has been reading to him runs:

> a very tall woman, tall much beyond the measure of tall women, called at the door. She had on a very long brown cloak and a very white cap, without bonnet; her face was excessively brown, but it had plainly once been fair. She led a little bare-footed child about 2 years old by the hand, and said her husband, who was a tinker, was gone before with the other children. I gave her a piece of bread. Afterwards on my road to Ambleside, beside the bridge at Rydale, I saw her husband sitting by the roadside, his two asses feeding beside him, and the two young children at play upon the grass. The man did not beg. I passed on and about $\frac{1}{4}$ of a mile further I saw two boys before me, one about 10, the other about 8 years old, at play chasing a butterfly. They were wild figures, not very ragged, but without shoes and stockings; the hat of the elder was wreathed round with yellow flowers, the younger whose hat was only a rimless crown, had it stuck round with laurel leaves. They continued at play till I drew very near, and then they addressed me with the begging cant and the whining voice of sorrow. I said 'I served your mother this morning'. (The Boys were so like the woman who had called at the door that I could not be mistaken.) 'O!' says the elder, 'you could not serve my mother for she's dead,

[119] See Susan M. Levin, *Dorothy Wordsworth and Romanticism* (New Brunswick, NJ: Rutgers, the State University, 1987), for a discussion of the way Dorothy's words 'imprison and sometimes stifle her brother' (36).

and my father's on at the next town—he's a potter.' I persisted
in my assertion, and that I would give them nothing. Says the
elder, 'Come, let's away', and away they flew like lightning.
(*Journals*, i. 47)

The poem omits the 2-year-old, and the husband and two young
children. The woman is alone, and is compared to an Amazonian
queen or bandit's wife. Instead of telling the simple truth about her
husband the tinker, she makes up a story of 'woes' that the poet
claims could not exist in England. She has become a picturesque,
exotic, untrustworthy figure. In most other details, the poem follows
the journal entry closely. The first verse makes the woman a grander
figure than she is in the journal:

> She had a tall Man's height, or more;
> No bonnet screen'd her from the heat;
> A long drab-colour'd Cloak she wore,
> A Mantle reaching to her feet:
> What other dress she had I could not know;
> Only she wore a Cap that was as white as snow.[120]

Here Wordsworth is practising the art described in his 1800 Preface,
using a language not essentially different from prose, but adding
the pleasures of rhythm 'to impart passion to the words' (*Lyrical
Ballads*, 756). Later revisions to the poem detracted from this poetic
simplicity. One addition figures the boys as cherubs: 'Wings let
them have, and they might flit | Precursors of Aurora's Car'—the
kind of conventional poetic decoration the earlier Wordsworth
scorned (*Poems*, ed. Curtis, 151). William's tendency to formalize
and elaborate in revision is part of his gradual movement away from
the simplicity represented by Dorothy's journal entries. Here we can
trace a difficulty posed by the sister as source. Her stark writing
represented an extreme version of the nakedness of expression to
which he was drawn, but to be too tied to it would threaten his

---

[120] *Poems, in Two Volumes, and Other Poems 1800–1807*, ed. Jared Curtis (Ithaca, NY: Cornell University Press, 1983), 113.

own possession of poetic language. His revisions are, in a way, an extended effort to 'escape the very words' of his sister.

The other poem discussed in the 1802 entry, 'To a Butterfly', involves a different method of composition. Its origin is only indirectly in the journal. As Dorothy describes it, William gets the idea from their conversation about butterfly-chasing, presumably itself sparked off by going back to the 1800 entry with its description of the boys. Shared discussion of childhood memory leads to a swift burst of inspiration, and the poem is quickly written.

> Stay near me—do not take thy flight!
> A little longer stay in sight!
> Much converse do I find in Thee,
> Historian of my Infancy!
> Float near me; do not yet depart!
> Dead times revive in thee:
> Thou bring'st, gay Creature as thou art!
> A solemn image to my heart,
> My Father's Family!
>
> Oh! pleasant, pleasant were the days,
> The time, when in our childhood plays,
> My Sister Emmeline and I
> Together chased the Butterfly!
> A very hunter did I rush
> Upon the prey:—with leaps and springs
> I follow'd on from brake to bush;
> But She, God love her! feared to brush
> The dust from off its wings.
>
> (*Poems*, ed. Curtis, 203–4)

Dorothy's account of their discussion suggests they were exchanging memories of childhood experiences not shared. In the poem past separation from his sister is transformed into imagined togetherness, restoring the lost unity of the childhood family. This revival of dead times depends on Dorothy's imagined presence, but also on her difference—her delicate tenderness contrasting with his boisterous hunting. The final lines evoking that tenderness use her words, but make them sound like his observation rather than her report.

During the spring of 1802, then, Wordsworth's writing was especially bound up in his relationship with Dorothy. The concluding lines of 'The Sparrow's Nest', written at this time, celebrate her influence on him, an influence seen as starting in childhood:

> The Blessing of my later years
> Was with me when a Boy;
> She gave me eyes, she gave me ears;
> And humble cares, and delicate fears;
> A heart, the fountain of sweet tears,
> And love, and thought, and joy.
>
> (*Poems*, ed. Curtis, 213)

Thomas De Quincey used these lines to illustrate his view that Dorothy's greatest gift to her brother was to save him from excessive masculinity: 'to ingraft, by her sexual sense of beauty, upon his masculine austerity that delicacy and those graces which else ... it would not have had'.[121] What Dorothy offers here, though, is not just access to the feminine but to perception itself: providing the poet with his sense organs, she becomes almost his creator. If she creates him, she makes him a lyric poet, a writer on flowers, butterflies, and birds, who can ignore, or even mock, aspirations to sublimity. The poet who in 'Tintern Abbey' had felt 'a sense sublime | Of something far more deeply interfused, | Whose dwelling is in the light of setting suns' (*Lyrical Ballads*, 119), now addressed himself cheerily to the small celandine:

> Eyes of some men travel far
> For the finding of a star;
> Up and down the heavens they go,
> Men that keep a mighty rout!
> I'm as great as they, I trow,
> Since the day I found thee out,

---

[121] *Recollections of the Lake Poets*, ed. Wright, 201.

> Little flower!—I'll make a stir,
> Like a great Astronomer.
>
> (*Poems*, ed. Curtis, 80)

In spring 1802, as well as enjoying poetic partnership with Dorothy, Wordsworth was planning his marriage to Mary Hutchinson in the October. While this clearly broke in on the close sibling relationship, Dorothy remained. Wordsworth spent his life surrounded by feminine care and companionship. As far as Coleridge was concerned, this was part of the reason he failed to get on with *The Recluse*. Writing to Thomas Poole in 1803, Coleridge rejoiced that Wordsworth had returned to this project after a time of what he called 'Self-involution':

> I saw him more and more benetted [*sic*] in hypochondriacal Fancies, living wholly among *Devotees*—having every the minutest Thing, almost his very Eating & Drinking, done for him by his Sister, or Wife—& I trembled, lest a Film should arise, and thicken on his moral Eye.—The habit too of writing such a multitude of small Poems was in this instance hurtful to him—such Things as that Sonnet of his in Monday's Morning Post, about Simonides & the Ghost—I rejoice therefore with a deep & true Joy, that he has at length yielded to my urgent & repeated—almost unremitting—requests & remonstrances—& will go on with the Recluse exclusively.—A Great Work, in which he will sail; on an open Ocean, & a steady wind; unfretted by short tacks, reefing, & hawling & disentangling the ropes—great work necessarily comprehending his attention & Feelings within the circle of great objects & elevated Conceptions (*Letters of Samuel Taylor Coleridge*, ii. 1013)

Wordsworth's daily dependence on sister and wife is linked here with his neglecting the great work for small pieces. The metaphor of *The Recluse* as oceangoing vessel recalls by contrast the Wordsworthian sonnet Coleridge deplores, which celebrates the poet Simonides' refusal to board a ship which is later wrecked. Coleridge's remarks encourage us to read this as Wordsworth's praise of inaction, his own refusal to embark. While Coleridge is clearly writing from a double jealousy—he would like to have the feminine help himself, and also he wants Wordsworth back—others have shared a sense that Wordsworth, under Dorothy's influence, could become a bit too comfortable. The problem is not that he wrote lyrics instead of *The Recluse*, but that the lyrics sometimes became whimsical.[122]

At their best, though, Wordsworth's lyrics express a joy in nature and community that is achieved through his relationship with Dorothy. *The Prelude* attests to her influence in a different way. Written mainly in two periods—the two-book *Prelude* in 1799, the remaining books during 1804–5, this 'poem to Coleridge' became a substitute for writing *The Recluse*, and a revision of Milton in which the growth of the poet's mind became the epic subject. As part of the dialogue with Coleridge, the poem continues the move towards independence found in 'Tintern Abbey'. In *The Prelude* Wordsworth developed the myth of himself 'as a self-generated poet whose origins are solely in his own childhood'.[123] If Wordsworth freed himself from dependence on his brother poet in this way, it was the myth of the combined influence of the mother, nature, and the sister that allowed him to do so. Wordsworth's development of a strong poetic self has long been seen as due both to his initial closeness to these feminine forces and his successful movement away from them. For Geoffrey Hartman, the greatness of *The Prelude* is in its movement towards transcendence, as Wordsworth 'came to realize that Nature itself led him beyond Nature'.[124] Dorothy, as his link to nature, is also transcended. The sister who, in 'The Sparrow's Nest', gave him eyes and ears, is not central to the narrative of the growth of the poet's mind, a work which creates and emphasizes his singleness of soul. While 'Home at Grasmere' has William and Dorothy as Adam and Eve, the opening of *The Prelude* uses its Miltonic references

---

[122] Jonathan Wordsworth finds the Wordsworth of 1802 complacent because of Dorothy's uncritical acceptance: 'She was a force for good in that her responsiveness was a stimulus to the outgoing poetry . . . but she did nothing to allay the self-regard.' *Borders of Vision*, 158.

[123] Magnuson, *Coleridge and Wordsworth*, 171.

[124] 'A Poet's Progress: Wordsworth and the *Via Naturaliter Negativa*', in *The Prelude*, 598–613; 599.

differently. It undoes the expulsion of the first couple from Eden: while 'the world was all before them' because they were banished, for Wordsworth, 'the world is all before me' as he returns to the paradise of his youth.[125] What is striking here is that the poet is alone, in contrast to the first pair, expelled together. The sister does not appear till the later books of *The Prelude*. In Book 6, lines 210–29, he recalls the joy of reunion with her and associates himself with Sidney, another poet inspired by love for his sister (*Prelude*, 196). The tribute to her in Book 10 is striking for its emphasis on her role as the preserver of his selfhood: she 'maintained for me a saving intercourse | With my true self', and 'in the midst of all, preserved me still | A poet' (ll. 914–15, 918–1199; *Prelude*, 408). She is both the ground of his separate selfhood and the force that modifies it: her influence softens his soul, which was 'too reckless of mild grace', or, in the 1850 version, 'In her original self too confident' (Bk. 13, l. 228; Bk. 14, l. 249; *Prelude*, 470, 471).

At the conclusion of *The Prelude*, the poet addresses Coleridge with the famous pledge that the two of them will become 'Prophets of Nature', teaching 'how the mind of man becomes | A thousand times more beautiful than the earth | On which he dwells' (Bk. 13, ll. 442, 446–8; *Prelude*, 482). Nature is transcended by mind, the feminine by the masculine, and this 'sublime self-assurance', as Anne Mellor remarks, depends on 'the arduous repression of the Other in all its forms: of the mother, of Dorothy, of other people, of history, of nature'. This position remains, as she says, highly precarious.[126] Dorothy, as mother substitute, sister soul, and connection to nature, was the necessary, and necessarily repressed ground of his sense of being a singular soul, independent of Coleridge, able at the end to escape Coleridge's definitions and himself define their shared mission.

The contrast between the self-effacing transparency of the sister's journals and the egotistical sublime of the brother's autobiographical

---

[125] J. Wordsworth, *Borders of Vision*, 104.
[126] *Romanticism and Gender* (New York: Routledge, 1993), 149.

poem fits the description given in Chodorow's psychoanalytical theory of the differences between masculine and feminine development
that result in the boy's culturally valued drive towards separation
and differentiation from the mother, and the girl's less differentiated, more relational sense of self.[127] Critics differ in the value
they place on Dorothy's expression of her subjectivity. Margaret
Homans, though noting that Dorothy's 'selflessness almost seems
to be a deliberate refutation of Wordsworthian egotism', tends to
emphasize the sister's lack of 'the strong sense of identity necessary
to writing Romantic poetry'. Susan J. Wolfson writes of Dorothy's
'myth of negative vocation', which surfaces in the poems she did
write, mainly in her later years.[128] In 'Irregular Verses', written in
1827, Dorothy Wordsworth lists the psychological blocks to her
development as a poet:

> bashfulness, a struggling shame
> A fear that elder heads might blame
> —Or something worse—a lurking pride
> Whispering my playmates would deride
> Stifled ambition, checked the aim
> If e'er by chance 'the numbers came.'
> —Nay even the mild maternal smile,
> That oft-times would repress, beguile
> The over-confidence of youth,
> Even that dear smile, to own the truth
> Was dreaded by a fond self-love;
> ''Twill glance on me—and to reprove
> Or,' (sorest wrong in childhood's school)
> 'Will *point* the sting of ridicule.'[129]

---

[127] See the discussion of Dorothy's consciousness in Levin, *Dorothy Wordsworth*,
15–17. For a discussion of the contrast between William's and Dorothy's autobiographical modes, see Mellor, *Romanticism and Gender*, 144–69.

[128] Homans, *Women Writers*, 75, 70, Wolfson, 'Dorothy Wordsworth in Conversation with William', in Anne Mellor (ed.), *Romanticism and Feminism* (Bloomington,
Ind.: Indiana University Press, 1988), 142.

[129] 'The Collected Poems of Dorothy Wordsworth', in app. to Levin, *Dorothy
Wordsworth*, 203.

The remembered maternal presence that, for her brother, was the bedrock of the poetic self appears here as its inhibitor. Others resist Dorothy Wordsworth's view of herself as a failed poet, valuing the expression of an 'interactive, absorptive, constantly changing' self, that can be traced in poems such as 'Floating Island at Hawkeshead' and in the journals.[130] Fay's positive valuation of the collaborative life, as opposed to its literary products, allows her to see Dorothy Wordsworth as renouncing, rather than failing to achieve, 'the male romantic project'. Mellor is most forthright in insisting on the value of the fluid subjectivity recorded in Dorothy Wordsworth's *Journals*: 'We need to be able both to recognize this alternative model of subjectivity and to grant it equal status with her brother's if we are accurately to describe the range of "Romantic self-consciousness".'[131] This is right, but it is no accident that it has taken so long for such a range to be acknowledged. What Fay calls 'the desire to be twinned with William's poethood', which made Dorothy Wordsworth 'submerge herself and her achievement in the fullness of *his* mind and his poetry',[132] fostered his development of the myth of the self-generated poet, a myth that has served to exclude women's writing from consideration from the canon of Romantic poetry.

The eighteenth-century novel and Romantic poetry both had their dominant writing brothers, and in each case a sister was pivotal to their relationship. In the Fieldings–Richardson triangle it is the sister who is caught in the middle, feeling the pull of both brothers and attempting in her writing to assert her independence. To the extent that she succeeds, it is her relation with a wider community of sisters that allows her to develop a distinct viewpoint. In the Wordsworths–Coleridge triangle, William Wordsworth is the one in the middle, needing his sister's influence in order to keep himself independent of Coleridge and create the egotistical sublime. In

---

[130] Mellor, *Romanticism and Gender*, 154. See ibid. 154–6 for a discussion of 'Floating Island at Hawkeshead'.
[131] Fay, *Becoming Wordsworthian*, 124; Mellor, *Romanticism and Gender*, 154.
[132] Fay, *Becoming Wordsworthian*, 211.

both cases, these central sibling relationships encapsulate something about the literary history of the different modes of writing. In the novel, women's prominent role was recognized from the beginning, even as their contributions were too readily assumed to belong unproblematically to an easily defined feminine realm. Like Sarah Fielding, the woman novelist of the eighteenth century was a sister sharing in a new venture, acknowledged, and condescended to, for her distinct voice. The reception of Romantic poetry proceeded very differently. As it became dominated by the notion of the poet as solitary self in search of the sublime, the work of women poets of the Romantic era was understood, until relatively recently, to be somehow outside the Romantic movement. The properly Romantic sister was not a fellow writer but a sister soul, there to serve her brother's self and writing.

4

Women in the Literary Family

Nobody doubted that women belonged in the family. It was as daughters and sisters, wives and mothers, that they were understood to find their meaning. This has so shaped public acknowledgement of women that it is no surprise to find literary women being celebrated in relation to their kin. To remember a woman writer in the way that Mary Herbert, for example, was remembered in the seventeenth century—as 'Sydneys sister Pembrokes mother'—was to embed her position as poet and patroness within a literal set of kinship relations to men.[1] It excluded her from the metaphorical line understood to be founded by, among others, her brother. During the following centuries the family, whether aristocratic or not, continued to be the setting for women writers' lives and, in many cases, the site of intersection between literal and literary relationships. At the same time kinship terms were rhetorically deployed in various ways, expressing, and helping to construct, a sense of how women stood in relation to that emergent, prestigious, and metaphorical family, the literary tradition. Women's shifting place in a shifting world of letters can be traced through the changing use of kinship terms in discussions of their writing.

Generative literary mothers, as we have seen, were difficult to acknowledge. Literary daughters were an easier case. They reflected 'proper' gender relations in a society in which '[a]ll men ideally

---

[1] William Browne, 'On the Countesse Dowager of Pembroke', cited in Margaret P. Hannay, *Philip's Phoenix: Mary Sidney, Countess of Pembroke* (New York: OUP, 1990), 206.

approximated to the condition of fathers; all women were thereby relegated to the childlike position of daughters'.[2] Filial deference is widespread in women's responses to male writers. A call to the father is implicit in Elizabeth Thomas's address to Dryden, who 'rais'd' her muse 'grov'ling from the Earth':

> You taught her Numbers; and you gave her Feet;
> And you set Rules, to bound Poetic Heat:
> If there is ought in me deserves that Name,
> The Spark was light [*sic*] at mighty *Dryden*'s Flame . . .[3]

Mary Jones, by contrast, feels she has no right to be daughter to the writer she imitates:

> Like some tall oak, behold his branches shoot!
> No tender scions springing at his root.
> Whilst lofty *Pope* erects his laurell'd head,
> No lays, like mine, can live beneath his shade.[4]

Much bolder, Maria Jane Jewsbury explicitly claims Wordsworth as her 'spirit's father'.[5] The father–daughter relation provided an obvious analogy for relations between male and female writers, but as we have seen in Burney's reception history, the literary daughter was liable to be scolded for forgetting her place if she aspired to inherit the father's estate. Daughters were not supposed to be heirs.

The obstacles to understanding women as mothers and founders or daughters and heirs of literary tradition did not stand in the way of seeing writing women as sisters, a metaphor suggesting shared occupation rather than inheritance, and so able to acknowledge an author without according her a canonical place. The woman writer's place in the literary family was most often understood as that of sister, whether

---

[2] Norma Clarke, *Ambitious Heights: Writing, Friendship, Love—The Jewsbury Sisters, Felicia Hemans, and Jane Welsh Carlyle* (London: Routledge, 1990), 22.

[3] [Elizabeth Thomas], *Miscellany Poems on Several Subjects* (London: Tho. Combes, 1722), 22.

[4] Mary Jones, *Miscellanies in Prose and Verse* (Oxford: Dodsley, Clements, and Frederick, 1750), 'An Epistle to Lady Bowyer', 1–2.

[5] Clarke, *Ambitious Heights*, 61.

to a brother writer or, more commonly, to a group of writing sisters. Throughout the eighteenth century, references to a sisterhood of authors fall into two distinct groups: women writers are either muses or hacks. Members of the same trade were routinely described as brothers, and the metaphor was easily extended into the trade of writing: references to brother poets, brother writers, and brother authors are common throughout this period, often with a facetious implication. Mr Spectator mentions a 'Brother of the Quill'; the writing hero of a picaresque novel meets a 'Brother Author'; a pamphlet written in support of David Garrick refers scornfully to 'some *starved brother author* in Grub-Street'.[6] Women belonging to a group or trade were also defined in kinship terms, though the range of sisters was narrower than that of brothers. Sisterhood was most commonly applied to nuns, to prostitutes, and to waiting-women. It was also—though very rarely—applied to writers, and early references tend to carry clear Grub Street implications. The other group of references is equally linked to shared occupation, but in an exalted sphere. The muses were understood as sisters. Women writers, in the gallant and limiting discourse that always formed one strand of the response to them, were muses themselves. It followed that the imagery of sisterhood applied to them, and could be adopted by them to suggest female solidarity.

Delarivier Manley uses both kinds of reference. She was one of the 'Nine Muses' who each wrote a poem 'On the Death of John Dryden, Esq.' for a memorial collection (actually, only eight different signatures appear—Manley wrote two of the poems). In the character of Melpomene, the tragic muse, she opened the collection with the call: 'Come all my Sisters now in Consort join'. Melpomene speaking to her sister muses merges with Manley calling on her sister writers.[7] One of these was Catharine Trotter, the 'Mrs C.T.'

[6] [Richard Steele], *Spectator* no. 552, Wed. 3 Dec. 1712, in *The Spectator*, ed. D. F. Bond (Oxford: Clarendon Press, 1965), iv. 478; *The Adventures of Dick Hazard* (London: W. Reeve, 1755), 191; *An appeal to the public in behalf of the manager* (London: Wilson and Fell, 1763), 36.

[7] *The Nine Muses: Or, Poems Written By Nine Several Ladies* ... (London: Richard Basset, 1700); repr. in *Drydeniana XIV: On the Death of Dryden, Folio Verse, 1700* (New York: Garland, 1975).

who wrote the tribute from Calliope, the heroic muse. Trotter and Manley, along with Mary Pix, another contributor to the collection, constituted a small but highly visible group of women writing for the stage at the turn of the century. They claimed descent from Aphra Behn, and were satirized in a 1696 comedy, *The Female Wits*. Manley and Trotter had exchanged high-flown compliments in dedications and prefaces. Later, though, relations between them soured, because of political differences (Trotter supported the Whigs, Manley the Tories), and Manley used 'Calista', the name Trotter had been given in *The Female Wits*, to portray her in *The Adventures of Rivella* (1714). It is in the autobiographical *Adventures of Rivella* that Manley refers to sister writers again, but with different connotations. Calista/Trotter is named as Rivella/Manley's 'Sister Authoress'. There is no warmth of fellowship in the appellation. Rather, the phrase insists on identifying Trotter—who, by this time, had married Patrick Cockburn and retired from writing for money—as merely another dependent professional, just as the description of Calista as 'the most of a *Prude* in her outward Professions, and the least of it in her inward Practice' casts a slur on the sexual reputation that Trotter (unlike Manley) had managed to maintain.[8]

During the middle years of the eighteenth century, the muse began to predominate over the hack, as the notion emerged of a writing sisterhood conceived in genteel, complimentary, and sentimental terms. Sisterhood could be seen as an appropriate metaphor for women's separate place in the canon. John Duncombe's much-anthologized poem *The Feminiad* (1754), written to celebrate virtuous female literary achievement, opens with a declaration that the laurels belong not only to men but to a sisterhood of women:

> Shall lordly man, the theme of ev'ry lay,
> Usurp the muse's tributary bay;
> In kingly state on *Pindus'* summit sit,

[8] Delarivier Manley, *The Adventures of Rivella*, in *The Novels of Mary Delarivière Manley*, ed. Patricia Köster (Gainseville, Fla.: Scholars' Facsimiles and Reprints, 1971), ii. 800, 802.

> Tyrant of verse, and arbiter of wit?
> By *Salic* law the female right deny,
> And view their genius with regardless eye?
> Justice forbid! and every muse inspire
> To sing the glories of a sister-quire![9]

The women whose achievements Duncombe celebrates come from a wide social range, from the domestic servant Mary Leapor to Anne, Viscountess Irwin; but the image of a sister choir tends to place them on a level in the same genteel space, with any thought of writing for money (in which some of his subjects were certainly engaged) firmly ignored. As Duncombe presents them, these writers are ladies, not sister authoresses joined in a low trade. The reference to a sister choir connects them rather to the muses, who were commonly described as a choir; here, however, the women are not themselves the muses, but a writing sisterhood formed in their image. The muses themselves make several appearances in Duncombe's poem: they educate woman, they inspire the poem celebrating female achievement, and they are a pattern for that achievement. A sisterhood of graces and muses is responsible for forming British women and turning them into a sisterhood of intellectuals:

> And, as with lavish hand each sister Grace
> Shapes the fair form and regulates the face,
> Each sister Muse, in blissful union join'd,
> Adorns, improves, and beautifies the mind.
> Ev'n now fond fancy in our polish'd land
> Assembled shows a blooming, studious band.
>
> (*Feminiad*, 8–9)

At the end of the poem the poet's muse praises him for celebrating women and herself addresses learned women as 'our sister choir' (Feminiad, 29).

The woman writer as sister muse became a familiar figure in late eighteenth-century poetry. Clearly there is something odd and

---

[9] John Duncombe, *The Feminiad: A Poem* (London: M. Cooper, 1754), 5–6.

unsatisfactory about connecting female intellectuals and poets with muses: it implies an inspirational and decorative rather than active role for them, and associates them with a general and conventional feminine charm rather than with any particular achievement. The figure of the muse worked to obscure the female poet's commercial and professional role—her connection to the hack; but in creating a ladylike aura round the expanding trade in poetry it actually contributed to the developing respectability of writing as a bourgeois profession, and of the lady writer as a distinct part of that profession. By the beginning of the nineteenth century, both these developments were well advanced. The novel, too, had undergone its own journey towards prestige, with the result that writers of prose fiction, who were not apt to be confused with muses, could respectably be sister authors. The phrase is used by Austen in *Northanger Abbey*. Cutting short an ironic diatribe about the disadvantages of knowledge for women, she explains:

> The advantages of natural folly in a beautiful girl have been already set forth by the capital pen of a sister author;—and to her treatment of the subject I will only add in justice to men, that though to the larger and more trifling part of the sex, imbecility in females is a great enhancement of their personal charms, there is a portion of them too reasonable and too well informed themselves to desire any thing more in a woman than ignorance.[10]

The sister author in this passage is usually understood to be Burney, but may rather be Edgeworth.[11] In either case the young Austen,

[10] Jane Austen, *Northanger Abbey*, bk. 1, ch. 14, ed. Marilyn Butler (Harmondsworth: Penguin, 1995), 99.

[11] Burney is considered the sister author because of Indiana Lynmere in *Camilla*, who is beautiful but vain and superficial. The novel satirizes Miss Margland, who advises that Indiana should not learn too much in case she spoils her beauty and cannot attract a man. *Camilla*, ed. Edward A. Bloom and Lilian D. Bloom (London: OUP, 1972), 46. See *Northanger Abbey*, ed. Butler, 219. Another likely candidate seems to me to be Maria Edgeworth, whose *Belinda* features sardonic treatment of Clarence Harvey's belief that the beautiful Virginia will be an ideal wife because of her ignorance, and is later startled to learn that this unspoilt child of nature cannot read. Austen may be referring

delighting in puncturing masculine egotism, has found an ally in an older woman novelist whom she can call sister.

During the Romantic period, sisterhood was an important metaphor for women poets, helping them to establish a sense of shared tradition (though they had to contend with people's habit of reading women and their relationships literally: a poem praising Felicia Hemans and Mary Ann Browne as poetic sisters gave rise to a persistent tradition that they were sisters in life).[12] Marlon Ross contrasts the sisterly, mutually supportive attitude of female poets to the rivalry of male poets, remarking of Felicia Hemans that she is pleased to be influenced by women because 'her task is to prove that women can be poets, not that she can outdo other poets'.[13] Stuart Curran finds fifty tributes from one Romantic woman poet to another.[14] In this, women were continuing a tradition of public mutual support that was as old as women's publishing. It is important not to overstate the devotedness of sisters, however. For one thing, sisterly solidarity could be a saleable pose. For another, female poets could be rivals as much as their brothers were: Anna Seward, for example, certainly harboured feelings of rivalry towards Charlotte Smith, whose sonnets she dubbed 'everlasting lamentables'.[15] Indeed, then as now, the notion of sisterhood prompted debates about the usefulness of separatism. Maria Edgeworth was in favour of establishing a journal for women's writing, and suggested that she and Anna Letitia Barbauld should edit it. Barbauld refused, pointing out that differences

to ch. 26, in which Edgeworth sets out in detail how 'simplicity' (or in Austen's robuster phrasing, 'natural folly'), attracts Harvey. *Belinda*, ed. Kathryn J. Kirkpatrick (Oxford: OUP, 1994), 362–89.

[12] Virginia Blain, ' "Thou with Earth's Music Answerest to the Sky": Felicia Hemans, Mary Ann Browne, and the myth of poetic sisterhood', *Women's Writing*, 2/3 (1995), 251–69.

[13] Marlon Ross, *The Contours of Masculine Desire: Romanticism and the Rise of Women's Poetry* (New York: OUP, 1989), 303.

[14] 'Romantic Women Poets: Inscribing the Self', in I. Armstrong and V. Blain (eds.), *Women's Poetry in the Enlightenment: The Making of a Canon, 1730–1820* (Basingstoke: Macmillan Press, 1999), 161.

[15] Cited in Judith Hawley, 'Charlotte Smith's Elegiac Sonnets: Losses and Gains', Ibid. 187.

of opinion among contributors would make for a paper full of 'discordant materials':

> there is no bond of union among literary women, any more than among literary men, different sentiments & different connections separate them much more than the joint interest of their sex would unite them. Miss Hannah More would not write along with you or me & we should probably hesitate at joining Miss Hayes [*sic*] or, if she were living, Mrs Godwin.[16]

Another reason to be wary of too simply celebrating poetic sisterhood is that the notion of it often went hand in hand with a growing sense, in the Romantic era, that women poets were united by shared melancholy, a troubled relation to their vocation, even a tragic destiny. The image of the melancholy poetess, popularized in Charlotte Smith's sonnets, clearly had a strong influence on the poetic development of Martha Hanson, writing in the early nineteenth century. For the epigraph to her own two-volume collection of poetry, she chose lines from Smith in which the poet reports the muse's favour towards her but concludes that:

> far, far happier is the lot of those
> Who never learn'd her dear delusive art;
> Which, while it decks the head with many a rose,
> Reserves the thorn to fester in the heart.[17]

The first thirteen pages of Hanson's second volume were devoted to 'Stanzas, occasioned by the death of Mrs. Charlotte Smith'. Smith's sorrows are as prominent as her talents in these stanzas, and it is sorrow, finally, that is presented as the bond between the two women. Smith's poetry enchanted her follower 'in childhood's sunny days', and 'taught my infant hands, to strike the Lyre', but this picture of enabling female influence is overtaken by one of shared affliction

---

[16] Cited in Adeline Johns-Putra, *Heroes and Housewives: Women's Epic Poetry and Domestic Ideology in the Romantic Age* (Bern: Peter Lang, 2001), 18.

[17] Martha Hanson, *Sonnets and Other Poems* (London: J. Mawman, Poultry, and T. Lake, Uxbridge, 1809), i, title page.

(*Sonnets,* ii. 5). As a happy child Hanson could not fully understand Smith's poetry; as a sorrowing adult she can:

> And had soft Sympathy the pow'r to heal,
> A Sister's Pitying Sympathy, had cured
> The griefs thy gentle Spirit here endured:
> For though the magick of thy tuneful strain,
> Never my humble powers shall attain,
> Affliction's hand has ratified the claim,
> That dares to greet thee with a Sister's name.
>
> (*Sonnets,* ii. 7–8)

Doubtful of her right to claim sisterhood on the basis of poetic achievement, Hanson claims it on the basis of sorrow. Unhappiness in effect authorizes her to imitate Smith: only the unhappy woman has a right to the female poetic tradition.

Such ideas became widespread in the early nineteenth century. Paradoxically, the most womanly and therefore admirable female writer was understood to be the one who most acutely felt a sense of conflict between being a woman and being a poet. The insult likely to be thrown openly at the female poet in the seventeenth century—that she could not be both a virtuous woman and a poet—had, by the Romantic period, become for many women a strong internalized notion, so that even as they were publicly praised precisely for bringing together womanliness and poetry, they expressed fundamental doubts about the happiness of the combination. Felicia Hemans, one of the most widely admired poets of the nineteenth century, whose work was praised as 'a perfect embodiment of woman's soul',[18] dwelt in her writing on the idea of the emptiness of artistic fame for a woman. 'Properzia Rossi' is a dramatic monologue in the voice of a woman the headnote describes as 'a celebrated female sculptor of Bologna, possessed also

---

[18] Frederic Rowton, cited in Stephen C. Behrendt, ' "Certainly not a Female Pen": Felicia Hemans's Early Public Reception', in Nanora Sweet and Julie Melnyk (eds.), *Felicia Hemans: Reimagining Poetry in the Nineteenth Century* (Basingstoke: Palgrave, 2001), 101.

of talents for poetry and music', who (like the Sappho of legend)
'died in consequence of an unrequited attachment'. As Properzia
works on the sculpture of Ariadne (another rejected woman, spurned
by Theseus) she muses on her creative energy:

> It comes,—the power
> Within me born, flows back; my fruitless dower
> That could not win me love. Yet once again
> I greet it proudly, with its rushing train
> Of glorious images:—they throng—they press—
> A sudden joy lights up my loneliness,—
> I shall not perish all!
>   The bright work grows
> Beneath my hand, unfolding, as a rose,
> Leaf after leaf, to beauty; line by line,
> I fix my thought, heart, soul, to burn, to shine,
> Thro' the pale marble's veins.[19]

For all her eloquent evocation of creative joy, Properzia's conclusion
is that her gift is 'fruitless' without the love of her beloved. Happiness
and fame are firmly opposed. As women gain great commercial success, and as poetry becomes feminized, the notion gains ascendancy
of a true poetic genius which women reach, if at all, at too great a
cost to their true womanly natures, defined in Hemans's poem by
their need for a man's love, and elsewhere also by their vocation for
self-denial in the service of others. The fear that a woman writing
would do violence to her nature coloured and distorted the sisterly
support writers could offer each other. Geraldine Jewsbury had what
in some ways was a powerfully enabling upbringing for a woman
writer—looked after by a much older sister who was herself an
ambitious writer. As Norma Clarke points out, 'Not many women
writers had been mothered by a woman who was a writer as well
as a sister'; but Maria Jane Jewsbury's mentoring reflected her own
ambivalence about a woman's writing career. 'The wreath of fame is

---

[19] *Records of Woman* (1828; Oxford: Woodstock Books, 1991), 49.

often a fiery crown, burning the brows that wear it', she warned her 15-year-old sister.[20]

The imagery of poetic sisterhood fed the development of a separate tradition—almost a separate canon—for women writers that was constructed in the many anthologies devoted to women's writing in the eighteenth and nineteenth centuries.[21] The relation of sisters to a poetic brotherhood carried other meanings. As we saw in the previous chapter, the relationship with a brother could be a crucial one in the lives of literary women. Their place among writers figured as brothers was also vital. The idea of male and female writers as brothers and sisters might well encourage an emphasis on the sister's specially feminine qualities; but this metaphor also had the potential to suggest a fellowship between writers of different sexes, or even rivalry on equal terms. From the Restoration onwards, the idea surfaces—if only intermittently—that the brotherhood of writers might be joined by sisters.

As writers were mostly men and brotherhood the established metaphor, an obvious tactic for a woman writer was to try and join the group by hailing her male contemporaries in fraternal terms. Aphra Behn made a typically bold claim to kinship with the male writers of her day. As a woman in a shifting, struggling, mainly male group of playwrights, poets, and hacks, she wanted to be accepted by her 'brothers of the pen', a metaphor she uses twice in her published work. The first time is in the title of 'A Letter to a Brother of the Pen in Tribulation', one of a number of poems addressed to members of her circle, whose function is to create a sense of camaraderie among a supportive, pleasure-loving group of actors and writers: mythologizing struggling professionals as a band of witty friends. It is a jokey poem, teasing 'Damon' (possibly the playwright Edward Ravenscroft) because he has had to take the usual, nasty treatment for venereal disease: mercury in a sweating

[20] Clarke, *Ambitious Heights*, 10, 70.
[21] See Margaret Ezell, *Writing Women's Literary History* (Baltimore: Johns Hopkins University Press, 1993), chs. 3 and 4.

tub. Intimate and gently mocking, she laughs at him for having to do penance in a tub:

> Poor *Damon!* Art thou caught? Is't even so?
> Art thou become a **Tabernacler* too?
> Where sure thou dost not mean to Preach or
> Pray,
> Unless it be the clean contrary way:
> This holy *(a)* time I little thought thy sin
> Deserv'd a *Tub* to do its Pennance in.
> O how you'll for th' *Aegyptian Flesh-pots* wish,
> When you'r half-famish'd with your Lenten dish,
> Your *Almonds, Currans, Biskets* hard and dry,
> Food that will Soul and Body mortifie:
> Damn'd Penetential Drink, that will infuse
> Dull Principles into thy Grateful Muse.

The shared intimacy of a close-knit group is established by the poem's explanatory footnotes, which are there to let the wider readership of the published poem share the banter between literary friends. The asterisk cues an explanation of Damon's joking association of the tabernacle, or house of worship, with the sweating-tub, while the note to *(a)* clarifies the reference to Lent. The poem goes on to indicate that it is as a fellow professional writer that the speaker misses Damon:

> —Pox on't that you must needs be fooling now,
> Just when the Wits had greatest *(b)* need of you.
> Was Summer then so long a coming on,
> That you must make an Artificial one?
> Much good may't do thee; but 'tis thought thy Brain
> E'er long will wish for cooler Days again.
> For Honesty no more will I engage:
> I durst have sworn thou'dst had thy Pusillage.
> Thy Looks the whole Cabal have cheated too;
> But thou wilt say, most of the Wits do so.
> Is this thy writing *(c)* Plays? Who thought thy Wit
> An interlude of Whoring would admit?

The footnote to *(b)* explains why Aphra Behn, professional writer, is concerned at Damon's absence: '*I wanted a Prologue to a Play,*' which the stricken poet cannot provide. (This may be referring to Ravenscroft's failure to let Behn have a prologue and epilogue for her 1673 play, *The Dutch Lover*). The footnote to *(c)*, '*He pretended to Retire to Write,*' blows the cover on a poet's lying excuse for his disappearance. The joke about Damon's innocent looks, which have fooled his friends into thinking he still had his 'Pusillage' (virginity) serves equally to create the sense of a knowing and gossipy 'cabal'. The poem then turns to considering the effect Damon's pox will have on his poetry, turning him into an angry satirist of women:

> To Poetry no more thou'lt be inclined,
> Unless in Verse to damn all Woman-kind:
> And 'tis but Just thou shouldst in Rancor grow
> Against that Sex that has Confin'd thee so. . . .

There is an edge to this banter that comes from the reader's consciousness that the speaker herself is one of 'that Sex'. As the poem continues, it becomes clear that the cosy relationship with Damon depends on the speaker's violent dissociation from other women, as she announces that she could curse the female who has infected her friend, and advises him to curse all the women he has had sex with:

> Now I could curse this Female, but I know,
> She needs it not, that thus cou'd handle you.
> Besides, that Vengeance does to thee belong,
> And 'twere Injustice to disarm thy Tongue.
> Curse then, dear Swain, that all the Youth may hear,
> And from thy dire Mishap be taught to fear.
> Curse till thou hast undone the Race, and all
> That did contribute to thy Spring and Fall.[22]

[22] *The Works of Aphra Behn*, ed. Janet Todd, i. *Poetry* (London: William Pickering, 1992), 72–3. For the possible identification of Damon with Ravenscroft, see Todd's note, ibid. 396.

She saves herself from her own curse on the female race by separating herself from any sexual relation with Damon: she stands outside that relation, productive of disease and curses, claiming fellowship instead. He is her brother: together they belong to a group of wits who live riotously, help each other with their writing, occasionally get into a mess in their sexual lives, and tease each other about it. It's not exactly true to say that the poet is occupying a masculine subject-position here: rather, she is claiming to speak as a woman who can be one of the boys.

Behn, with her difficult, varied, and prolific literary career, could be taken as representative of the woman who attempts to join a brotherhood of writing. In her last years, she sometimes expressed disappointment that the intimate fellowship imagined in 'A Letter to a Brother' had not in fact been granted to her. The bitter preface to *The Lucky Chance* (1686) reproaches male writers for refusing to accept her as one of them:

> All I ask, is the privilege for my masculine part the poet in me (if any such you will allow me) to tread in those successful paths my predecessors have so long thrived in, to take those measures that both the ancient and modern writers have set me, and by which they have pleased the world so well. If I must not, because of my sex, have this freedom, but that you will usurp all to yourselves, I lay down my quill, and you shall hear no more of me—no, not so much as to make comparisons, because I will be kinder to my brothers of the pen than they have been to a defenceless woman.[23]

As we saw in the previous chapter, the attempt to be the sister of brother writers continued to be problematic in the generations after Behn's death. Many women writers had significant relationships with their brothers: Jane Barker's brother educated her in medicine and introduced her to a literary circle of Cambridge students; Anna Letitia Aikin (later Barbauld) did much of her early writing with

---

[23] Aphra Behn, *The Rover and Other Plays*, ed. Jane Spencer (Oxford: World's Classics, 1995), 191.

her brother; Frances Sheridan's brothers helped with her education. Behn's claim to join a symbolic literary fraternity, however, was only rarely echoed by her female successors.

One such echo can be seen in Catharine Cockburn's attempt to forge a poetic bond with Alexander Pope; but it was couched in conditionals and hedged with denials. 'I might lay some claim to you as a brother poet,' she wrote, 'but it would be a very empty one, since I can plead no affinity with your excellent talents that way; and an indifferent poet is a very scurvy character.' Her letter to him was written 'about the year 1738', thirty years after the former Catharine Trotter had retired from professional writing for the theatre. It was never sent. It was, however, included in the two-volume edition of her works that she was preparing in her final years, and which was published in 1751, two years after her death. This edition, with its life of the author by Thomas Birch, presented the one-time playwright as a respectable woman of letters, emphasizing the religious and philosophical writing to which she had devoted what time she could spare from her family. Her tentative claim to fellowship with Pope was her way of placing herself in 'the middle class' of writers, below the famous poet in genius but far above the Grub Street hacks who envied and attacked him.[24] It is a measure of Catharine Cockburn's move into religious, philosophical, and ladylike respectability that a woman who years ago had been dubbed Delarivier Manley's sister authoress could now—however tenuously—present herself as sister to Alexander Pope.

There were women who, without explicitly calling Pope brother, could address him as friend or rival, without the diffidence of Cockburn or Mary Jones, and without the deference women poets showed earlier to Dryden or later to Wordsworth. High social rank gave Anne Finch, Countess of Winchilsea, and Lady Mary Wortley Montagu, the right to address the poet on equal terms. Finch could adopt a friendly but teasing tone while warning Pope that he

[24] *The Works of Mrs. Catharine Cockburn* (London: J. and P. Knapton, 1751), vol. i. p. xxxix.

should stop impugning women's literary abilities: 'Yet Alexander, have a care | And shock the sex no more'.[25] Montagu, at one point Pope's friend and later one of his bitterest enemies, traded virulent attacks with him. The reasons for their quarrel have never been fully clear, but Montagu's biographer, Isobel Grundy, offers the likeliest explanation, that the threat of a female poetic rival contributed to Pope's feelings. It is likely 'that sexual issues inflamed a quarrel based in authorship issues; that [Montagu] was desirable and unattainable, and made him feel humiliated; that he felt her poetic creativity trespassed on the prerogative of his'.[26] Montagu was probably co-author of *Verses Address'd to the Imitator of Horace*, which used Pope's disabilities as a fruitful source of insult, finally telling him to go 'with the Emblem of thy crooked Mind | marked on thy Back, like *Cain*, by God's own Hand', and 'Wander like him, accursed through the Land'.[27] By writing such an attack Montagu stepped outside the privileges of her rank and found herself in 'a wilderness inhabited by warring tribes of pamphleteers', subject to all sorts of insult herself.[28] Still, there were some enemies of Pope ready to defend her as a woman of 'a great deal of Wit and Learning ... she is Mr. Pope's very own Sister in Poetry, and writes almost as well as himself'.[29]

By the later eighteenth century, there were male writers ready to greet their sisters in poetry. The word muse, so frequently applied to writing women, was a way, however flowery and sentimental, of acknowledging kinship between male and female writers. The anonymous author of a poem to a young lady, published in a collection of miscellaneous amateur verse that came out in twelve instalments over 1799–1800, addresses its subject as a possible writer herself: the verse, the writer speculates, 'haply greets a sister

[25] 'To Mr Pope', *The Anne Finch Wellesley Manuscript Poems*, ed. Barbara McGovern and Charles H. Hinnant (Athens, Ga.: University of Georgia Press, 1998), 69.
[26] Isobel Grundy, *Lady Mary Wortley Montagu: Comet of the Enlightenment* (Oxford: OUP, 1999), 274.
[27] Cited ibid., 339.   [28] Ibid., 340.
[29] Thomas Bentley, *A Letter to Mr. Pope, Occasioned by Sober Advice from Horace*, cited ibid. 351.

muse'. As the title of the poem indicates, it is written 'to a young Lady, enamoured of a young Gentleman, very slow in returning her affection'; no doubt it is her situation as unrequited lover that makes her seem likely to be a poet.[30] With much more certainty, George Butt addressed Anna Seward as a 'sister muse' in his epistle on the death of Lady Millar, celebrating a woman who encouraged virtuous poets by reference to the female poet who alone can properly praise her. He does not 'presume to guard the fame | Which Seward's verse sustains'. Seward, 'Skill'd in the pensive lay', belongs to a sacred group: 'we poets', who would not give up our literary bliss for any money, 'Whatever tax we pay.'[31] Minor sentimental and magazine verse at the end of the eighteenth century had at least one virtue: there, if nowhere else, brother poets acknowledged that they had sisters.

The metaphor of poets as brothers and sisters calls up the idea of sibling rivalry between them. The notion of the woman poet as man's rival changes between the seventeenth and nineteenth centuries, from an idea to be gallantly mooted without serious consideration, to a genuine possibility, one that male poets could find a threat and that female poets contemplated with mixed feelings. The change can be traced through successive evocations of Corinna—a name that stood for the woman poet as sister rival just as the name Sappho suggested the woman poet as (repressed) poetic mother. Corinna, a Theban (or Boetian) poet who is famous in legend but about whose life little is certainly known, was said to have defeated Pindar in poetic contests. She could stand, then, for the woman writer as successful rival to men. Corinna was also the name of a courtesan celebrated in Ovid's poetry, and from there was taken into the English tradition as a name for the poet's beloved, whether in complimentary song (as in Herrick or Campion) or in obscene verse (as in Rochester). As Anne McWhir has shown, the shared name led to an association between the two Corinnas, and reinforced the connection between women as

---

[30] *The Meteors* (London: A. and J. Black, and H. D. Symonds, 1800), i. 40–1.

[31] George Butt, *Poems* (Kidderminster: G. Gower, 1793), 220, 221.

writers and as sexual objects.[32] Dryden, writing to praise Elizabeth Thomas for her poetry in 1699, was careful to distinguish between the two uses of the name:

> since you do me the Favour to desire a Name from me, take that of Corinna if you please; I mean not the Lady with whom Ovid was in Love, but the famous Theban Poetess, who overcame Pindar five Times, as Historians tell us. I wou'd have call'd you Sapho [*sic*], but that I hear you are handsomer.[33]

Dryden can give Thomas the name of the poet Corinna, gallantly naming her after the woman who outdid Pindar, because there is no question of anyone imagining that she will overcome him: she is not a real rival. His compliment that she is handsomer than Sappho serves to cut her off from a matrilineal tradition: Sappho was a name applied at the time to Behn, against whose 'loose' example Dryden warned Thomas in another letter.[34]

Thomas encouraged people to think of her as 'Dryden's Corinna', but the name backfired on her when Pope included her in *The Dunciad* as 'Curl's Corinna', producer of filth for the filthy publisher. Edmund Curll himself capitalized on the association by publishing posthumous volumes of her memoirs and letters as *Pylades and Corinna*, including a portrait of Thomas, a 'PICTURE of CORINNA', copies of which were advertised at sixpence.[35] Swift's poem 'Corinna' also mocks a woman, 'half Whore, half Wife', who 'Turns Auth'ress, and is *Curll*'s for Life'—probably indicating a type composed from elements of several women writers of the day rather than any one individual. In the later 'A Beautiful Young Nymph going to Bed', Corinna is the name of the prostitute.[36] For most of the eighteenth

---

[32] Anne McWhir, 'Elizabeth Thomas and the two Corinnas: Giving the Woman Writer a Bad Name', *ELH* 62 (1995), 105–19.

[33] *The Letters of John Dryden*, ed. Charles E. Ward (Durham, NC: Duke University Press, 1942), 126.

[34] Dryden told Thomas that he was sure she would avoid 'the Licenses which Mrs. Behn allowed herself, of writing loosely, and giving (if I may have leave to say so) some Scandal to the Modesty of her Sex', ibid. 127.

[35] McWhir, '*Elizabeth Thomas*', 105–10.   [36] Ibid. 112–13.

century, it was Corinna the slut—or, in politer poetry, Corinna the flirt—who predominated, with Corinna the writer forgotten, so that the name actually suggests the anthithesis of the poetic fame to which, by the middle of the century, the virtuous woman might legitimately aspire. In Duncombe's *Feminiad*, Corinna is the name given to the superficial woman against whom the sister choir of women poets is defined. Those ladies who 'rival men' in study are the ones whose beauty, being of the mind, will last 'When all Corinna's roses fade away'.[37]

Early in the nineteenth century, Corinna as writer was revived in Germaine de Staël's novel *Corinne; ou, l'Italie* (1807). *Corinne* had a strong influence on English women writers of the nineteenth century, establishing the opposition between literary fame and happiness in love that was to make a writing vocation appear a tragic fate for a woman. Staël's influence on Felicia Hemans's poem 'Corinna at the Capitol' (1829) is evident, and when the poem was reprinted in *Songs of the Affections* the name was changed to Corinne. The Theban poet, however, remains the main referent. Hemans describes the scene of Corinna's triumph over Pindar:

> Daughter of th'Italian heaven!
> Thou, to whom its fires are given,
> Joyously thy car hath roll'd
> Where the conqueror's pass'd of old;
> And the festal sun that shone,
> O'er three hundred triumphs gone,*
> Makes thy day of glory bright,
> With a shower of golden light.[38]

The asterisk refers the reader to a quotation from Byron's *Childe Harold IV*, 'The trebly hundred triumphs'. As Susan J. Wolfson shows, this reference is part of a pattern of allusion to and dialogue

---

[37] Duncombe, *Feminiad*, 29–30.
[38] 'Corinna at the Capitol', cited in Susan J. Wolfson, 'Hemans and the Romance of Byron', in Sweet and Melnyk (eds.), *Felicia Hemans*, 171.

with Byron in Hemans's work.[39] Indeed Hemans, like the Corinna of her poem, was a serious rival to Byron in a way that eighteenth-century Corinnas had not been to their brother poets. Like Corinna, she had success in literary competitions, in her case winning the Royal Society of Literature's first poetry prize for 'Dartmoor' in 1821.[40] Of course Byron did not enter the competition, and the excited reaction of her son Arthur, reported in one of her letters—'Now I am sure Mamma is a better poet than Lord Byron!'—says more about her place in her own family than her public esteem.[41] However, her popularity certainly rivalled his; there were some who attributed her 'Modern Greece' to him; and she was praised as a 'female genius' who offered a tenderness and womanliness that provided an antithesis to Byronic dangers. His early appreciation of her poetry turned to dislike of 'Mrs Hewoman's', 'your feminine He-man'—a reaction to a combination of political differences and the experience of a woman's rival popularity.[42]

In the early nineteenth century, then, the woman poet could be a rival sister to brother poets, achieving popularity and high critical praise as a special, womanly kind of writer. At the same time the self-image of women poets became coloured by the myth of Corinne, the triumphant poet whose art cannot make her happy because she has lost her chance of love and domestic happiness. The woman poet's success and self-division were both exemplified in Felicia Hemans. As Stephen Behrendt has shown, Hemans's success came from a progressive feminization of her image along with the early nineteenth-century feminization of public taste in poetry.[43] The poet as feminine woman gave her fame, but it was a fame that did not last.

---

[39] Wolfson, ibid. 155–80.

[40] For a discussion of this and other literary prizes as attracting entrants mainly from among women and lower-class writers, see Barbara D. Taylor, 'The Search for a Space: A Note on Felicia Hemans and the Royal Society of Literature', ibid. 115–23.

[41] Harriett Hughes, *The Works of Mrs. Hemans* (1839), cited in Clarke, *Ambitious Heights*, 47.

[42] Wolfson, 'Hemans and the Romance of Byron', 161.

[43] '"Certainly Not a Female Pen": Felicia Hemans's Early Public Reception', in Sweet and Melnyk (eds.), *Felicia Hemans*, 95–114.

Daughter, Sister, Aunt, Mother: Jane Austen

Meanwhile, it was in the novel, a form that had always been especially associated with women, that the basis was being laid for the much more secure canonization of a woman writer understood as specially feminine. With Jane Austen we reach a very significant turning point in the history of women's reception into the English canon: a woman writer who became known not just as a sister but as an inheriting daughter and generative mother within the national tradition. Often called the first major woman writer in English, Austen is certainly the first to have a sustained and unchallenged canonical place. Whereas Burney received immediate acclaim as the heiress of Fielding and Richardson, only to be relegated to the literary sidelines after her death, Austen was more gradually but more securely canonized, a process that involved her being constructed as kin not only to novelists but to Homer and Shakespeare. Analysts of Austen's reception have emphasized the slow beginnings of her fame. Brian Southam notes that her great popularity and the real volume of critical attention to her work came after the Austen-Leigh *Memoir* of 1870, and John Halperin that she was relatively little discussed during the nineteenth century.[44] However, as they also note, there was an early strain of Austen criticism that placed her in the highest of literary company.

Walter Scott's 1816 review of *Emma* judged Austen to be one of the new fiction writers who concentrated on 'nature' and daily life rather than the excitements of romance, finding her 'almost alone' in being able to make the mundane as interesting as the extraordinary, and comparing her work to Flemish painting.[45] This review, now seen as the first serious critical attention given her,

---

[44] B. C. Southam, 'Introduction', in Southam (ed.), *Jane Austen: The Critical Heritage, i. 1811–1870* (London: Routledge, 1968), 1; John Halperin, 'Introduction: Jane Austen's Nineteenth-Century Critics: Walter Scott to Henry James', in Halperin (ed.), *Jane Austen: Bicentenary Essays* (Cambridge: CUP, 1975), 3–42.

[45] Southam (ed.), *Austen: Critical Heritage,* i. 63, 67.

has become famous not so much for what it says as for who is saying it: it represents the assessment of her chief contemporary brother novelist. His later scattered remarks and journal comments, where he compares his own 'Big Bow-wow strain' to her 'exquisite touch', links her to Maria Edgeworth and Susan Ferrier as writers who prove women's superiority to men in the delineation of 'real society', and acknowledges 'a finishing-off in some of her scenes that is really quite above everybody else',[46] complete the picture of Scott and Austen as the Fielding and Richardson of their day, or the brother and sister of the early nineteenth-century novel.

More explicitly, critics shortly after Austen's death began a series of comparisons that elevated not only the writer but her medium. Richard Whately, reviewing *Northanger Abbey* and *Persuasion* for the *Quarterly Review* in 1821, referred to the most illustrious of precedents in his praise of her narrative use of speech:

> she has not been forgetful of the most important maxim, so long ago illustrated by Homer, and afterwards enforced by Aristotle, of saying as little as possible in her own person, and giving a dramatic air to the narrative, by introducing frequent conversations; which she conducts with a regard to character hardly exceeded even by Shakespeare himself. Like him, she shows as admirable a discrimination in the characters of fools as of people of sense

The same epic and dramatic writers are invoked in defence of Austen's 'minuteness of detail'. 'Let any one cut out from the Iliad or from Shakespeare's plays everything … which is absolutely devoid of importance and interest *in itself*; and he will find that what is left will have lost more than half its charms.'[47] Twenty years later, the comparison with Shakespeare was made again, in the course of Macaulay's damning review of *The Diaries and Letters of Madame d'Arblay*. While Burney/Mme d'Arblay

---

[46] Ibid. 106.   [47] Ibid. 97–8, 98.

created characters in the coarser 'humours' mode, Austen wrote in a finer tradition:

> Shakespeare has no equal or second. But among the writers who, in the point we have noticed [the ability to create complex character], have approached nearest to the manner of the great master, we have no hesitation in placing Jane Austen, a woman of whom England is justly proud.[48]

G. H. Lewes, Austen's keenest mid-nineteenth-century champion, picked up on this comparison and extended it, using it to place Austen among brothers more prestigious than Scott. He put her alongside Cervantes, Fielding, and Goethe as authors whose skill with characters recalled Shakespeare and Molière.[49] In an 1847 review he identified Fielding and Austen as 'the greatest novelists in our language', placing both above Scott, who, 'if he was an Ariosto . . . was not a Shakspeare [*sic*]'. Austen, on the other hand,

> has been called a prose Shakspeare; and, among others, by Macaulay. In spite of the sense of incongruity which besets us in the words *prose* Shakspeare, we confess the greatness of Miss Austen, her marvellous dramatic power, seems more than anything in Scott akin to the greatest quality in Shakspeare.[50]

Unlike Virginia Woolf, who in *A Room of One's Own* (1929) was to imagine 'Judith Shakespeare' both as the poet's suicidal contemporary, who never managed to write, and as the great woman writer of a distant future, Lewes considered the position of sister to the great poet as already achieved in the nineteenth century. In an unsigned 1851 essay, he called Austen Shakespeare's 'younger sister'.[51]

[48] *Edinburgh Review*, 76 (Jan. 1843), 561.

[49] In an essay in *New Quarterly Review* (Oct. 1845), cited in Halperin, 'Introduction', 40–1.

[50] 'Recent Novels: French and English', *Fraser's Magazine*, 37 (Dec. 1847), 687; in Southam (ed.), *Austen: Critical Heritage*, i. 124. Southam points out that the phrase 'prose Shakspeare', attributed to Macaulay, is not in fact used in Macaulay's known comments: see ibid. 125.

[51] Halperin, 'Introduction', 18.

These praises demonstrate a familiar critical strategy, the elevation of one writer by the depreciation of others who have been associated with her, in this case Scott and Burney. The downgrading of Burney is especially significant because of the implication it carries for women's place in literary history. An anonymous writer for the *Retrospective Review* in 1823 compared Austen and Burney as representative 'female writers' of different times, 'one still, we believe, in existence, but belonging, as a writer, to the last century; and the other, though coeval with ourselves, now no more', concluding that while the older writer's work can be summed up as 'the style of portrait-painting relished by our fathers', the younger one's novels 'have enshrined themselves in the heart, and live for ever in the thoughts'.[52] In this essay, Austen replaces Burney, as if the literary world can accommodate only one really important woman writer. A more complex idea of women's place in the literary family is offered by Macaulay, in the essay mentioned above and also discussed in Chapter 1. Here, Austen's ability to approach the master, Shakespeare, serves as a counterpoint to the main theme of Burney's misguided attempt to follow Johnson. While the two female novelists are differently placed in relation to patrilineal tradition, they are at the same time accorded a matrilineal link. In fact, deploying a rhetoric similar to that used by Virginia Woolf many years later, Macaulay sees the older, inferior woman writer as making it possible for greater women to follow her. Burney

> vindicated the right of her sex to an equal share in a fair and noble province of letters. . . . Several among the successors of Madame D'Arblay have equalled her; two, we think [Edgeworth and Austen], have surpassed her. But the fact that she has been surpassed, gives her an additional claim to our respect and gratitude; for in truth we owe to her, not only Evelina, Cecilia, and Camilla, but also Mansfield Park and the Absentee.[53]

[52] Cited in Southam (ed.), *Austen: Critical Heritage*, i. 107, 111.
[53] *Edinburgh Review*, 76 (Jan. 1843), 569–70.

In Macaulay's implicit literary genealogy, Austen belongs but is not confined to a female line. In its understanding of greatness as following the master, its sidelining of female tradition, and its acknowledgement of the token woman who can enter into the inheritance of men, his essay exemplifies the terms in which literary histories were written in the nineteenth and twentieth centuries, terms which have not yet been discarded.

The elevation of Austen at Burney's expense is one manifestation of what Clifford Siskin has called the 'Great Forgetting that became the Great Tradition', a process, he argues, in which the novel became an important part of the new discipline of Literature through the suppression of its links to women and the sentimental. Austen, as a parodist of many of the sentimental women novelists of her time and before, contributed to 'the taming of writing, through the sub-suming of the sentimental within newly comfortable forms, [which] inevitably entailed the disciplinary disappearance of many women writers'. This meant that she played a part in the early nineteenth-century elevation and masculinization of the novel while becoming the genre's exemplary feminine writer, 'both remembered *and* an enigma'.[54] Clara Tuite similarly argues that the 'institutionalization of English literature studies coincides historically with the beginnings of the modern canonization of Austen ... and works to produce ... the mutually implicating and mutually canonizing relationship between Austen and the novel genre'.[55]

This sense of Austen as enigma, as the great woman writer whose rise entails the fall of those preceding her, persists in criticism today. Feminist critics have been divided over whether to restore her lost links to a matrilineal tradition, insisting on the positive and non-parodic elements in her response to earlier and contemporary women novelists, or to see her as a daddy's girl, affirming patriarchal values as she takes her place within a patrilineal tradition. Sometimes, even

---

[54] Siskin, *The Work of Writing: Literature and Social Change in Britain, 1700–1830* (Baltimore: Johns Hopkins University Press, 1998), 195, 207, 200.

[55] Tuite, *Romantic Austen: Sexual Politics and the Literary Canon* (Cambridge: CUP, 2002), 190–1.

now, it seems as if high praise of Austen necessitates the sweeping condemnation of the women writers around her. In 'Sublimely Bad', an essay reviewing a modern edition of Eliza Fenwick's 1796 novel, *Secresy: or the Ruin on the Rock*, Terry Castle treats the novel's faults as exemplifying those of all women writing novels before Austen, and sees their bad writing as evidence of the psychological problems faced by women who have been 'cut off from discourse'. The 'appalling, seemingly pathological relations that obtain in [early women's fiction] between parents and children' are considered neither as literary stereotype nor social analysis, but as a symptom of the writers' 'autistic' alienation from their literary fathers.[56] In Castle's essay, Austen figures rather as she does in Woolf's *A Room of One's Own*, as the mysterious great woman writer who somehow escapes the anger that deforms her sisters' work. By a 'miracle about which we know little: the outwitting of autism', Austen escaped any sense of alienation. Even her juvenile work shows 'the touch of grace, the inability to feel frightened'. The mystery is solved for Castle by an appeal to Austen's father. Certainly, if Austen is the first woman to enjoy a central place within the patriarchal family of English literary history, we might expect her to be on excellent terms with her metaphorical fathers, and perhaps her biological father too; but it is going a bit far to attribute her success so largely to the grace (of God?) that the latter brought:

> One suspects that the admirable Reverend Austen, whose love
> for his brilliant daughter shines forth in all of her compositions,
> had something to do with this grace: did something well enough
> to make writing seem the most natural thing on earth.[57]

Castle here turns Austen's work into an expression of the father: it is he who shines forth in her work.

While this romanticized view of Austen's father may be unwarranted, it is worth considering the ways Austen's family situation

---

[56] Castle, 'Sublimely Bad', in *Boss Ladies, Watch Out! Essays on Women, Sex, and Writing* (London: Routledge, 2002), 141, 140.
[57] Ibid. 142, 143.

enabled her to assume the place she took in the literary family. The Austen family's enjoyment of novels, amateur theatricals, and wordgames, and its shared love of satirical fun, evidently fostered the young writer's comic talents.[58] Most accounts of her life agree on the helpful role played by her father, who offered early encouragement of her writing, and appreciated the irreverence of her wit.[59] Austen's mother has aroused mixed responses. Claire Tomalin gives the most positive assessment of her influence, as a verse writer herself, a 'mother who could make magic with words', and a woman whose 'sharp tongue for neighbours' was 'appreciated by her daughter and passed on to her'.[60] She notes, however, the tensions in their relationship caused by Mrs Austen's hypochondria,[61] and others have suggested that Mrs Austen may have preferred her elder daughter Cassandra, and may have inspired unpleasant mothers in Austen's fiction.[62] Alison Sulloway sees Mrs Austen's imagination and satirical wit as important formative influences on her daughter, but speculates that the relationship was fraught with the mother's jealousy of a daughter 'usurping the male privilege of writing'.[63] Austen's elder brothers James and Henry were early writing role-models with their satirical periodical *The Loiterer*. James is said to have helped with his sister's education by directing her reading, while Henry later acted as her literary agent.[64] However, the most important part in nurturing Austen as writer is generally agreed to have been played by her sister Cassandra. Their niece, Anna Lefroy, remarked that

> They were everything to each other. They seemed to lead a
> life to themselves within the general family life shared only

[58] See e.g., John Halperin , *The Life of Jane Austen* (Brighton: Harvester Press, 1984), 27–35.

[59] Ibid. 63; Claire Tomalin, *Jane Austen: A Life* (London: Penguin, 1998), 65–7; George Holbert Tucker, 'Jane Austen's Family', in J. David Grey (ed.), *The Jane Austen Handbook* (London: Athlone Press, 1986), 144.

[60] Tomalin, *Jane Austen*, 103. See also Alison Sulloway, *Jane Austen and the Province of Womanhood* (Philadelphia: University of Pennsylvania Press, 1989), 91.

[61] Tomalin, *Jane Austen*, 145–6; see also Halperin, *Life*, 64.

[62] Halperin, *Life*, 63–4.

[63] Sulloway, *Jane Austen*, 92.   [64] Halperin, *Life*, 21–2.

with each other. I will not say their true, but their *full*, feelings
and opinions were known only to themselves. They alone fully
understood what each had suffered and felt and thought.[65]

Following this lead, Austen's biographers have found Cassandra to
be the most important person in the novelist's life, who provided
the most intimate and understanding audience, and the emotional
security that allowed Austen to write as she did.[66] Whatever Austen's
relation to the 'sister choir' of women writers, it is clear that in her
personal life sisterhood helped her to write.

However we assess the relative influence of different elements of
Austen's family life, it was the ground for a novelist who was to take
a place within the national literary family that no woman had had
before. Part of this is the effect of later reception, but part is that
of her own assumption of a literary inheritance. The breadth of her
English inheritance is striking. In addition to her use, both parodic
and serious, of such obvious precursors as Richardson, Fielding,
Lennox, Burney, Smith, Radcliffe, and Edgeworth, she absorbed
and used the work of many other novelists of the late eighteenth
century.[67] The Bible and Book of Common Prayer influenced
her sentence construction.[68] She loved and made use of Crabbe,
Cowper, and Johnson.[69] She has been seen as an Augustan in the

[65] Mary Augusta Austen-Leigh, *Personal Aspects of Jane Austen* (London: John Murray, 1920), 147–8.

[66] Tucker, 'Jane Austen's Family', 150; Halperin, *Life*, 23. Terry Castle, in an essay that balances the one praising the influence of Austen's father, accords Cassandra the major role as 'the essential ballast in Austen's life . . . the caretaker of her mind and body, and guarantor of her imaginative freedom', and writes that Austen was able to create works 'among the supreme humane inventions of the English language' because 'she loved and was loved' by Cassandra. 'Was Jane Austen Gay?', in *Boss Ladies*, 134.

[67] Kenneth L. Moler, *Jane Austen's Art of Allusion* (Lincoln, Nebr.: University of Nebraska Press, 1968); Margaret Anne Doody, 'Jane Austen's Reading', in Grey (ed.), *Jane Austen Handbook*, 347–3. For Austen's relation to jacobin and anti-jacobin fiction of the 1790s see Marilyn Butler, *Jane Austen and the War of Ideas* (Oxford: Clarendon Press, 1975).

[68] Doody, 'Austen's Reading', 347; Isobel Grundy, 'Jane Austen and Literary Traditions', in Edward Copeland and Juliet McMaster (eds.), *The Cambridge Companion to Jane Austen* (Cambridge: CUP, 1997), 196.

[69] Grundy, 'Austen and Literary Traditions', 197–9.

line of Pope.[70] Jocelyn Harris has detailed her use of earlier writers, especially Chaucer, Milton, and Shakespeare.[71] She took freely from prose fiction and from other traditions, and from both men and women, though her famous defence of the novel in *Northanger Abbey* concentrated on the vindication of fiction and of work by women. The parodic nature of Austen's early work in particular raises questions about her attitude to her inheritance. Jo Alyson Parker portrays her as initially unsure how to deal with feminocentric fiction: in *Northanger Abbey* she is 'uncertain about what to make of her authorial inheritance, simultaneously embracing and faulting the matrilineal literary tradition', while in her later novels she develops a greater confidence and 'revises Fielding's canonical texts, decentering their implicitly masculine set of values'.[72] Margaret Doody, in contrast, finds a sophisticated surety in Austen's juvenilia, with its 'disconcerting, uncompromising laughter', and considers Austen as a naturally Rabelaisian writer the refinement of whose later novels came from a need to compromise with the early nineteenth-century marketplace.[73] While Austen's disagreements with and criticisms of her predecessors are certainly vital, and while it is fascinating to speculate on the kind of writing she would have developed in a different cultural climate, those critics are surely right who emphasize the overall ease of her relationship to her literary inheritance, what Harris calls 'her confident, even cheerful intertextuality'.[74]

This ease of absorption and allusion is one reason critics have seen Austen as an Augustan, understanding art as a form of sophisticated imitation. Both Harris and Doody look back to Dryden, that early

[70] Reuben A. Brower, 'From the *Iliad* to Jane Austen, via *The Rape of the Lock*', in Halperin (ed.), *Austen: Bicentenary Essays*, 43–60.

[71] Harris, *Jane Austen's Art of Memory* (Cambridge: CUP, 1989).

[72] Parker, *The Author's Inheritance: Henry Fielding, Jane Austen, and the Establishment of the Novel* (DeKalb, Ill.: Northern Illinois University Press, 1998), 60, 181.

[73] Doody, introd. to Jane Austen, *Catharine and Other Writings*, ed. Margaret Anne Doody and Douglas Murray (Oxford: OUP, 1993), p. xxxiv.

[74] Jocelyn Harris, 'Jane Austen and the Burden of the (Male) Past: The Case Reexamined', in Devoney Looser (ed.), *Jane Austen and the Discourses of Feminism* (Houndmills: Macmillan, 1995), 88.

definer of the right way of taking up a literary inheritance, when expressing Austen's relation to hers. 'I detect no trace of anxiety in her', writes Harris, 'for to paraphrase Dryden on Jonson, she "invades Authors like a Monarch, and what would be theft in other Poets, is only victory in her"'.[75] Doody, dealing with Austen's use of late eighteenth-century novelists, writes: 'It is tempting to paraphrase Dryden on Ben Jonson's relation to the Ancients: You may track her everywhere in their snow.'[76] Reuben Brower revives a metaphor used by Dryden when he writes that 'in Jane Austen the mind and art of Pope found its reincarnation'.[77] Linked to this chain of English greats, inheriting their mode of inheritance, Austen nevertheless represents a major shift in tradition. As both Doody and Harris emphasize, this writer who boasted of being 'the most unlearned and uninformed female who ever dared to be an authoress'[78] sticks almost exclusively to her English predecessors, showing scarcely a trace of interest in the classical tradition that for them was so central.[79] While Burney was affected by an uneasy sense of lacking classical learning, yet was reluctant to gain it, Austen seems to have assumed that Milton's daughters did not need Latin. Her ability to take so confident a place in the English literary line was contingent on the independent prestige that line had gained by the early nineteenth century, a development to which Burney herself, and Richardson before her, had contributed. The line from Dryden to Austen is one of increasing confidence in the status of the national literary tradition, so that it became possible to be its heiress without reference to the classical line which for Dryden was its necessary precursor—and even without reference to Dryden himself, who may not have been read by Austen.[80]

[75] Harris, *Austen's Art of Memory*, pp. x–xi.
[76] Doody, 'Austen's Reading', 362.
[77] Brower, 'From the *Iliad* to Austen', 59.
[78] *Jane Austen's Letters*, ed. R. W. Chapman (Oxford: OUP, 1979), 443.
[79] Doody, 'Austen's Reading', 355–7.
[80] Ibid. 356.

Entering the canon meant, as Dryden knew well, not just inheriting but making the inheritance one's own and passing it on. For Dryden and the Augustans, the emphasis fell on the way true literary imitation involves producing something fresh. By Austen's time, the Romantic stress was on the importance of originality: every author, as Wordsworth put it, 'as far as he is great and at the same time *original*', having 'the task of *creating* the taste by which he is to be enjoyed'.[81] Austen's art has been well demonstrated to be one of allusion and memory, but the extent of her refashioning of her inheritance is such as to make her an original in Wordsworthian terms, creating a new taste. She is the first of the modern novelists, practising a form of realism and demonstrating an approach to character that profoundly influenced the nineteenth- and twentieth-century approaches to fiction. Austen left no literary manifestos, and her references to her art tend to be ironically self-deprecating. It is clear enough, however, that her artistic intentions were to make fiction more natural and probable, and that she progressed from expressing this mainly through parody to the development of subtler forms of character rendition. Because she achieves her total effects through a complex of subtle narrative strategies it is difficult to pin down her particular innovations. However, one particular Austenian contribution that has become recognized as key to her work is her development of free indirect discourse.

Free indirect discourse (variously known as free indirect speech, free indirect style, *style indirect libre*, *Erlebte Rede*, represented thought and dialogue, and coloured narrative) incorporates the thought or speech of a character into the third-person narrative, changing the grammatical forms accordingly.[82] It allows for a close blending

---

[81] 'Essay, Supplementary to the Preface' (1815), in *William Wordsworth*, ed. Stephen Gill (Oxford: OUP, 1984), 657–8.

[82] For a discussion of free indirect speech, *style indirect libre*, and *Erlebte Rede*, see Roy Pascal, *The Dual Voice: Free Indirect Speech and its Functioning in the Nineteenth-Century European Novel* (Manchester: MUP, 1977). 'Represented speech and thought' is the preferred term in Ann Banfield's Chomskyan account, *Unspeakable Sentences: Narration*

between the narrative voice and the characters', creating the illusion of being in the mind of the character, and at the same time it can exploit the residual distance between character's and narrator's voice to create an ironic perspective, by colouring the third-person narrative with words typical of particular characters and understood to be thought or spoken by them. This blend of identification with and distance from a character can be used for creating both empathy and intellectual distance.

Free indirect discourse is now so firmly established in all kinds of narrative writing that it is not generally noticed as a technique at all, but it was relatively new in Austen's day, and it is one of the main features of a narrative that offers the reader the familiar pleasures of identification with fictional characters. Its relative absence in earlier fiction is an important part of what makes the early novel appear alien and less immediately attractive than later fiction to readers today. Virtually unknown before the seventeenth century, it appears with the development of narrative fiction and emerges at around the same time in different European countries. Ann Banfield has argued convincingly that it is fundamentally a written technique rather than a written representation of the oral, and that its emergence is a part of the move from an oral to a written tradition.[83] While various eighteenth-century uses of free indirect discourse have been identified, Austen is generally acknowledged as the first to develop it fully as a central novelistic device.[84]

The technique is intermittently used in many of the popular novels of the late eighteenth century. In particular, Austen takes

---

and Representation in the Language of Fiction (London: Routledge and Kegan Paul, 1982). Graham Hough distinguishes between 'free indirect style', when the character's 'actual mode of expression' is used, and 'coloured narrative', where the narrative voice is affected by the character's 'point of view', but allows that in practice the two shade into each other. 'Narrative and Dialogue in Jane Austen', *Critical Quarterly*, 12 (1970), 204, 205.

[83] Banfield, *Unspeakable Sentences*, 225–54.

[84] Pascal, *Dual Voice*, mentions Rousseau and Henry Fielding as 18th-cent. authors using the technique, but dates its extensive development to the early 19th cent., with Goethe and Austen as its first major proponents: for Austen, see ibid. 45–60. David Lodge names Austen 'the first English novelist to use [free indirect speech] extensively'. 'Jane Austen's Novels: Form and Structure', in Grey (ed.), *Austen Handbook*, 175.

hints for the style from Burney, who uses it in *Cecilia* to represent her heroine's reflections. This is Cecilia analysing her feelings:

> Mr Harrel's house, which had never pleased her, now became utterly disgustful; she was wearied and uncomfortable, yet, willing to attribute her uneasiness to any other than the true cause, she fancied the house itself was changed, and that all its inhabitants and visitors were more than usually disagreeable: but this idle error was of short duration, the moment of self-conviction was at hand, and when Delvile presented her the letter he had written for Mr Belfield, it flashed in her eyes!
>
> This detection of the altered state of her mind opened to her views and her hopes a scene entirely new, for neither the exertion of the most active benevolence, nor the steady course of the most virtuous conduct, sufficed any longer to wholly engage her thoughts, or constitute her felicity; she had purposes that came nearer home, and cares that threatened to absorb in themselves that heart and those faculties which hitherto had only seemed animated for the service of others.
>
> Yet this loss of mental freedom gave her not much uneasiness, since the choice of her heart, though involuntary, was approved by her principles, and confirmed by her judgment. Young Delvile's situation in life was just what she wished, more elevated than her own, yet not so exalted as to humble her with a sense of inferiority; his connections were honourable, his mother appeared to her the first of women, his character and disposition seemed formed to make her happy, and her own fortune was so large, that to the state of his she was indifferent.[85]

It is characteristic of free indirect style that it can be difficult to distinguish between narrator's objective comment and character's subjective thought. In the second paragraph, we need to attribute the references to Cecilia's unselfishness to the narrator if the heroine is not to be horribly smug. In the third paragraph, on the other hand, the reflections on Delvile's situation in life are clearly Cecilia's:

---

[85] *Cecilia*, ed. Peter Sabor and Margaret Doody (Oxford: OUP, 1988), 252.

her thought and narrative voice are blended. The first paragraph is more complex. Initially there seems to be a fair distance between Cecilia's consciousness and the narrative's, as the narrative comments on her fancies and her inability to recognize the real reason for her feelings. However, this quickly changes as she reaches the 'moment of self-conviction', in the light of which the preceding comments on her fancies and error could equally be her own reflections. In this paragraph, Cecilia is recalling an earlier moment of revelation, when she suddenly understood her feelings for Delvile. Anticipating Austen, whose Emma was to find that '[i]t darted through her, with the speed of an arrow, that Mr Knightley must marry no one but herself!', Burney dramatizes the heroine's realization that she is in love.[86]

Going much further than Burney and other earlier writers in making free indirect discourse a dominant part of the narrative, Austen develops her presentation of human consciousness as faulty, self-deceptive, comic, and yet sympathetic. Much discussion of her use of the technique has focused on *Emma*, where she presents much of the narrative through the medium of the heroine's consciousness.[87] This creates subtle ironic pleasures in the gap between Emma's point of view and the facts of the narrative, a gap that is indicated to the reader in constant hints yet may not be fully evident on a first reading. Emma keeps on making mistakes, even when she is consciously trying to learn from previous errors. When she thinks she has detected Harriet's dawning attraction for Frank Churchill, her determination not to encourage her as she had done in the matter of Mr Elton allows the two of them to remain quite ignorant of each others' meaning. She does not learn that Harriet is thinking of Mr Knightley. Ironically, the misjudgement arises out of careful thought:

> She then took a longer time for consideration. Should she proceed no farther?—should she let it pass, and seem to

[86] *Emma*, ed. James Kinsley (Oxford: World's Classics, 2003), 320.
[87] See e.g. David Lodge, 'Jane Austen's Novels: Form and Structure', in Grey (ed.), *Austen Handbook*, 165–78; Wayne C. Booth, *The Rhetoric of Fiction* (Chicago: University of Chicago Press, 1961).

suspect nothing?—Perhaps Harriet might think her cold and angry if she did; or perhaps if she were totally silent, it might drive Harriet into asking her to hear too much; and against any thing like such an unreserve as had been, such an open and frequent discussion of hopes and chances, she was perfectly resolved.—She believed it would be wiser for her to say and know at once, all that she meant to say and know. Plain dealing was always best. She had previously determined how far she would proceed, on any application of the sort; and it would be safer for both, to have the judicious law of her own brain laid down with speed.—She was decided, and thus spoke—

'Harriet, I will not affect to be in doubt of your meaning. . . .'
(*Emma*, 268)

Thinking she is going in for plain dealing, Emma is doing anything but, and it is amusing to observe how her tentative approaches to uncertainty, in the repeated 'should she' and 'perhaps', lead her straight back to the comforts of being 'perfectly resolved' and 'decided' on another course of potentially disastrous action. At the same time, the minute presentation from her own point of view of just how she goes wrong while trying to go right, builds up sympathy for her.

Free indirect discourse is also important in *Persuasion*, where each social group, each family, ultimately each individual, tend to be absorbed in their own concerns and unable to feel each other's. Anne, unimportant within her own family, moving between Kellynch, Uppercross, and Bath at others' convenience, is well placed to understand this. Like everyone around her she is caught in her own desires and liable to allow them to colour everything she sees, but she is aware of it, and able to take an ironic perspective on herself. At Bath, standing with Lady Russell looking out on the street, she sees Wentworth and is sure Lady Russell is watching him too: 'She could thoroughly comprehend the sort of fascination he must possess over Lady Russell's mind, the difficulty it must be for her to withdraw her eyes, the astonishment she must be feeling that eight or nine years should have passed over him, and in foreign climes and active service too, without robbing him of one personal grace!' Lady Russell's remark a moment later that in fact she has been studying curtains in the house opposite prompts Anne to sigh and smile 'in pity and disdain, either at her friend or herself'.[88] If in *Emma* the emphasis is on the intellect and its errors, in *Persuasion* there is more rendering of sensation. A crowded social world and the heroine's inner feelings are constantly juxtaposed. Listening to Wentworth, who is talking of Benwick's sudden second attachment and almost but not quite broaching the subject of their own relationship, Anne keeps up the surface of conversation while the agitation of her feelings is conveyed through her own confused impressions of the surrounding scene:

> Anne, who, in spite of the agitated voice in which the latter part [of Wentworth's speech] had been uttered, and in spite of all the various noises of the room, the almost ceaseless slam of the door, and ceaseless buzz of persons walking through, had distinguished every word, was struck, gratified, confused, and beginning to breathe very quick, and feel an hundred things in a moment. It was impossible for her to enter on such a subject; and yet, after a pause, feeling the necessity of speaking, and having not the smallest wish for a total change, she only deviated so far as to say,
> 'You were a good while at Lyme, I think?' (*Persuasion*, 391)

In scenes like this Austen presents subjective experience both more vividly and more subtly than previous novelists, and her influence on the rendering of consciousness in later fiction has been profound.

Austen is the first English woman writer to have been widely recognized as generative, not only in a matrilineal but in a mixed tradition. Male writers have been identified as her heirs.[89] In F. R. Leavis's notoriously selective 'Great Tradition' of English novelists, she was

[88] *Persuasion*, in *Northanger Abbey and Persuasion*, ed. John Davie (Oxford: Oxford English Novels, 1971), 387, 388.
[89] '[I]n narrative method James is surely Jane Austen's lawful heir'; '[Trollope's] world is the heir of Miss Austen's' (Obituary assessment of Anthony Trollope in *The Times*, 1882). Norman Page, 'Influence on Later Writers', in Grey (ed.), *Austen Handbook*, 232.

placed at the head of a line that ran from her through George Eliot
to Henry James and Joseph Conrad, to D. H. Lawrence.[90] Norman
Page credits her domestic realism, irony, moral seriousness, and concentration on heroines with giving rise to 'a vigorous and significant
tradition that is exemplified in the work of such major novelists as
George Eliot, Elizabeth Gaskell, Henry James, and E. M. Forster',
and sums up her influence as 'a positive creative force in the novel
in England'.[91] Her influence in the development of free indirect
discourse is particularly important here, leading her to be identified especially as Henry James's progenitor. David Lodge sees this
narrative method as producing

> an intensification of what Henry James called the sense of felt
> life—a more intimate relationship between fictional discourse
> and the processes of human consciousness. And not until
> Henry James himself, perhaps, was there a novelist in the
> English language who equaled the skill and subtlety with
> which Jane Austen carried out this difficult technical feat.[92]

It is in relation to James that Austen has been called mother—the
first time, as far as I am aware, that a female writer has been explicitly
credited with having a metaphorical son in the way that male
writers are commonly understood to have them. The relationship
was not, like those between father and son, invoked as a matter
of course in critical discussion, but elaborated within a fiction:
Rudyard Kipling's story 'The Janeites'. The title echoes the name
given to Austen enthusiasts in the late nineteenth and early twentieth
centuries, a byword for a kind of sentimental adulation of the novelist
deplored by more serious critics.[93] Kipling's Janeites, however, are
not confined to the lost pastoral of idyllic gentility that Austen was
taken, in Janeite tradition, to represent. They are soldiers in the

[90] F. R. Leavis, *The Great Tradition: George Eliot, Henry James, Joseph Conrad* (1948; London: Chatto and Windus, 1962), 27.

[91] 'Influence on Later Writers', in Grey (ed.), *Austen Handbook*, 229, 230.

[92] 'Jane Austen's Novels', 177–8.

[93] For a discussion of Janeitism see Claudia L. Johnson, 'Austen Cults and Cultures', in Copeland and McMaster (eds.), *Cambridge Companion to Austen*, 211–26.

Great War trenches, for whom 'Jane' is a way of coping with the Front. The woman whose writing was famous for not including war provides the names given to their guns. Her name allows entry into a freemasonry in which army rank is set aside. She is also made the means of surviving war: while most of the Janeites die in battle, the survivor, Humberstall, finds his way onto a full hospital train because the sister in charge recognizes him as a fellow spirit by his reference to Austen's Miss Bates. The story treats the Janeites with a fundamentally sympathetic humour, and its epigraph not only makes Austen a national icon but hints at a likeness between her and Christ the Redeemer as it proclaims: 'Glory, love and honour unto England's Jane!'[94] Within the story, the Janeites discuss the question of Jane's progeny. Humberstall reports the conversation:

> But, as I was sayin', 'Ammick says what a pity 'twas Jane 'ad died barren. 'I deny that,' says Mosse. 'I maintain she was fruitful in the 'ighest sense o' the word.' An' Mosse knew about such things, too. 'I'm inclined to agree with 'Ammick,' says young Gander. 'Any'ow, she's left no direct an' lawful progeny....' 'Pahardon me, gents,' Macklin says, 'but this *is* a matter on which I *do* 'appen to be moderately well-informed. She *did* leave lawful issue in the shape o' one son; an' 'is name was 'Enery James.'
>
> 'By what sire! Prove it,' says Gander, before 'is senior officers could get in a word.
>
> 'I will,' says Macklin, surgin' on 'is two thumbs. An, mark you, none of 'em spoke! I forget whom he said was the sire of this 'Enery James-man; but 'e delivered 'em a lecture on this Jane-woman for more than a quarter of an hour.[95]

The literary father is not left out of account in quite the same way that paternal genealogies manage to do without the mother. It is assumed that James must have had a sire; but whoever he

<hr>

[94] 'The Janeites', in *Debits and Credits* (London: Macmillan and Co., 1926), 147. The line echoes the opening line of the hymn, 'All glory, laud and honour, to thee Redeemer King!'
[95] Ibid. 153–4.

was, he is dismissed as unmemorable, and the maternal line reigns. Kipling's story indicates the difficulty of acknowledging the literary mother in its comic treatment of Macklin, who is 'bosko absoluto' as he pronounces on Jane's relation to James, and falls down in a drunken stupor at the end of his speech. The contrast between this and the straightforward references—or, sometimes, solemn tributes—to literary fathers in critical literature is telling. Comedy cloaks an awkwardness about the literary mother, but it does not cancel out the acknowledgement. There is a level at which Kipling is quite serious here about providing James, a writer he greatly admired, and whose naturalization as a British citizen he had welcomed, with this maternal link to the best of English tradition. Women writers have often been seen in relation to their literal family connections: Sidney's sister, Pembroke's mother. Austen has been granted the more prestigious metaphorical connection to the patriarchal family of English literature: Shakespeare's sister, James's mother.

Kipling draws attention to a connection which James himself was far less ready to acknowledge. His own remarks on Austen blend appreciation for her writing with denial of the conscious artistry behind it. Austen is a garden bird whose song flows from simple nature: 'with all her light felicity, [she] leaves us hardly more curious of her process, or of the experience in her that fed it, than the brown thrush who tells his story from the garden bough'; or else another creature just as lacking in self-awareness, a lady working at her tapestry. Her great virtue, 'the extraordinary grace of her facility' amounts to

> unconsciousness: as if, at the most, for difficulty, for embarrassment, she sometimes, over her work basket, her tapestry flowers, in the spare, cool drawing-room of other days, fell a-musing, lapsed too metaphorically, as one may say, into wool-gathering, and her dropped stitches, of these pardonable, of these precious moments, were afterwards picked up as little touches of human truth, little glimpses of steady vision, little master-strokes of imagination.

James's tendency to depreciate Austen, his suggestion that she is overrated, is partly a reaction to the commercial success of the sentimentalized 'Janeite' view of her. The publishing industry, he complains, finds 'their "dear", our dear, everybody's dear, Jane so infinitely to their material purpose'.[96] It seems also to betray, as Halperin suggests, James's wish to deny influence: 'he is often reticent and at times even misleading on the subject of the real formative influences upon his own art'.[97] A woman's formative influence, not surprisingly, rouses particular anxiety in her metaphorical sons. The literary mother seems too close to the Mighty Mother of myth. That is one explanation for the particularly violent dislike of Austen expressed by some male writers. D. H. Lawrence, for example, later named by F. R. Leavis as the culmination of the Great Tradition she started, called her an 'old maid', who was 'thoroughly unpleasant, English in the bad, mean, snobbish sense of the word'.[98] Mark Twain found her 'entirely impossible. It seems a great pity to me that they allowed her to die a natural death!' Some of this is enjoyment of a pose—in Twain's case 'the rough-neck American democrat in collision with the genteel English spinster'[99]—and some is explicable as reaction to the complacent conservative patriotism and reverent excesses of those who called 'Jane' divine. ('One shudders to speak' of anyone not admiring her, said Montague Summers in 1917.)[100] Some is the reaction of novelists with a strong investment in their masculinity to the idea of being in literary descent from a woman. Kipling's Austen as fruitful mother is replaced by Lawrence's barren old maid; and Mark Twain surely expresses matricidal feelings as he compulsively rereads what he hates, and tries to kill a literary ancestry that will not go away: 'her books madden me so that I

[96] 'The Lesson of Balzac' (1905), in *The House of Fiction*, ed. Leon Edel (London: Rupert Hart-Davis, 1957).

[97] Halperin, 'Introduction', 35.

[98] *Lady Chatterley's Lover* and *A Propos of Lady Chatterley's Lover*, ed. Michael Squires (Cambridge: CUP, 1993), 333.

[99] Southam (ed.), *Austen: The Critical Heritage*, ii. 1870–1940, 232.

[100] Brian Southam, 'Janeites and Anti-Janeites', in Grey (ed.), *Austen Handbook*, 240.

can't conceal my frenzy . . . Every time I read "Pride and Prejudice"
I want to dig her up and hit her over the skull with her own
shin-bone.'[101]

At the other end of the appreciative spectrum, but also bearing
marks of the fear of strong female influence, is the sentimental
appellation 'aunt Jane'. Here, an epithet that belonged to Austen's
private family life is turned into her public designation—quite
openly, in Richard Simpson's review of the Austen-Leigh *Memoir*.
On the one hand, Simpson adds his voice to those comparing Austen
to Shakespeare: on the other, he implicitly reduces her stature with
the sugary suggestion that we should 'borrow from Miss Austen's
biographer the title which the affection of a nephew bestows upon
her, and recognise her officially as "dear aunt Jane" '.[102] In a literary
tradition made up of fathers, sons, and brothers, with a few daughters
and sisters, an aunt can be added without threatening the status quo.
The aunt as aunt has no children of her own. In life, Austen belonged
to a distinct and common class of woman, the spinster dependent
on her brothers, whose closest connection to a later generation
was to those brothers' children—sidelined from inheritance and
generation. What she made of this position had the potential to
transform the notion of the aunt. When her niece Anna Austen (later
Lefroy) started writing fiction, Austen read her work and wrote letters
of encouragement and advice that now stand as her most important
commentary on the novelist's art. The published critical essays and
the public mentoring of sons typical of male writers contrast with
Austen's private, family-based encouragement for a woman writer
of the next generation. With the publication of Austen's letters, a
new image of the aunt became available; one adopted, for example,
by Fay Weldon in her own homage to Austen, *Letters to Alice*.[103]
However, this new expression of female literary influence is not what
was invoked when Simpson recommended all Austen's readers to

---

[101] Southam (ed.), *Critical Heritage*, ii. 232.
[102] Cited in Halperin, 'Introduction', 34.
[103] *Letters to Alice: On First Reading Jane Austen* (London: Coronet, 1985).

adopt her as their dear aunt. To apply the term 'aunt Jane' to her in a literary context was a way of containing her, making her safe: it amounted, despite the affection and admiration that prompted it, to a denial of her generative power in the metaphorical line.

There were many metaphors for literary activity and relationships between writers: the circle, with its connotations of friendship and equality; the race or contest; the war, as Johnson described it, between rising and established wits; the trade, in which writers incurred debts to one another; the republic of letters. These—unlike familial metaphors—did not automatically assign the female writer a fixed position based on her gender. They offered, potentially, freer access to the literary world. But literary history has always been obsessed with the metaphor of the line; and writers have been accepted into the canon through being assigned a place in a line of inheritance based on kinship. From 1660 to 1830 many different lines were drawn, creating a number of different traditions, or what Dryden called clans. There was the Spenser–Milton–Dryden–Pope line of poets, or later, the Shakespeare–Milton–Wordsworth one. Scott saw Fielding as his father in fiction, Dryden in poetry. A line of criticism ran from Dryden to Johnson. The cooperation or competition between contemporaries, understood as brotherhood, became absorbed into the familial metaphor even as it deflected attention from the father; and the brothers of one generation became the fathers of the next. The tradition of English Literature was structured like a patriarchal family.

In this book I have explored some of the relationships that made up that family. I have tried to show how writers' relations both to real-life and metaphorical kin helped create and express the positions they were accorded in the new discourses of literary history. There are other stories of literary relations than the ones I have told here: the father–daughter partnership of Richard Lovell and Maria Edgeworth, and the strange, stormy, parodic relationship of Charlotte Charke to her Poet Laureate father, Colley Cibber; Matthew Lewis's anxieties about his mother's writing; the careers of the sisters and sister novelists Harriet and Sophia Lee; and many more. I hope that this work will encourage others to explore the ties between kinship and the creation of literary canons.

Women's place in the literary family has been a particular concern for me. Metaphors of kinship and family, I have argued, served both to include and subordinate women in the canon. In so far as women's work became canonical, it was through being assigned a familial place, whether a subordinate one within the patriarchal line, or in some imagined alternative familial arrangement. As women's writing became more voluminous and visible, there was a struggle over women's place in the literary family. While male Romantic poets conceived of the sister as sister soul, reflection of the brother and conduit for the expression of his feminine side, female Romantic poets were constructing themselves as a separate sisterhood or as rival sisters to their brothers. In fiction, whose early matrilineage through Aphra Behn had been repudiated, a new maternal line of Burney–Edgeworth–Austen was drawn. The woman writer might claim inheritance from the father, as Burney did, and even, eventually, like Austen, be seen as the mother of sons as well as daughters. But the continued rarity of the maternal metaphor, while the paternal one remains commonplace, reminds us of the imbalance built into our notions of generation, kinship, and inheritance. New configurations of writers, different kinds of canon, will need other metaphors.

Bibliography

PRIMARY SOURCES

The Adventures of Dick Hazard (London: W. Reeve, 1755).

Addison, Joseph, and Steele, Richard, *The Spectator*, ed. D. F. Bond, 5 vols. (Oxford: Clarendon Press, 1965).

Aikin, Lucy, *Epistles on Women, Exemplifying Their Character and Condition in various ages and nations. With Miscellaneous Poems* (London: J. Johnson, 1810).

An appeal to the public in behalf of the manager (London: Wilson and Fell, 1763).

Austen, Jane, *Northanger Abbey and Persuasion*, ed. John Davie (Oxford: Oxford English Novels, 1971).

_____ *Jane Austen's Letters*, ed. R. W. Chapman (Oxford: OUP, 1979).

_____ *Catharine and Other Writings*, ed. Margaret Anne Doody and Douglas Murray (Oxford: OUP, 1993).

_____ *Northanger Abbey*, ed. Marilyn Butler (Harmondsworth: Penguin, 1995).

_____ *Emma*, ed. J. Kinsley (Oxford: World's Classics, 2003).

Barbauld, Anna Letitia, *The Works of Anna Laetitia Barbauld. With a Memoir by Lucy Aikin*, 2 vols. (London: Longman, Hurst, Rees, Orme, Brown, and Green, 1825).

_____ *The Poems of Anna Letitia Barbauld*, ed. William McCarthy and Elizabeth Kraft (Athens, Ga.: University of Georgia Press, 1994).

Behn, Aphra, *Poems Upon Several Occasions* (London: R. and J. Tonson, 1684).

_____ *The Works of Aphra Behn*, ed. Janet Todd. 7 vols. (London: Pickering and Chatto, 1992–6).

_____ *The Rover and Other Plays*, ed. Jane Spencer (Oxford: World's Classics, 1995).

Boswell, James, *Life of Johnson*, ed. R. W. Chapman, corr. J. D. Fleeman (Oxford: OUP, 1970).

Brereton, Jane, *Merlin: A Poem* (London: Edward Cave, 1735).

———*Poems on Several Occasions* (London: Edward Cave, 1744).

Burke, Edmund, *Reflections on the Revolution in France*, ed. Conor Cruise O'Brien (London: Pelican, 1968).

Burney, Frances, *The Wanderer; or, Female Difficulties*, 5 vols. (London: Longman, Hurst, Rees, Orme and Brown, 1814).

———*Memoirs of Doctor Burney*, 3 vols. (London: Edward Moxon, 1832).

———*Dr Johnson and Fanny Burney: Being the Johnsonian Passages from the works of Mme d'Arblay*, ed. *Chauncy Brewster Tinker* (London: Andrew Melrose, 1912).

———*Journals and Letters of Fanny Burney (Madame d'Arblay)*, 12 vols., ed. Joyce Hemlow et al. (Oxford: Clarendon Press, 1972–84).

———*Camilla*, ed. Edward A. Bloom and Lilian D. Bloom (London: OUP, 1972).

———*Evelina: or the History of a Young Lady's Entrance into the World*, ed. Edward A. and Lilian D. Bloom (Oxford: World's Classics, 1982).

———*Cecilia, or Memoirs of an Heiress*, ed. Peter Sabor and Margaret Doody (Oxford: OUP, 1988).

———*The Complete Plays of Frances Burney*, i. *Comedies; ii. Tragedies*, ed. Peter Sabor (London: William Pickering, 1995).

———*The Early Journals and Letters of Fanny Burney*, Volume iii: *The Streatham Years*, Part I, 1778–1779, ed. Lars E. Troide and Stewart J. Cooke (Oxford: Clarendon Press, 1994).

Butt, George, *Poems* (Kidderminster: G. Gower, 1793).

The Challenge . . . Or, the Female War (London: E. Whitlock, 1679).

Charke, Charlotte, *A Narrative of the Life of Mrs. Charlotte Charke, Youngest Daughter of Colley Cibber, Esq. Written by herself* (London: Hunt and Clarke, 1827).

———*A Narrative of the Life of Mrs. Charlotte Charke* (Gainesville, Fla.: Scholars' Facsimiles and Reprints, 1969).

Cockburn, Catharine, *The Works of Mrs. Catharine Cockburn*, 2 vols. (London: J. and P. Knapton, 1751).

Coleridge, Samuel Taylor, *Letters of Samuel Taylor Coleridge*, 3 vols., ed. E. L. Griggs (Oxford: Clarendon Press, 1956).

———*The Notebooks of Samuel Taylor Coleridge*, 4 vols., ed. Kathleen Coburn (London: Routledge and Kegan Paul, 1957).

_____*The Collected Works of Samuel Taylor Coleridge*, 16 vols., ed. J. C. C. Mays. (Princeton: PUP, 1970–2001).

Congreve, William, *The Complete Works of William Congreve,* ed. Montague Summers, 4 vols. (Soho: Nonesuch Press, 1923).

_____*The Complete Plays of William Congreve*, ed. Herbert Davis (Chicago: University of Chicago Press, 1967).

_____*The Double-Dealer*, ed. J. C. Ross (London: Ernest Benn, 1981).

Cowley, Abraham, *The Poetical Works of Abraham Cowley*, 4 vols. (Edinburgh: Apollo Press, 1777).

De Quincey, Thomas, *Recollections of the Lakes and the Lake Poets* (Harmondsworth: Penguin, 1978).

Dryden, John, *The Satires of Decimus Junius Juvenalis. Translated into English Verse* (2nd edn., London: Jacob Tonson, 1697).

_____*The Dramatick Works of John Dryden*, Esq., 6 vols. (London: J. Tonson, 1717).

_____*Essays of John Dryden*, ed. W. P. Ker, 2 vols. (Oxford: Clarendon Press, 1900).

_____*The Works of John Dryden*, ed. H. T. Swedenberg et al., 20 vols. (Berkeley and Los Angeles: University of California Press, 1956–).

_____*The Letters of John Dryden*, ed. Charles E. Ward (Durham, NC: Duke University Press, 1942).

_____*The Poems and Fables of John Dryden*, ed. James Kinsley (Oxford: OUP, 1970).

Dryden, John, Jr, *The Husband His own Cuckold. A Comedy. As it is Acted at the Theater in Little Lincolns-Inn Fields, By His Majesty's Servants* (London: J. Tonson, 1696).

Drydeniana XIV: On the Death of Dryden, Folio Verse, 1700 (New York: Garland, 1975).

Duncombe, John, *The Feminiad: A Poem* (London: M. Cooper, 1754).

Edgeworth, Maria, *Belinda*, ed. Kathryn J. Kirkpatrick (Oxford: OUP, 1994).

Fenton, Elijah, *Poems on Several Occasions* (London: Bernard Lintot, 1717).

Fielding, Henry, *Joseph Andrews*, ed. Douglas Brooks (Oxford: OUP, 1971).

_____*The History of Tom Jones, a Foundling*, ed. Martin C. Battestin and Fredson Bowers (Oxford: Clarendon Press, 1974).

Fielding, Henry, *The Jacobite's Journal and Related Writings*, ed. W. B. Coley (Oxford: Clarendon Press, 1974).

___ *Miscellanies by Henry Fielding, Esq.*, ii, ed. Hugh Amory, introd. Bertrand A. Goldgar (Oxford: Clarendon Press, 1993).

___ and Fielding, Sarah, *The Correspondence of Henry and Sarah Fielding*, ed. Martin C. Battestin and Clive T. Probyn (Oxford: Clarendon Press, 1993).

Fielding, Sarah, *Familiar Letters between the Principal Characters in* David Simple (London: A. Millar, 1747).

___ *The History of the Countess of Dellwyn*, 2 vols. (London: A. Millar, 1759).

___ *Remarks on Clarissa, Addressed to the Author*, introd. Peter Sabor [Augustan Reprint Society, 231–2] (Los Angeles: William Andrews Clark Memorial Library, 1985).

___ *The Lives of Cleopatra and Octavia* ed. Christopher D. Johnson (London: Associated University Presses, 1994).

___ *The Adventures of David Simple* and *Volume the Last*, ed. Peter Sabor (Lexington, Ky.: University Press of Kentucky, 1998).

[___ and Collier, Jane], *The Cry: A New Dramatic Fable*, 3 vols. (London: R. and J. Dodsley, 1754).

Finch, Anne, Countess of Winchilsea, *The Poems of Anne, Countess of Winchilsea*, ed. Myra Reynolds (Chicago: University of Chicago Press, 1903).

___ *The Anne Finch Wellesley Manuscript Poems*, ed. Barbara McGovern and Charles H. Hinnant (Athens, Ga.: University of Georgia Press, 1998).

Gray, Thomas, *The Poems of Gray, Collins and Goldsmith*, ed. Roger Lonsdale (London: Longman, 1969).

Gregory, John, *A Father's Legacy to his Daughters* (London: G. Nocholson, [1809]).

Hanson, Martha, *Sonnets and Other Poems*, 2 vols. (London: J. Mawman, Poultry, and T. Lake, Uxbridge, 1809).

Hazlitt, William, review of *The Wanderer*, *Edinburgh Review*, 24 (Feb. 1815), 320–38.

___ *Lectures on the English Comic Writers*, ed. R. Brimley Johnson (London: OUP, 1951).

Hemans, Felicia, *Records of Woman* (Oxford: Woodstock Books, 1991).

James, Henry, *The House of Fiction*, ed. Leon Edel (London: Rupert Hart-Davis, 1957).

Johnson, Samuel, *Lives of the English Poets*, ed. George Birkbeck Hill, 3 vols. (Oxford: Clarendon Press, 1905).

——*Lives of the English Poets*, ed. Arthur Waugh, 2 vols. (London: OUP, 1961).

——*Johnson's Lives of the Poets: A Selection*, ed. J. P. Hardy (Oxford: Clarendon Press, 1971).

Jones, Mary, *Miscellanies in Prose and Verse* (Oxford: Dodsley, Clements, and Frederick, 1750).

Jonson, Ben, *Complete Poems*, ed. George Parfitt (Harmondsworth: Penguin, 1980).

Kelly, Gary (gen. Ed.), *Bluestocking Feminism: Writers of the Bluestocking Circle, 1738–1785*, 6 vols. (London: Pickering and Chatto, 1999).

Kipling, Rudyard, *Debits and Credits* (London: Macmillan and Co., 1926).

Lawrence, D. H., *Lady Chatterley's Lover and A Propos of Lady Chatterley's Lover*, ed. Michael Squires (Cambridge: CUP, 1993).

Lee, Sophia, *The Recess*, ed. April Alliston (Lexington, Ky.: University Press of Kentucky, 2000).

Le Fanu, Alicia, *Memoirs of the Life and Writings of Mrs. Frances Sheridan* (London: G. and W. B. Whittaker, 1824).

Lennox, Charlotte, *The Female Quixote*, ed. Margaret Dalziel (Oxford: World's Classics, 1989).

Manley, Delarivier, *The Royal Mischief* (London: R. Bentley, F. Saunders, J. Knapton, and R. Wellington, 1696).

——*The Novels of Mary Delarivière Manley*, 2 vols., ed. Patricia Köster (Gainseville, Fla.: Scholars' Facsimiles and Reprints, 1971).

The Meteors, 2 vols. (London: A. and J. Black, and H. D. Symonds, 1800).

Milton, John, *Poetical Works*, ed. Douglas Bush (London: OUP, 1969).

Moore, Thomas, *Memoirs of the Life of the Right Honourable Richard Brinsley Sheridan* (London: Longman, Hurst, Rees, Orme, Brown, and Green, 1825).

Philips, Katherine, *Poems by the Most Deservedly Admired Mrs. Katherine Philips* (London: H. Herringman, 1667).

Pope, Alexander, *The Poems of Alexander Pope* [The Twickenham Edition], 11 vols. (London: Methuen and Co., 1939–69).

—— *Correspondence of Alexander Pope*, ed. George Sherburn, 6 vols. (Oxford: Clarendon Press, 1956).

—— *The Dunciad in Four Books*, ed. Valerie Rumbold (Essex: Pearson Education Ltd., 1999).

—— *Selected Letters*, ed. Howard Erskine-Hill (Oxford: OUP, 2000).

Reeve, Clara, *The Progress of Romance*, 2 vols. (Colchester: W. Keymer, 1785).

Richardson, Samuel, *The Correspondence of Samuel Richardson*, 6 vols. ed. Anna Laetitia Barbauld (London: Richard Phillips, 1804).

—— *Selected Letters of Samuel Richardson*, ed. John Carroll (Oxford: Clarendon Press, 1964).

Scott, Sir Walter, *Letters of Sir Walter Scott*, ed. H. J. C. Grierson, 12 vols. (London: Constable, 1932–7).

Shelley, Mary, *The Journals of Mary Shelley 1814–1844*, 2 vols., ed. Paula R. Feldman and Diana Scott-Kilvert (Oxford: Clarendon Press, 1987).

—— *Selected Letters of Mary Wollstonecraft Shelley*, ed. Betty T. Bennett (Baltimore: Johns Hopkins University Press, 1995).

—— *Novels and Selected Works of Mary Shelley*, 9 vols. (London: William Pickering, 1996).

Shelley, Percy Bysshe, *Poetical Works*, ed. Thomas Hutchinson, corr. G. M. Mathews (London: OUP, 1970).

Sheridan, Frances, *The Plays of Frances Sheridan*, ed. Robert Hogan and Jerry C. Beasley (London: Associated University Presses, 1984).

Sheridan, Richard Brinsley, *The Rivals, A Comedy*, ed. from the Larpent MS by Richard Little Purdy (Oxford: Clarendon Press, 1935).

—— *The Letters of Richard Brinsley Sheridan*, ed. Cecil Price (Oxford: Clarendon Press, 1966).

—— *The Dramatic Works of Richard Brinsley Sheridan*, ed. Cecil Price, 2 vols. (Oxford: Clarendon Press, 1973).

—— *The School for Scandal and Other Plays*, ed. Michael Cordner (Oxford: OUP, 1998).

—— and Sheridan, Frances, *Sheridan's Plays, now printed as he wrote them, and his mother's unfinished comedy A Journey to Bath*, ed. W. Fraser Rae (London: David Nutt, 1902).

Sidney, Sir Philip, *The Poems of Sir Philip Sidney*, ed. William A. Ringler, Jr. (Oxford: Clarendon Press, 1962).

Spence, Joseph, *Observations, Anecdotes, and Characters of Books and Men*, ed. James M. Osborn 2 vols. (Oxford: Clarendon Press, 1966).

Spenser, Edmund, *The Works of Mr Edmund Spenser*, 6 vols.(London: Jacob Tonson, 1715).

[Thomas, Elizabeth], *Miscellany Poems on Several Subjects* (London: Tho. Combes, 1722).

Thrale, Hester Lynch, *Thraliana: The Diary of Mrs Hester Lynch Thrale (Later Mrs Piozzi) 1776–1809*, ed. Katharine C. Balderston, 2 vols. (2nd edn., Oxford: Clarendon Press, 1951).

Virgil, *The Aeneid of Virgil, Books I–IV*, ed. T. E. Page (London: Macmillan and Co., 1894).

_____ *The Aeneid: A New Prose Translation by David West* (London: Penguin, 1990).

Warton, Thomas, *Thomas Warton's History of English Poetry*, 4 vols., ed. David Fairer (London: Routledge/Thoemmes Press, 1998).

Whyte, Samuel, and Whyte, E. A., *Miscellanea Nova* (Dublin, 1800; repr. New York: Garland, 1974).

Williams, Ioan (ed.), *Novel and Romance 1700–1800: A Documentary Record* (London: Routledge and Kegan Paul, 1970).

Wollstonecraft, Mary, *A Vindication of the Rights of Woman*, ed. M. B. Kramnick (Harmondsworth: Pelican, 1975).

_____ *Collected Letters of Mary Wollstonecraft*, ed. Ralph M. Wardle (Ithaca, NY: Cornell University Press, 1979).

_____ *Mary and The Wrongs of Woman*, ed. Gary Kelly (Oxford: World's Classics, 1980).

_____ *The Works of Mary Wollstonecraft*, ed. Janet Todd and Marilyn Butler, 7 vols. (London: William Pickering, 1989).

Wordsworth, Dorothy, *Journals of Dorothy Wordsworth*, 2 vols. ed. E. de Selincourt (London: Macmillan, 1952).

_____ and Wordsworth, William, *The Letters of William and Dorothy Wordsworth*, 7 vols. ed. Ernest de Selincourt, rev. C. L. Shaver (Oxford: Clarendon Press, 1967–88).

Wordsworth, William, *The Prelude: 1797, 1805, 1850*, ed. Jonathan Wordsworth, M. H. Abrams, and Stephen Gill (New York: W. W. Norton and Co., 1979).

Wordsworth, William, *Poems, in Two Volumes, and Other Poems 1800–1807,* ed. Jared Curtis (Ithaca, NY: Cornell University Press, 1983).

—— *William Wordsworth,* ed. Stephen Gill (Oxford: OUP, 1984).

—— *Lyrical Ballads and Other Poems, 1797–1800,* ed. James Butler and Karen Green (Ithaca, NY: Cornell University Press, 1992).

Young, Edward, *Conjectures on Original Composition* (London: A. Millar and R. and J. Dodsley, 1759).

SECONDARY SOURCES

Aaron, Jane, *A Double Singleness: Gender and the Writings of Charles and Mary Lamb* (Oxford: Clarendon Press, 1991).

Alliston, April, *Virtue's Faults: Correspondences in Eighteenth-Century British and French Women's Fiction* (Stanford, Calif.: Stanford University Press, 1996).

Amarasinghe, Upali, *Dryden and Pope in the Early Nineteenth Century: A Study of Changing Literary Taste 1800–1830* (Cambridge: CUP, 1962).

Armstrong, Isobel, and Blain, Virginia (eds.), *Women's Poetry in the Enlightenment: The Making of a Canon, 1730–1820* (Basingstoke: Macmillan Press, 1999).

Austen-Leigh, Mary Augusta, *Personal Aspects of Jane Austen* (London: John Murray, 1920).

Baker, Sheridan, 'Did Fielding Write "A Vision"?', *Eighteenth-Century Studies,* 22 (Summer 1989), 548–51.

Ballaster, Ros, *Seductive Forms: Women's Amatory Fiction from 1684 to 1740* (Oxford: Clarendon Press, 1992).

Banfield, Ann, *Unspeakable Sentences: Narration and Representation in the Language of Fiction* (London: Routledge and Kegan Paul, 1982).

Barber, Bernard, and Hirsch, Walter (eds.), *The Sociology of Science* (New York: Free Press of Glencoe, 1962).

Barchas, Janine, 'Sarah Fielding's Dashing Style and Eighteenth-Century Print Culture', *ELH* 63 (1996), 633–56.

Barnard, John (ed.), *Pope: The Critical Heritage* (London: Routledge and Kegan Paul, 1973).

Bate, W. Jackson, *The Burden of the Past and the English Poet* (London: Chatto and Windus, 1971).

Bateson, F. W., *Wordsworth: A Reinterpretation* (London: Longmans, Green and Co., 1954).

Battersby, Christine, *Gender and Genius: Towards a Feminist Aesthetics* (London: Women's Press, 1989).

Battestin, Martin C., 'Henry Fielding, Sarah Fielding, and "the dreadful Sin of Incest"', *Novel*, 13/1 (Fall 1979), 6–18.

——with Battestin, Ruthe R., *Henry Fielding: A Life* (London: Routledge, 1989).

Bell, Ian A., *Henry Fielding: Authorship and Authority* (London and New York: Longman, 1994).

Benzie, W., *The Dublin Orator: Thomas Sheridan's Influence on Eighteenth-Century Rhetoric and Belles Lettres* (Leeds: University of Leeds, School of English, 1972).

Blain, Virginia, ' "Thou with Earth's Music Answerest to the Sky": Felicia Hemans, Mary Ann Browne, and the myth of poetic sisterhood', *Women's Writing*, 2/3 (1995), 251–69.

Bloom, Harold, *A Map of Misreading* (New York: OUP, 1975).

——*The Anxiety of Influence: A Theory of Poetry* (2nd edn., New York: OUP, 1997).

Booth, Wayne C., *The Rhetoric of Fiction* (Chicago: University of Chicago Press, 1961).

Bowers, Toni, *The Politics of Motherhood: British Writing and Culture 1680–1760* (Cambridge: CUP, 1996).

Bree, Linda, *Sarah Fielding* (New York: Twayne Publishers, 1996).

Brissender, R. F., and Eade, J. C. (eds.), *Literary Transmission and Authority: Dryden and Other Writers* (Cambridge: CUP, 1993).

Brooke-Davies, Douglas, *Pope's Dunciad and the Queen of Night: A Study in Emotional Jacobitism* (Manchester: MUP, 1985).

Burrows, J. F. ' "A Vision" as a Revision?', *Eighteenth-Century Studies*, 22/4 (Summer 1989), 551–65.

——' "I lisped in Numbers": Fielding, Richardson, and the Appraisal of Statistical Evidence', *Scriblerian*, 33 (1991), 234–41.

——and Hassall, A. J., '*Anna Boleyn* and the Authenticity of Fielding's Feminine Narratives', *Eighteenth-Century Studies*, 21 (1988), 427–53.

Buss, Helen, Macdonald, D. L., and McWhirr, Anne (eds.), *Mary Wollstonecraft and Mary Shelley: Writing Lives* (Ontario: Wilfred Laurier University Press, 2001).

Butler, Judith, *Gender Trouble: Feminism and the Subversion of Gender* (London: Routledge, 1990).

Butler, Marilyn, *Jane Austen and the War of Ideas* (Oxford: Clarendon Press, 1975).

Cameron, Deborah, *Feminism and Linguistic Theory* (2nd edn. London: Macmillan, 1992).

Campbell, Jill, *Natural Masques: Gender and Identity in Fielding's Plays and Novels* (Stanford, Calif.: Stanford University Press, 1995).

Castle, Terry, 'Lab'ring Bards: Birth *Topoi* and English Poetics 1660–1820', *Journal of English and German Philology* 78/2 (1979), 193–208.

——— *The Female Thermometer: Eighteenth-Century Culture and the Invention of the Uncanny* (Oxford: Oxford University Press, 1995).

——— *Boss Ladies, Watch Out! Essays on Women, Sex, and Writing* (London: Routledge, 2002).

Chew, Samuel P., Jr., '*The Dupe*: A Study in the "Low"', *Philological Quarterly*, 18 (1939), 196–203.

Chisholm, Kate, *Fanny Burney: Her Life* (London: Vintage, 1999).

Chodorow, Nancy, *The Reproduction of Mothering: Psychoanalysis and the Sociology of Gender* (Berkeley and Los Angeles: University of California Press, 1978).

Cixous, Helene, 'The Laugh of the Medusa', trans. Keith Cohen and Paula Cohen, in Warhol and Herndl (eds.), *Feminisms*.

Clarke, Norma, *Ambitious Heights: Writing, Friendship, Love—The Jewsbury Sisters, Felicia Hemans, and Jane Welsh Carlyle* (London: Routledge, 1990).

——— *Dr Johnson's Women* (London: Hambledon, 2000).

——— *The Rise and Fall of the Woman of Letters* (London: Pimlico, 2004).

Clemit, Pamela, *The Godwinian Novel: The Rational Fictions of Godwin, Brockden Brown, Mary Shelley* (Oxford: Clarendon Press, 1993).

Cooke, Stewart J., '"Good Heads and Good Hearts": Sarah Fielding's Moral Romance', *English Studies in Canada*, 21 (1995), 268–82.

Copeland, Edward and McMaster, Juliet (eds.), *The Cambridge Companion to Jane Austen* (Cambridge: CUP, 1997).

Cressy, David, 'Kinship and Kin Interaction in Early Modern England', *Past and Present*, 113 (1986), 38–69.

Cutting-Gray, Joanne, *Woman as 'Nobody' and the Novels of Fanny Burney* (Gainesville, Fla.: University Press of Florida, 1992).

Damrosch, Leopold Jr, *The Imaginative World of Alexander Pope* (Berkeley and Los Angeles: University of California Press, 1987).

Darby, Barbara, *Frances Burney, Dramatist: Gender, Performance, and the Late-Eighteenth-Century Stage* (Lexington, Ky.: University Press of Kentucky, 1997).

Davidoff, Leonore and Hall, Catherine, *Family Fortunes: Men and Women of the English Middle Class 1780–1850* (London: Hutchinson, 1987).

Davis, Lloyd, 'Redemptive Advice: Dorothy Leigh's *The Mother's Blessing*', in Jo Wallwork and Paul Salzman (eds.), *Women Writing 1550–1750; Meridian*, 18/1 (2001), 59–72.

DeJean, Joan, *Fictions of Sappho 1547–1937* (Chicago: University of Chicago Press, 1989).

DeMaria, Robert, Jr. *The Life of Samuel Johnson: A Critical Biography* (Oxford: Blackwell, 1993).

Digeon, Aurélion, *The Novels of Henry Fielding* (1925; repr. New York: Russell, 1962).

Dinnerstein, Dorothy, *The Rocking of the Cradle, and the Ruling of the World* (London: Souvenir Press, 1978) (1st pub. 1976 as *The Mermaid and the Minotaur*).

Donoghue, Emma, *Passions between Women: British Lesbian Culture 1668–1801* (London: Scarlet Press, 1993).

Donoghue, Frank, *The Fame Machine: Book Reviewing and Eighteenth-Century Literary Careers* (Stanford, Calif.: Stanford University Press, 1996).

Doody, M. A., 'Swift among the Women', *Yearbook of English Studies*, 18 (1988), 68–92.

_____ *Frances Burney: The Life in the Works* (New Brunswick, NJ: Rutgers University Press, 1988).

Easlea, Brian, *Fathering the Unthinkable: Masculinity, Scientists and the Nuclear Arms Race* (London: Pluto Press Ltd, 1983).

Eaves, T. C. Duncan, and Kimpel, Ben D., *Samuel Richardson: A Biography* (Oxford: Clarendon Press, 1971).

Eger, Elizabeth (ed.), *Bluestocking Feminism: Writers of the Bluestocking Circle 1738–1785*, i. *Elizabeth Montagu* (London: Pickering and Chatto, 1999).

Eisenstein, Hester and Jardine, Alice (eds.), *The Future of Difference* (New Brunswick, NJ: Rutgers University Press, 1985).

Ellison, Julie, *Delicate Subjects: Romanticism, Gender and the Ethics of Understanding* (Ithaca, NY: Cornell University Press, 1990).

Epstein, Julia, *The Iron Pen: Frances Burney and the Politics of Women's Writing* (Bristol: Bristol Classical Press, 1989).

Erickson, Amy Louise, *Women and Property in Early Modern England* (London: Routledge, 1993).

Erickson, J. P., '*Evelina* and *Betsy Thoughtless*', *Texas Studies in Literature and Language*, 6 (1964), 86–103.

Ezell, Margaret, *Writing Women's Literary History* (Baltimore: Johns Hopkins University Press, 1993).

——*Social Authorship and the Advent of Print* (Baltimore: Johns Hopkins University Press, 2001).

Faulkner, Thomas C., and Blair, Rhonda L., 'The Classical and Mythographic Sources of Pope's Dulness', *Huntington Library Quarterly*, 43 (1980), 213–46.

Fay, Elizabeth A., *Becoming Wordsworthian: A Performative Aesthetics* (Amherst, Mass.: University of Massachusetts Press, 1995).

Feldman, Paula R., and Kelly, Theresa M. (eds.), *Romantic Women Writers: Voices and Countervoices* (Hanover, Canada: University Press of New England, 1995).

Fletcher, Anthony, *Gender, Sex and Subordination* (New Haven: Yale University Press, 1995).

Fliegelman, Jay, *Prodigals and Pilgrims: The American Revolution Against Patriarchal Authority, 1750–1800* (Cambridge: CUP, 1982).

Flint, Christopher, *Family Fictions: Narrative and Domestic Relations in Britain, 1688–1798* (Stanford, Calif.: Stanford University Press, 1998).

Francus, Marilyn, 'The Monstrous Mother: Reproductive Anxiety in Swift and Pope', *ELH*, 61 (1994), 829–52.

Franklin, Sarah, and McKinnon, Susan (eds), *Relative Values: Reconfiguring Kinship Studies* (Durham, NC: Duke University Press, 2001).

Friedman, Susan Stanford, 'Creativity and the Childbirth Metaphor: Gender Difference in Literary Discourse', *Feminist Studies*, 13/1 (Spring 1987), 49–82.

Frost, William, 'Dryden and the Classics: With a Look at his "Aeneis"', in Earl Miner (ed.), *John Dryden* [Writers and their background] (London: G. Bell and Sons, 1972), 267–96.

Garner, S. N., Kehane, Claire, and Sprengnether, Madelon (eds.), *The (M)other Tongue: Essays in Feminist Psychoanalytic Interpretation* (Ithaca, NY: Cornell University Press, 1985).

Gautier, Gary, 'Henry and Sarah Fielding on Romance and Sensibility', *Novel*, 31 (1998), 195–214.

—— *Landed Patriarchy in Fielding's Novels: Fictional Landscapes, Fictional Genders* [Studies in British Literature vol. 35] (Lewiston: Edwin Mellon Press, 1998).

Gelber, Michael Werth, *The Just and the Lively: The Literary Criticism of John Dryden* (Manchester: MUP, 1999).

Gelpi, Barbara, *Shelley's Goddess: Maternity, Language, Subjectivity* (New York: OUP, 1992).

Gibbs, Lewis, *Sheridan* (London: J. M. Dent and Sons Ltd., 1947).

Gill, Stephen, *William Wordsworth: A Life* (Oxford: Clarendon Press, 1989).

Gittings, Robert, and Manton, Jo, *Dorothy Wordsworth* (Oxford: Clarendon Press, 1985).

Gonda, Caroline, *Reading Daughters' Fictions 1709–1834: Novels and Society from Manley to Edgeworth* (Cambridge: CUP, 1996).

Gosse, Edmund, *Life of William Congreve* (London: Walter Scott, 1888).

Grassby, Richard, *Kinship and Capitalism: Marriage, Family, and Business in the English-Speaking World, 1580–1740* (Cambridge: Woodrow Wilson Center Press and CUP, 2001).

Greenfield, Susan C., and Barash, Carol (eds.), *Inventing Maternity: Politics, Science, and Literature, 1650–1865* (Lexington, Ky.: University of Kentucky Press, 1999).

Grey, J. David (ed.), *The Jane Austen Handbook* (London: Athlone Press, 1986).

Griffin, Dustin H., *Alexander Pope: The Poet in the Poems* (Princeton: PUP, 1978).

—— *Regaining Paradise: Milton and the Eighteenth Century* (Cambridge: CUP, 1986).

Grundy, Isobel, *Lady Mary Wortley Montagu: Comet of the Enlightenment* (Oxford: OUP, 1999).

Guerinot, J. V. (ed.), *Pope: A Collection of Critical Essays* (Englewood Cliffs, NJ: Prentice-Hall, 1972).

Haggerty, George E., *Unnatural Affections: Women and Fiction in the Later Eighteenth Century* (Bloomington, Ind.: Indiana University Press, 1998).

Halperin, John (ed.), *Jane Austen: Bicentenary Essays* (Cambridge: CUP, 1975).

____ *The Life of Jane Austen* (Brighton: Harvester Press, 1984).

Hammond, Brean (ed.), *Pope* (London: Longman, 1996).

____ *Professional Imaginative Writing in England, 1670–1740: 'Hackney for Bread'* (Oxford: Clarendon Press, 1997).

Hammond, Paul, and Hopkins, David (eds.), *John Dryden: Tercentenary Essays* (Oxford: Clarendon Press, 2000).

Hannay, Margaret P., *Philip's Phoenix: Mary Sidney, Countess of Pembroke* (New York: OUP, 1990).

Harman, Claire, *Fanny Burney: A Biography* (London: HarperCollins, 2000).

Harris, Jocelyn, *Jane Austen's Art of Memory* (Cambridge: CUP, 1989).

Hodges, John C., *William Congreve the Man: A Biography from New Sources* (New York: MLA and London: OUP, 1941).

____ (ed.), *William Congreve: Letters and Documents* (London: Macmillan, 1964).

Hofkosh, Sonia, *Sexual Politics and the Romantic Author* (Cambridge: CUP, 1998).

Holmes, Richard, *Coleridge: Early Visions* (London: Penguin, 1990).

Hóly, Ladislav, *Anthropological Perspectives on Kinship* (London: Pluto Press, 1996).

Homans, Margaret, *Women Writers and Poetic Identity: Dorothy Wordsworth, Emily Brontë, and Emily Dickinson* (Princeton: PUP, 1980).

Horney, Karen, *Feminine Psychology*, ed. Harold Kelman (New York: W. W. Norton and Co., 1967).

Horowitz, Maryanne Cline, 'The "Science" of Embryology before the Discovery of the Ovum', in Marilyn J. Boxer and Jean H. Quataert (eds.), *Connecting Spheres: Women in the Western World, 1500 to the Present* (Oxford: OUP, 1987), 86–94.

Hough, Graham, 'Narrative and Dialogue in Jane Austen', *Critical Quarterly*, 12 (1970), 210–29.

Houlbrooke, Ralph A., *The English Family 1450–1700* [Themes in British Social History] (London: Longman, 1984).

Hume, R. D., *The Development of English Drama in the Late Seventeenth Century* (Oxford: Clarendon Press, 1976).

Hunt, Lynn, *The Family Romance of the French Revolution* (London: Routledge, 1992).

Ingrassia, Catherine, 'Women Writing/Writing Women: Pope, Dulness, and "Feminization" in the *Dunciad*', *Eighteenth-Century Life*, 14 (1990), 40–58.

Jacobus, Mary, *Romanticism, Writing and Sexual Difference: Essays on The Prelude* (Oxford: Clarendon Press, 1989).

Johnson, Barbara, 'My Monster/My Self', *Diacritics*, 12 (1982), 2–20.

Johnson, Mark (ed.), *Philosophical Perspectives on Metaphor* (Minneapolis: University of Minnesota Press, 1981).

——— *The Body in the Mind: The Bodily Basis of Meaning, Reason and Imagination* (Chicago: University of Chicago Press, 1987).

——— *Moral Imagination: Implications of Cognitive Science for Ethics* (Chicago: University of Chicago Press, 1993).

Johns-Putra, Adeline, *Heroes and Housewives: Women's Epic Poetry and Domestic Ideology in the Romantic Age* (Bern: Peter Lang, 2001).

Jones, Kathleen, *A Passionate Sisterhood: The Sisters, Wives and Daughters of the Lake Poets* (London: Virago, 1998).

Jones, Vivien (ed.), *Women and Literature in Britain 1700–1800* (Cambridge: CUP, 2000).

Keller, Evelyn Fox, 'From Secrets of Life to Secrets of Death', in Mary Jacobus, Evelyn Fox Keller, and Sally Shuttleworth (eds.), *Body/Politics: Women and the Discourses of Science* (New York: Routledge, 1990), 177–191.

——— *Refiguring Life: Metaphors in Twentieth-Century Biology* (New York: Columbia University Press, 1995).

Kennedy, Deborah, 'Hemans, Wordsworth, and the "Literary Lady"', *Victorian Poetry*, 35/3 (1997), 267–85.

Kewes, Paulina, 'Between the "Triumvirate of Wit" and the Bard: The English Dramatic Canon, 1660-1820', in Cedric C. Brown and Arthur F. Marotti (eds.), *Texts and Cultural Change in Early Modern England* (London: Macmillan, 1997), 200–24.

——— *Authorship and Appropriation: Writing for the Stage in England, 1660–1710* (Oxford: Clarendon Press, 1998).

Keymer, Tom, 'Jane Collier, Reader of Richardson, and the Fire Scene in *Clarissa*', in Albert J. Rivero (ed.), *New Essays on Samuel Richardson* (Houndmills: Macmillan, 1996), 141–61.

——— and Mee, Jon (eds.), *The Cambridge Companion to English Literature 1740–1830* (Cambridge: CUP, 2004).

King, Kathryn, *Jane Barker, Exile: A Literary Career 1675–1725* (Oxford: Clarendon Press, 2000).

Kinsley, James, and Kinsley, Helen (eds.), *Dryden: The Critical Heritage* (London: Routledge and Kegan Paul, 1971).

Knellwolf, Christa, *A Contradiction Still: Representations of Women in the Poetry of Alexander Pope* (Manchester: MUP, 1998).

Kövecses, Zoltán, *Metaphor: A Practical Introduction* (Oxford: OUP, 2002).

Kowaleski-Wallace, Elizabeth, *Their Fathers' Daughters: Hannah More, Maria Edgeworth, and Patriarchal Complicity* (New York: OUP, 1991).

Kramnick, Jonathan Brody, *Making the English Canon: Print-Capitalism and the Cultural Past, 1700–1770* (Cambridge: CUP, 1998).

Kristeva, Julia, *Revolution in Poetic Language*, tr. Margaret Waller, introd. Leon S. Roudiez (New York: Columbia University Press, 1984).

——— *The Kristeva Reader*, ed. Toril Moi (Oxford: Basil Blackwell, 1986).

Labbe, Jacqueline M., *Romantic Visualities: Landscape, Gender and Romanticism* (London: Macmillan, 1998).

Lacan, Jacques, and the école freudienne, *Feminine Sexuality*, tr. Jacqueline Rose, ed. Juliet Mitchell and Jacqueline Rose (London: Macmillan, 1982).

Lakoff, George, *Women, Fire and Dangerous Things: What Categories Reveal about the Mind* (Chicago: University of Chicago Press, 1987).

Leavis, F. R., *The Great Tradition: George Eliot, Henry James, Joseph Conrad* (1948; London: Chatto and Windus, 1962).

Lefanu, Alicia, *Memoirs of the Life and Writings of Mrs. Frances Sheridan* (London: G. and W. B. Whittaker, 1824).

Levin, Susan M., *Dorothy Wordsworth and Romanticism* (New Brunswick, NJ: Rutgers, the State University, 1987).

Levine, David, *Family Formation in an Age of Nascent Capitalism* (New York: Academic Press, 1977).

Levine, George, and Knoepflmacher, U. C. (eds.), *The Endurance of Frankenstein* (Berkeley and Los Angeles: University of California Press, 1979).

Lindsay, Alexander, and Erskine-Hill, Howard (eds.), *William Congreve: The Critical Heritage* (London: Routledge, 1989).

Lodge, David, *The Modes of Modern Writing* (London: Edward Arnold, 1977).

Loftis, John, *Sheridan and the Drama of Georgian England* (Oxford: Basil Blackwell, 1976).

Lokke, Kari E., *Tracing Women's Romanticism: Gender, History and Transcendence* (London: Routledge, 2004).

Lonsdale, Roger, *Dr Charles Burney: A Literary Biography* (Oxford: Clarendon Press, 1965).

Looser, Devoney (ed.), *Jane Austen and the Discourses of Feminism* (Houndmills: Macmillan, 1995).

Lootens, Tricia, *Lost Saints: Silence, Gender and Victorian Literary Canonization* (Charlottesville, Va.: University Press of Virginia, 1996).

Lynch, Deidre, *The Economy of Character: Novels, Market Culture, and the Business of Inner Meaning* (Chicago: University of Chicago Press, 1998).

MacCannell, Juliet Flower, *The Regime of the Brother: After the Patriarchy* (London: Routledge, 1991).

McFarland, Thomas, 'The Symbiosis of Coleridge and Wordsworth', *Studies in Romanticism*, 11 (1972), 263–303.

——*Romanticism and the Forms of Ruin: Wordsworth, Coleridge, and Modalities of Fragmentation* (Princeton: PUP, 1981).

Macfarlane, Alan, *Marriage and Love in England: Modes of Reproduction, 1300–1840* (Oxford: Basil Blackwell, 1986).

McGovern, Barbara, *Anne Finch and Her Poetry: a Critical Biography* (Athens, Ga., and London: University of Georgia Press, 1992).

Mack, Maynard, *Collected in Himself: Essays Critical, Biographical and Bibliographical on Pope and Some of His Contemporaries* (London: Associated University Presses, 1982).

——*Alexander Pope: A Life* (New Haven: Yale University Press, 1985).

McKeon, Michael, 'Writer as Hero: Novelistic Prefigurations and the Emergence of Literary Biography', in William H. Epstein (ed.), *Contesting the Subject: Essays in the Postmodern Theory and Practice of Biography and Biographical Criticism* (West Layfayette: Purdue University Press, 1991), 17–41.

McWhir, Anne, 'Elizabeth Thomas and the Two Corinnas: Giving the Woman Writer a Bad Name', *ELH* 62 (1995), 105–19.

Magnuson, Paul, *Coleridge and Wordsworth: A Lyrical Dialogue* (Princeton: PUP, 1988).

Mandel, Laura, *Misogynous Economies: The Business of Literature in Eighteenth-Century Britain* (Lexington, Ky.: University Press of Kentucky, 1999).

Matlak, Richard E., *The Poetry of Relationship: The Wordsworths and Coleridge, 1797–1800* (Basingstoke: Macmillan, 1997).

Mellor, Anne (ed.), *Romanticism and Feminism* (Bloomington, Ind.: Indiana University Press, 1988).

——*Mary Shelley: Her Life, Her Fiction, Her Monsters* (New York: Routledge, 1989).

——*Romanticism and Gender* (New York: Routledge, 1993).

——*Mothers of the Nation: Women's Political Writing in England, 1780–1830* (Bloomington, Ind.: Indiana University Press, 2002).

Mendelson, Sara, and Crawford, Patricia, *Women in Early Modern England 1550–1720* (Oxford: Clarendon Press, 1998).

Merton, Robert K., 'Priorities in Scientific Discovery: A Chapter in the Sociology of Science', in Bernard Barber and Walter Hirsch (eds.), *The Sociology of Science* (New York: Free Press of Glencoe, 1962), 447–85.

Michie, Allen, *Richardson and Fielding: The Dynamics of a Critical Rivalry* (London: Associated University Presses, 1999).

Michie, Helena, *The Flesh Made Word: Female Figures and Women's Bodies* (New York: OUP, 1987).

Miner, Earl, *The Cavalier Mode from Jonson to Cotton* (Princeton: PUP, 1971).

Moers, Ellen, *Literary Women* (London: Women's Press, 1980).

Moi, Toril, *What is a Woman? And Other Essays* (Oxford: OUP, 1999).

Moler, Kenneth L., *Jane Austen's Art of Allusion* (Lincoln, Nebr.: University of Nebraska Press, 1968).

Moorman, Mary, *William Wordsworth, A Biography: The Early Years, 1770–1803* (Oxford: Clarendon Press, 1957).

Morris, Brian (ed.), *William Congreve* (London: Ernest Benn, 1972).

Morwood, James, *The Life and Works of Richard Brinsley Sheridan* (Edinburgh: Scottish Academic Press, 1985).

Myers, Mitzi, 'De-Romanticizing the Subject: Maria Edgeworth's "The Bracelets", Mythologies of Origin, and the Daughter's Coming to Writing'. In Feldman and Kelley (eds.), *Romantic Women Writers*, 88–110.

Newlyn, Lucy, *Coleridge, Wordsworth and the Language of Allusion* (1986; 2nd edn. Oxford: Oxford University Press, 2001).

Nicholson, Linda J., *Gender and History: The Limits of Social Theory in the Age of the Family* (New York: Columbia University Press, 1986).

Nickel, Terri, ' "Ingenious Torment": Incest, Family and the Structure of Community in the Work of Sarah Fielding', *Eighteenth Century: Theory and Interpretation*, 36 (1995), 234–47.

Nicolson, Marjorie and Rousseau, G. S., *This Long Disease, My Life: Alexander Pope and the Sciences* (Princeton: PUP, 1968).

Novak, Maximillian E., *William Congreve* (New York: Twayne, 1971).

Nussbaum, Felicity, *The Autobiographical Subject: Gender and Ideology in Eighteenth-Century England* (Baltimore: Johns Hopkins University Press, 1989).

—— 'Effeminacy and Femininity: Domestic Prose Satire and *David Simple*', *Eighteenth-Century Fiction*, 11/4 (July 1999), 421–44.

O'Toole, Fintan, *A Traitor's Kiss: The Life of Richard Brinsley Sheridan* (London: Granta Books, 1997).

Page, Norman, *The Language of Jane Austen* (Oxford: Basil Blackwell, 1972).

Parker, Jo Alyson, *The Author's Inheritance: Henry Fielding, Jane Austen, and the Establishment of the Novel* (De Kalb, Ill.: Northern Illinois University Press, 1998).

Pascal, Roy, *The Dual Voice: Free Indirect Speech and its Functioning in the Nineteenth-Century European Novel* (Manchester: MUP, 1977).

Pask, Kevin, *The Emergence of the English Author: Scripting the Life of the Poet in Early Modern England* (Cambridge: CUP, 1996).

Pateman, Carole, *The Disorder of Woman: Democracy, Feminism and Political Theory* (Cambridge: Polity Press, 1989).

Pearson, Jacqueline, *Women's Reading in Britain 1750–1835: A Dangerous Recreation* (Cambridge: CUP, 1999).

Perry, Ruth, 'Women in Families: The Great Disinheritance', in V. Jones (ed.), *Women and Literature in Britain*, 111–31.

—— *Novel Relations: The Transformation of Kinship in English Literature and Culture 1748–1818* (Cambridge: CUP, 2004).

Peterson, Linda H., *Traditions of Victorian Women's Autobiography: The Poetics and Politics of Life Writing* (Charlottesville, Va.: University Press of Virginia, 1999).

Pettit, Alexander, 'David Simple and the Attenuation of "Phallic Power"', *Eighteenth-Century Fiction*, 11 (Jan 1999), 169–84.

Poole, Kristen, ' "The fittest closet for all goodness": Authorial Strategies of Jacobean Mothers' Manuals', *Studies in English Literature 1500–1900*, 35 (1995), 69–88.

Powell, John, Blakely, Derek W., and Powell, Tessa, *Biographical Dictionary of Literary Influences: The Nineteenth Century, 1800-1914* (Westport, Conn.: Greenwood Press, 2001).

Prescott, Sarah, *Women, Authorship and Literary Culture 1690–1740* (London: Palgrave Macmillan, 2003).

Rainbolt, Martha, 'Their Ancient Claim: Sappho and Seventeenth- and Eighteenth-Century British Women's Poetry', *Seventeenth Century*, 12 (1997), 111–34.

Raven, James, and Forster, Antonia, *The English Novel 1770–1829: A Bibliographical Survey of Prose Fiction Published in the British Isles, i. 1770–1799* (Oxford: OUP, 2000).

Regan, John V., 'Orpheus and the *Dunciad*'s Narrator', *Eighteenth-Century Studies*, 9 (1975), 87–101.

Ricks, Christopher, 'Allusion: the Poet as Heir', in R. F. Brissenden and J. C. Eade (eds.), *Studies in the Eighteenth Century III* (Canberra: Australian National University Press, 1976).

Rodden, John, *The Politics of Literary Reputation: The Making and Claiming of 'St. George' Orwell* (New York: OUP, 1989).

Roe, Nicholas, *Wordsworth and Coleridge: The Radical Years* (Oxford: Clarendon Press, 1988).

Rogers, Katharine M., *Feminism in Eighteenth-Century England* (Brighton: Harvester Press, 1982).

——— *Frances Burney: The World of 'Female Difficulties'* (New York: Harvester, 1990).

Rosenthal, Laura J., *Playwrights and Plagiarists in Early Modern England* (Ithaca, NY: Cornell University Press, 1996).

Ross, Marlon B., *The Contours of Masculine Desire: Romanticism and the Rise of Women's Poetry* (New York: OUP, 1989).

Rumbold, Valerie, *Women's Place in Pope's World* (Cambridge: CUP, 1989).

Ruoff, Gene. W., *Wordsworth and Coleridge: The Making of the Major Lyrics 1802–1804* (New Brunswick, NJ: Rutgers University Press, 1989).

Sanders, Lloyd C., *Life of Richard Brinsley Sheridan* (London: Walter Scott, n.d.).

Schellenberg, Betty A., 'From Propensity to Profession: Female Authorship and the Early Career of Frances Burney', *Eighteenth-Century Fiction*, 14 (2002), 345–70.

—— *The Conversational Circle: Re-reading the English Novel, 1740–1775* (Lexington, Ky.: University Press of Kentucky, 1996).

Schiebinger, Londa, *The Mind Has No Sex? Women in the Origins of Modern Science* (Cambridge, Mass: Harvard University Press, 1989).

Schneider, David, *A Critique of the Study of Kinship* (Ann Arbor: University of Michigan Press, 1984).

Seidel, Michael, *Satiric Inheritance, Rabelais to Sterne* (Princeton: PUP, 1979).

Sheldon, Esther K., *Thomas Sheridan of Smock Alley* (Princeton: PUP, 1967).

Sherburn, George, *The Early Career of Alexander Pope* (Oxford: Clarendon Press, 1934).

Sichel, Walter, *Sheridan from New and Original Material: Including a Manuscript Diary by Georgiana Duchess of Devonshire*, 2 vols. (London: Constable and Co. Ltd., 1909).

Siskin, Clifford, *The Work of Writing: Literature and Social Change in Britain, 1700–1830* (Baltimore: Johns Hopkins University Press, 1998).

Sitter, John E., 'Mother, Memory, Muse and Poetry after Pope', *ELH* 44 (1977), 312–36.

Southam, B. C. (ed.), *Jane Austen: The Critical Heritage*, 2 vols. (London: Routledge, 1968).

Spacks, P. M., *Imagining a Self: Autobiography and Novel in Eighteenth-Century England* (Cambridge, Mass.: Harvard University Press, 1976).

Spencer, Jane, 'Women Writers and the Eighteenth-Century Novel', in John Richetti (ed), *The Cambridge Companion to the Eighteenth-Century Novel* (Cambridge: CUP University Press, 1996), 212–35.

—— *Aphra Behn's Afterlife* (Oxford: OUP, 2000).

Stone, Lawrence, *The Family, Sex and Marriage in England 1500–1800* (London: Weidenfeld and Nicolson, 1977).

Sulloway, Alison, *Jane Austen and the Province of Womanhood* (Philadelphia: University of Pennsylvania Press, 1989).

Summers, Claude J., and Pebworth, Ted-Larry (eds.), *Literary Circles and Cultural Communities in Renaissance England* (Columbia, Mo.: University of Missouri Press, 2000).

Sunstein, Emily, *Mary Shelley: Romance and Reality* (Boston: Little, Brown, 1989).

Sweet, Nanora, and Melnyk, Julie (eds.), *Felicia Hemans: Reimagining Poetry in the Nineteenth Century* (Basingstoke: Palgrave, 2001).

Tadmor, Naomi, *Family and Friends in Eighteenth-Century England: Household, Kinship, and Patronage* (Cambridge: CUP, 2001).

Tandon, Bharat, *Jane Austen and the Morality of Conversation* (London: Anthem Press, 2003).

Tauchert, Ashley, *Mary Wollstonecraft and the Accent of the Feminine* (Basingstoke: Palgrave Macmillan, 2002).

Taylor, Barbara, *Mary Wollstonecraft and the Feminist Imagination* (Cambridge: CUP, 2003).

Taylor, D. Crane, *William Congreve* (New York: Russell & Russell, Inc., 1963).

Terry, Richard, *Poetry and the Making of the English Literary Past 1660–1781* (Oxford: OUP, 2001).

Thaddeus, Janice Farr, *Frances Burney: A Literary Life* (Basingstoke: Macmillan, 2000).

Thomas, Claudia N., 'Pope's *Iliad* and the Contemporary Context of his "Appeals to the Ladies"', *Eighteenth-Century Life*, 14/2 (1990), 1–17.

——*Alexander Pope and His Eighteenth-Century Women Readers* (Carbondale, Ill.: Southern Illinois University Press, 1994).

Todd, Janet, *Mary Wollstonecraft: A Revolutionary Life* (London: Weidenfeld and Nicholson, 2000).

Tomalin, Claire, *Jane Austen: A Life* (London: Penguin, 1998).

Trumbach, Randolph, *The Rise of the Egalitarian Family: Aristocratic Kinship and Domestic Relations in Eighteenth-Century England* (New York: Academic Press, 1978).

Tuite, Clara, *Romantic Austen: Sexual Politics and the Literary Canon* (Cambridge: CUP, 2002).

Turner, Mark, *Death is the Mother of Beauty: Mind, Metaphor, Criticism* (Chicago: University of Chicago Press, 1987).

Waldron, Mary, *Jane Austen and the Fiction of her Time* (Cambridge: CUP, 1999).

Wall, Wendy, *The Imprint of Gender* (Ithaca, NY: Cornell University Press, 1993).

Ward, Charles E., *The Life of John Dryden* (Chapel Hill, NC: University of North Carolina Press, 1961).

Warhol, Robin R. and Herndl, Diane Price (eds.), *Feminisms: An Anthology of Literary Theory and Criticism* (Basingstoke: Macmillan, 1997).

Warner, William, *Licensing Entertainment: The Elevation of Novel Reading in Britain, 1684–1750* (Berkeley and Los Angeles: University of California Press, 1998).

Weil, Rachel, *Political Passions: Gender, the Family and Political Argument in England 1680–1714* (Manchester: MUP, 1999).

Wiesenthal, Christian S., 'Representation and Experimentation in the Major Comedies of Richard Brinsley Sheridan', *Eighteenth-Century Studies*, 25 (1992), 309–30.

Williams, Aubrey, *Pope's Dunciad: A Study of Its Meaning* (London: Methuen, 1955).

Williams, Carolyn D., *Pope, Homer and Manliness: Some Aspects of Eighteenth-Century Classical Learning* (London: Routledge, 1993).

Wilson, Carol Shiner, and Haefner, Joel (eds.), *Re-Visioning Romanticism: British Women Writers, 1776–1837* (Philadelphia: University of Pennsylvania Press, 1994).

Wimsatt, W. K., Jr, *The Prose Style of Samuel Johnson* (Hamden, Conn.: Archon Books, 1972).

Winn, James Anderton, *John Dryden and His World* (New Haven: Yale University Press, 1987).

Winstead, Karen A., 'The Conversion of Margery Kempe's Son', *English Language Notes*, 32/2 (Dec. 1994), 9–12.

Wood, Nigel, *Dr Johnson and Fanny Burney* (Bristol: Bristol Classical Press, 1989).

Woodmansee, Martha, *The Author, Art and the Market: Rereading the History of Aesthetics* (New York: Columbia University Press, 1994).

Wordsworth, Jonathan, *William Wordsworth: The Borders of Vision* (Oxford: Clarendon Press, 1982).

Wu, Duncan, *Wordsworth: An Inner Life* (2002; Oxford: Blackwell, 2004).

Index

Abraham 9
absolutism 132
Adam 3, 9, 72, 176, 183
Addison, Joseph 39
Aikin, Lucy 2–4
  Epistles on Women 2–4
Akenside, Mark 96
Alliston, April 12
amatory fiction 138, 139
American Revolution 132
anxiety of influence 2, 13, 19–20, 131
Ariosto 161, 210
Aristotle 10–11, 21
d'Arblay, Mme *see* Burney, Frances
Arnold, Matthew 171
Austen, Cassandra (mother) 214
Austen, Cassandra (sister) 214–15
Austen, Revd George 213–14
Austen, Henry 214
  The Loiterer 214
Austen, James 214
  The Loiterer 214
Austen, Jane 12, 13, 208–30
  as aunt 228–9
  canonization of 208, 209–12, 215
  free indirect discourse in 219,
    221–4
  literary heirs of 223–4, 230
  literary inheritance of 215–18
  and matrilineal tradition 216, 230
  as mother of James 224–6
  originality of 218
  and patrilineal tradition 213
  on the sister author 193–4
  relation to Burney 211–12, 215
  relation to Scott 208–9
  relation to Shakespeare 208–11,
    226, 228

Emma 208, 221–2, 223
Northanger Abbey 193, 209, 216
Persuasion 209, 222–3
Austen-Leigh, James Edward 208
  Memoir of Jane Austen 208, 228
Austen-Leigh, Mary Augusta 215 n.

Ballaster, Ros 51 n., 86 n.
Banfield, Ann 218 n., 219
Barbauld, Anna Letitia 4, 194, 201
Barchas, Janine 148
Barlow, Ruth 121
Barnard, John 36 n.
Bate, W. Jackson 19
Bateson, F. W. 175 n.
Battestin, Martin 153 n.
Beech, Mary 94
Behn, Aphra 45, 46, 115, 140, 191
  and literary brotherhood 198–201
  as literary mother 11, 51, 78, 79,
    139, 230
  as successor to Sappho and
    Orinda 77
  The Dutch Lover 200
  'Letter to a Brother of the Pen' 198,
    201
  *Love-letters between a Nobleman and
    his Sister* 139
  The Lucky Chance 201
Behrendt, Stephen 196 n., 207
Bentley, Richard 88
Bentley, Thomas 203 n.
Bion
  elegy on Adonis 98
Birch, Thomas 202
Blain, Virginia 194 n.
Blair, Rhonda L. 84 n., 86 n.
Bloom, Harold 19

Boccaccio 21 n.
body
  associated with women 17, 74
Boileau
  Le Lutrin 148
Booth, Wayne C. 221 n.
Boswell, James 151 n.
Bowers, Toni 76
Bowles, William 29
Bradshaigh, Lady 151, 154 n.
Brady, Jennifer 20 n., 25 n., 34, 35 n.,
  41 n., 79
Bree, Linda 140 n., 141, 164 n.
Brereton, Charlotte 73, 114, 117–9
  'To the Memory of a Mother' 118
  'Written August 7, being the
    Anniversary of a Mother's
    Death' 119
Brereton, Jane 73, 114–19
  'Verses from a Mother to her
    Daughter' 117
Brereton, Thomas 114
Brooke, Frances 51
Brooke-Davies, Douglas 84 n.
Brower, Reuben A. 216 n., 217
Browne, Mary Ann 194
Browne, William 188 n.
brother-sister relations 13, 15, 134–7,
  201
Brown, Tom 24
Burke, Edmund 132
Burney, Charles 48, 53, 57, 60, 71
  suppression of *The Witlings* 63–4,
    67, 70
  History of Music 48
Burney, Elizabeth 63
Burney, Frances 15, 16, 46–72, 106,
  217, 230
  attitude to authorship 48–9, 67
  as daughter of Johnson 46–72
  free indirect discourse in 220–1
  and literary mothers 51, 60, 67–8
  and patronage 60, 62, 68–9
  and rival father-figures 60, 67

  as successor to Richardson and
    Fielding 47, 52–3, 55, 70, 208
  reception of 47, 51–3, 70–2, 189,
    209
  relation to Austen 193, 211–12,
    219–20
  relationship with her father 48–9,
    52
  relationship with Elizabeth
    Montagu 65–6, 68–9
  relationship with Hester Thrale 47,
    60, 68–9
  Camilla 193 n.
  Cecilia 47, 60, 70, 71, 220–1
  Diary and Letters 71, 209
  Evelina 47, 48, 50–4, 68
  Memoirs of Dr Burney 49
  The Wanderer 47, 70
  The Witlings 48, 60–4, 67, 68,
    69–70
Burney, Susanna 57
Burrows, J. F. 146 n., 147 n.
Butler, Marilyn 215 n.
Butler, Samuel 148
  Hudibras 148
Butt, George 204
Byron, George Gordon, Lord 207
  Childe Harold IV 206

Camden, William 23
Cameron, Deborah 16 n.
canon 4–5, 7
  and literary lines 22–3, 229
  masculinity of 17
  and patrilineage 9–10
  women's place in 11–12, 17, 127,
    191, 198, 208
  see also literary tradition, national
    literary tradition
Carnochan, W. B. 144 n.
Carter, Dr 117–18
  Sermons 117
Carter, Elizabeth 46, 115, 118
Castle, Terry 26 n., 75, 213

Cave, Edward 115, 118
Cervantes, Miguel de 148, 162, 210
  Don Quixote 148, 162
Charke, Charlotte 229
Chaucer, Geoffrey 1 n., 5, 23, 47, 216
  as father of English poetry 22
  as father of Spenser 18, 28
Chew, Samuel P. Jr 113 n.
Chodorow, Nancy 93, 185
Cibber, Colley 82, 86, 87, 229
Cixous, Helene 90
Clairmont, Claire 120
Clarke, Norma 46 n., 57 n., 189 n.,
  197–8, 198 n
Clemit, Pamela 120 n., 125 n.
Cockburn, Catharine *see* Trotter,
  Catharine
Cockburn, Patrick 191
Coleridge, Nancy 166
Coleridge, Samuel Taylor 131
  family position of 166
  on Imagination 165
  marriage 168
  relations with Dorothy
    Wordsworth 134–6, 165–9,
    171–3, 175–6, 186–7
  relations with William
    Wordsworth 134–6, 165–9,
    172–6, 182–7
  relationship with his mother 166
  Christabel 172
  'Dejection: An Ode' 165–6
  'Letter to Sara Hutchinson' 165
  The Brook 174
Collier, Arthur 153
Collier, Jane 136, 150 n., 161
Collier, Margaret 152–3
Collier, Jeremy 41
Collins, William 96
Colman, George 103
  Polly Honeycombe 103
Congreve, William 30, 44, 106, 109,
  114
  and literary ambition 41–3

as son of Dryden 5, 29, 33–43
and women's writing 31, 35, 46, 79
  The Double-Dealer 35, 79
  Incognita 33
  The Mourning Bride 39
  The Old Batchelour 33, 34, 38
  The Way of the World 41
Conrad, Joseph 224
Cooke, Stewart J. 164 n.
Corinna 204–7
Cowley, Abraham 74, 76
  'Upon Mrs. K. *Philips* her
    Poems' 74, 76–7
Cowper, William 215
Crabbe 215
creation
  Biblical account of 11
creativity 9–10
  and childbirth metaphor 26, 73–5
  and female fecundity 85
  and fraternal relations 131
  and maternity 127
  and paternal metaphor 20
  and spirit 11
  and women 11
Cressy, David 14 n.
Crisp, Samuel 48, 53, 60, 71
  literary advice to Burney 54–5
  jealousy of Johnson–Burney
    relationship 67
  suppression of *The Witlings* 63, 64,
    67, 70
  Virginia 54
Curll, Edmund 205
Curran, Stuart 194

Darby, Barbara 63
Davenant, Thomas 24, 34
Davidoff, Leonore 7
Davis, Lloyd 75 n.
DeJean, Joan 78–9
Delaney, Carol 9
De Quincey, Thomas 168, 181
Digeon, Aurélion, 146 n., 149

Dinnerstein, Dorothy 95
Doody, Margaret 49, 63, 215 n., 216, 217
Dryden, Charles 29
Dryden, Erasmus-Henry 29
Dryden, John 1, 18–45, 95, 96
  and childbirth metaphor 75
  critical writing of 18, 22, 76, 216–18
  and father-son metaphor 13, 18–20, 22–3, 26, 47, 132
  as father of English criticism 19, 45
  as father of Scott 2, 4
  and laureateship 23, 37
  literary relations with women 45–6, 189, 205
  masculine reputation of 37–8
  place in literary lines 229
  as son of Jonson 28
  relation to Johnson 45
  relation to Pope 43–5, 83
  relations with Congreve 5, 33–43
  relations with his son John 28–33
  Discourse on Satire 27, 29
  Of Dramatic Poesy 22
  Examen Poeticum 40
  The Hind and the Panther 24
  Mac Flecknoe 24–7, 44
  Satires of Juvenal and Persius 29
  Ode to Anne Killigrew 76
  'To my Dear Friend Mr. Congreve' 1, 35–8
Dryden, John Junior 29–33, 34
  The Husband His Own Cuckold 30–3
Duncombe, John 191–2
  The Feminiad 191–2, 206

Easlea, Brian 8
Eaves, T. C. Duncan 141 n., 142 n.
Edgeworth, Maria 194, 229
  relation to Austen 193, 209, 215, 230
  Belinda 193 n.
Edgeworth, Richard Lovell 229

Eger, Elizabeth 66 n.
Eliot, George 224
epic 3, 4, 148
epistolary writing 149
equality 131–2, 141, 155–8
Epstein, Julia 47 n.
Erickson, Amy Louise 14 n., 158 n.
Erickson, J. P. 51 n.
Erskine-Hill, Howard 38
Etherege, George 34
Eusden, Laurence 86
Eve, 72, 176, 183
Ezell, Margaret 198 n.

Fairfax, Edward 18
family
  and business organization 7
  and literary partnership 7, 100
  as setting for literary career 101
  and women's place 188
  see also Sheridan family
father–son relations 5, 13, 18, 27–33, 37–8
Faulkner, Thomas C. 84 n., 86 n.
Fay, Elizabeth A. 135 n., 186
fellowship 131
Female Wits 191
feminine language 90
Fenton, Elijah 1 n.
Fenwick, Eliza
  Secrecy 213
Ferrier, Susan 209
Fielding, Beatrice 136
Fielding, Catharine 136
Fielding, Henry 16, 47, 106, 216
  attitude to women novelists 139
  compared to Burney 52–3, 55
  encouragement of Charlotte Lennox 139
  literary reputation 5, 50, 53, 210
  masculine reputation 144
  as father of English novel 23, 164
  as founder of new province of writing 138

relations with Sarah Fielding 134,
136, 139–41, 144–53, 157,
161–4, 186
relations with Samuel
Richardson 134, 135–53, 164,
186
response to *Clarissa* 142–4, 149
Amelia 151, 161
Covent-Garden Journal 139
Jacobite's Journal 149
Joseph Andrews 136, 137, 141, 145
*A Journey from this World to the
Next* 145–6
Shamela 136, 141, 145
Tom Jones 135, 138, 140, 141, 142,
150–1, 154, 161
Fielding, Sarah 6, 16, 187
on brother-sister relations 155–8,
160–1
and feminine viewpoint 146–8
on fraternal equality 156–61
as literary innovator 162
relations with Henry Fielding 134,
136, 139–41, 144–53, 157,
161–4, 186
relations with Samuel
Richardson 134, 136–54, 159,
161–4, 186
and satire 147
Anna Boleyn's narrative 145–6
The Adventures of David Simple 140,
146–7, 155–8, 161
The Cry 136, 159–60, 161
Familiar Letters 146–7, 148–9, 161
The Governess 136, 150
*History of the Countess of
Dellwyn* 154
*The Lives of Cleopatra and
Octavia* 146, 160, 162–3
Remarks on Clarissa 136, 149–50,
163
Volume the Last 154, 158–9
Fielding, Ursula 136
Filmer, Sir Robert

Patriarcha 132
Finch, Anne 81, 115–16, 202–3
The Spleen 116
'To Mr Pope' 203 n.
Flecknoe, Richard 24
Fletcher, Anthony 14 n.
Fletcher, John 22, 36
Forster, E. M. 224
Francus, Marilyn 85
fraternal social contract 138
fraternity 131–4
free indirect discourse 218–24
French Revolution 132–3
Freud, Sigmund 132–3
Totem and Taboo 132
Fricker, Sara 168

Galen 10
Garrick, David 102
Gaskell, Elizabeth 224
Gelber, Michael Werth 19 n., 26 n.
Gelpi, Barbara 98
genealogy
biblical 9
and literary tradition 2, 5, 11, 22
Genesis 3, 9
generation
and literary authority 8, 10–11
men's relation to 17, 21
and motherhood 76
paternal 8, 21
women's relation to 11, 17
Gibbons, Brian 36 n.
Gill, Stephen 175
Gillman, Anne 168
Gillman, James 168
Gittings, Robert 164 n.
Godwin, William 70, 120
Goldgar, Bertrand A. 146 n.
Goldsmith, Oliver 54, 112
The Vicar of Wakefield 54
Gosse, Edmund 37–8, 41
Gower, John 23
Grassby, Richard 7, 22 n., 158 n.

Gray, Thomas 96
  The Progress of Poesy 96–7, 98
Griffin, Dustin 19 n., 20, 91–2
Griffith, Elizabeth 7, 51, 68
Griffith, Richard 7
Grundy, Isobel 203, 215 n.

Haggerty, George E. 156 n.
Hall, Catherine 7
Halperin, John 208, 214 n.,
  215 n., 227
Hammond, Brean 38, 91
Hanson, Martha 195–6
  Sonnets 195–6
Harris, James 153
Harris, Jocelyn 216–17
Hart, Walter 21
Hartman, Geoffrey 183
Hassall, A. J. 146 n., 147 n.
Hawley, Judith 194 n.
Hazlitt, William 70, 169, 173
Haywood, Eliza 51, 68, 86, 115
  The History of Betsy Thoughtless 51
Hemans, Felicia 194, 196–7, 206–7
  'Corinna at the Capitol' 206
  'Dartmoor' 207
  'Modern Greece' 207
  'Properzia Rossi' 196–7
Henley, 'Orator' 88
Herbert, Mary 188
Hervey, Stephen 29
Hodges, John C. 44 n.
Holmes, Richard 166 n.
Hóly, Ladislav 8 n.
Homans, Margaret 168, 175 n., 185
Homer 23, 148, 208
  as father of epic 137
  as father of Greek poetry 22
  as father of modern poets 20–1
  manliness of 42, 43
  place in line of poets 98
  translations of 42–4
  Iliad 40, 43–4
Hopkins, Charles 39
Hough, Graham 219 n.

Houlbrooke, Ralph A. 14 n.
Howard, Elizabeth 29
Howard, Sir Robert 31–2
Hughes, Harriett 207 n.
Hume, R. D. 38 n.
Hunt, Lynn 132
Hunting, R. S. 148
Hutchinson, Mary 134, 164, 177, 182
Hutchinson, Sara 164

Imlay, Fanny 121, 123, 128, 130
Imlay, Gilbert 121
Ingrassia, Catherine 82 n., 85 n.
inheritance
  and literary tradition 2, 4, 11–12, 15, 22, 44–6
  as metaphor 4, 11, 15, 18–20, 22, 37
  changing patterns of 14–15, 21–2, 158
  patrilineal model of 11–12, 15, 21–3
  spiritual 27–8
  see also literary inheritance, maternal literary inheritance, paternal literary inheritance
imitation 27, 50, 117, 218
Irwin, Anne 192
Isaac 9
Isles, Duncan 139 n.

Jacobus, Mary 175 n.
James II 23, 29
James, Henry 223 n., 224–7
Jewsbury, Geraldine 197
Jewsbury, Maria Jane 189, 197
Jocelin, Elizabeth
  The Mothers Legacie 123
Johnson, Barbara 127 n.
Johnson, Claudia L. 224 n.
Johnson, Samuel 15, 19, 211, 215
  attitude to literary profession 55, 64–7, 69
  and Censor in *The Witlings* 62, 67

critical remarks on Fieldings and
   Richardson 151–2
encouragement of women
   writers 46, 57, 59, 69
place in literary line 229
praise of Frances Sheridan 102,
   112
relation to Milton 58–9
relation to Samuel Crisp 67
relations with Burney 45–72
rivalry with Elizabeth Montagu 62,
   64–6
as son of Dryden 45
Dictionary 45
Life of Cowley 57
Life of Milton 58–9
Lives of the Poets 45, 55–6
Rambler 45
Jones, Ann Rosalind 90 n.
Jones, Emrys 91
Jones, Kathleen 164 n.
Jones, Mary 189, 202
Jonson, Ben 1, 22, 23–8, 36, 217
   and sons of Ben 18, 28
Jupiter 2
Juvenal 85

Keats, John 80, 98
Kenrick, Daniel 39 n.
Kenrick, William 51
Killigrew, Anne 35, 45, 76
Kimpel, Ben D. 141 n., 142 n.
kinship
   anthropological debate concerning
      8
   and economy 7
   historical changes in relations
      of 6–7, 9, 13–15
   and inheritance 9, 11
   as metaphor 4, 5, 6–9, 13, 131–4,
      188, 190, 230
   between writers 5–7, 13, 17, 30–3,
      73, 140, 188
   literary 4–6, 12, 131–4, 203
   see also family, patrilineage

Kipling, Rudyard 224, 226, 227
   'The Janeites', 224–6
Kristeva, Julia 16, 90

Lacan, Jacques 16 n.
Lacanian account of language 16–17
laureateship 23–4, 37, 86
Lawrence, D. H. 224, 227
Leapor, Mary 192
Leavis, F. R. 227
   The Great Tradition 223–4
Lee, Harriet 7, 229
Lee, Nathaniel 34
Lee, Sophia 7, 229
Le Fanu, Alicia 100, 110–112
   *Memoirs of the Life and Writings of
      Mrs Frances Sheridan* 100,
      110–11
Lefroy, Anna 214, 228
Lennox, Charlotte 46, 57, 139, 215
   The Female Quixote 139
Levin, Susan M. 178 n., 185 n.
Lewes, G. H. 210
Lewis, Matthew 229
linguistic theory 16–17, 90
Linley, Elizabeth 102
literary brotherhood 9, 13, 131–87,
      190, 198, 229
   and literary innovation 134, 137
   mediated through sister
      figure 134–7, 144–5, 152
literary brother-sister
   relations 134–87, 198–204, 209
literary borrowing 17
   as male use of feminine matter 109,
      172
literary daughterhood 46–51, 53–4,
      72, 188–9
literary fatherhood 17, 27–9, 31–3,
      36–8
   critical focus on 20
   as generative 8
   taken seriously 78
   understood historically 73
   see also paternal literary inheritance

literary inheritance
 father to daughter 4, 45–72, 189
 father to son 4–5, 9–10, 18–45, 86
 mixed 215, 223–4
 mother to daughter 4, 35, 114–30
 mother to son 4, 79, 86, 99–114,
  224–8
literary motherhood 17, 20, 35,
 78–80, 114–15, 226
 as generative 208
 submergence of 76
 understood in mythical terms 8, 73
 see also maternal literary inheritance
literary sisterhood 9, 134, 140,
 189–98, 215
literary sonship 29–33, 37–43
literary tradition
 classical 148
 as family 5, 13, 17, 188–9, 226
 masculinization of 20
 and matrilineal metaphor 76–80,
  115–19
 and patrilineal metaphor 2, 4, 10,
  18–22, 26–8, 35–8, 76
 women's relation to 2, 11, 45–54,
  58–9, 76–8, 117, 188–230
Locke, John
 Two Treatises of Government 132
Lodge, David 219 n., 221 n., 224
Lokke, Kari E. 127 n.
Longinus 25–6
Lonsdale, Roger 49 n.

Macaulay, Thomas Babington 71,
 209, 211–12
MacCannell, Juliet Flower 132, 138
McFarland, Thomas 135, 166–7, 168,
 173 n., 174 n.
Macfarlane, Alan 14 n.
McWhir, Anne 205–6
Mack, Maynard 43 n., 89 n., 94
Magnuson, Paul 135 n., 183 n.
Mainwaring, Arthur 34
male–female hierarchy 11

Malone, Edmond 37
Mandel, Laura 12
Manley, Delarivier 51, 115, 190–1,
 202
 The Adventures of Rivella 191
Manton, Jo 164 n.
Marivaux 50
Martial 85
Marvell, Andrew 24
Mary II, 37
maternal literary inheritance 4, 20–1,
 73, 79, 100, 114–19
 male anxiety about 107–9,
  138–40, 227–8
 materiality of 109
 recognition of 119
maternity
 idealization of 76, 99
 materiality of 21, 74, 75, 87, 108
 and monstrosity 73, 75–6, 85, 87,
  127–30
 myths of 17, 73–4, 95–6
 and poetic creativity 73–5, 90
 and pre-Oedipal period 90
 Romantic revaluation of 130
 and women's writing 75–6,
  118–19, 123, 127–8
Matlak, Richard E. 135 n., 169,
 173 n.
Mellor, Anne 76 n., 120 n., 127 n.,
 128, 184, 185 n., 186
mentoring 5, 13, 57, 59, 228
 father to daughter 46–7, 54
 father to son 27–8, 32–5
Merton, Robert K. 8 n.
Milton, John 3, 72, 88, 161, 216
 as literary father 4, 19–20, 44, 133
 as national poet 5
 place in line of poets 96, 98, 229
 relation to Romantic poets 13, 174,
  183
 relationship with his
  daughters 58–9, 217
 as son of Spenser, 18

Lycidas 80, 98
Paradise Lost 80, 85
Miner, Earl 19 n.
mind–body hierarchy 11, 27, 74
 and women 12, 17
Moers, Ellen 127 n.
Moler, Kenneth 215 n.
Molière 35, 60
 Les Femmes savantes 35, 60
Montagu, Elizabeth 65, 66
 and Lady Smatter in *The
  Witlings* 62–4, 66
 *Essay on the Writings and Genius of
  Shakespeare* 66
Montagu, Lady Mary Wortley 78,
  202–3
 *Verses Address'd to the Imitator of
  Horace* 203
Moore, Thomas 100, 108, 111
 *Memoirs of Richard Brinsley
  Sheridan* 101, 110 n., 111
Moorman, Mary 166, 169 n., 173 n.,
  174 n.
More, Hannah 56–7, 104
Morwood, James 106 n.
Moschus
 elegy on Bion 98
Moskal, Jeanne 125
mother goddess 83–5, 89–90, 96,
  98–9
mother–daughter relations 73, 114
mother–son relations 74, 99–100
Motteux, Peter 30
Mulso, Hester 154 n.
Murphy, Arthur 60
Muse 73
 as mother of poets 80, 82, 96–8
 as name applied to women
  writers 190–2, 203–4

national literary tradition 1, 9–10, 11,
  13, 208
 as family, 17, 213, 215, 229
 and maternal influence 95
 as patrilineage 85–6, 95, 96

status of 217
 see also canon, literary tradition
nature
 divinity of 99
 as mother 97, 99, 166
 as source of imaginative power 165
 transcendence of 184
neoclassicism 75, 85, 95, 133
Newlyn, Lucy 135 n., 175
Nickel, Terri 156 n., 157
Nicolson, Marjorie 94 n.
'Nine Muses' 190
 'On the Death of John Dryden,
  Esq,' 190–1
Novak, Maximilian E. 41, 42
novel
 and feminized forms of writing 138,
  139
 and literary brotherhood 134,
  137–8
 and the literary sister 138–40, 187
 masculinization of 71, 212
 matrilineal tradition of 51, 211–12
 mixed lineage of 46
 patrilineal tradition of 51, 53, 70,
  137–8
 status of 23, 50–1, 53, 70–1, 137,
  193, 212
 women's role in development of 187
Nussbaum, Felicity 156 n.

Ogilby, John 25, 43
Oldham, John 38
Oppenheimer, J. Robert 8
originality 133, 218
Orinda, *see* Philips, Katherine
Orpheus 79, 80–2
Osborn, James M. 45
O'Toole, Fintan 106, 112 n.
Otway, Thomas 34
Ovid 80, 204
 Metamorphoses 80

Page, Norman 223 n., 224
Parker, Jo Alyson 216

Pascal, Roy 218 n., 219 n.
Pask, Kevin 58
Pateman, Carole 132 n., 138
paternal literary inheritance 4–5,
    20–1, 27–8, 44–5
  women's share of 47–51, 53, 212
paternity
  spirituality of 21, 27, 44, 87
  see also generation
patriarchy 9–10, 132, 138
patrilineage 9–10, 83
  and maternal power 83, 96
patronage 31–2, 34–5, 46, 60, 68–9
Pennington, Lady Sarah
  An Unfortunate Mother's Advice
    123
Perry, Ruth 14–15, 158 n.
Philips, Edward 58–9
Philips, Katherine 74, 115
Pindar 97, 204–6
Pix, Mary 46, 191
poet
  as self-generated 183, 186
  as son of mother 79–80, 82, 86,
    96–8, 166
poetic identity 131, 175, 183–6,
    196–7
poetic tradition
  English, elevation of 22–3
  male lineage of 46, 80, 83, 96, 98
  and maternity 73, 83, 98
  and women 56, 196
  see also national literary tradition
Poole, Thomas 182
Pope, Alexander 19, 21 n., 46, 73,
    80–95, 115, 117
  and Goddess Dulness 82, 83–92
  illness of 43, 92–3
  and masculinity 43, 93
  and patrilineal literary tradition 95
  place in literary line 229
  relationship with his mother 92–3,
    95
  relationship with his nurse 94

and myth of monstrous mother 73,
    128, 130
  relationship with Lady Mary
    Wortley Montagu 78, 202
  as son of Dryden 29, 43–5
  women writers' attitudes to 189,
    202–3
  The Dunciad 17, 44, 73, 80–95,
    96, 128, 129–30, 148, 205
  Epistles to Several Persons 93
  The Rape of the Lock 81
  Windsor Forest 84
Pope, Edith 92
Prescott, Sarah 114, 118 n.
print culture 82
Probyn, Clive 153 n.
professionalization of literature 45,
    193
Prynne, William 24

Radcliffe, Ann 70, 215
Rae, W. Fraser 108, 114 n.
Rainbolt, Martha 78 n.
Ravenscroft, Edward 198, 200
Reeve, Clara 163
  The Progress of Romance 163 n.
reproduction 9
  and creativity 10
  myths of 17
  rival theories of 10, 21
Reynolds, Joshua 53
Rhodes, R. C. 109 n.
Richardson, Samuel 5, 47, 70, 102,
    115, 217
  attitude to women novelists 139
  compared to Burney 52–3, 55
  encouragement of Frances
    Sheridan 110
  as father of the novel 164
  and female correspondents as
    daughters 139, 153–4
  and feminine voice 144–5
  literary reputation 53
  and new species of writing 138, 162

relations with Henry Fielding 134,
135–54, 161–4, 186
relations with Sarah Fielding 134,
136–54, 159, 161–4, 186
reputation as friend to women 144,
152–3
Pamela 136, 138, 141, 144–5, 148,
162
Clarissa 135, 136, 141–3, 150, 154
Sir Charles Grandison 159, 161
Ricks, Christopher 19 n., 25 n., 44 n.
rivalry
between father figures 67
between male and female
writers 198, 203, 204–5, 207
fraternal 131, 136–8, 143–5
Robinson, Charles E. 124 n., 125 n.
Roe, Nicholas 135 n.
Rogers, Katharine M. 63, 144 n.
romance 138
Romanticism 165
and cult of mother 99
and the feminine 172, 175
and literary fathers 133
and literary brotherhood 133–4
and maternal influence 140
and originality 218
and place of the sister 140, 187, 230
and women poets 194–6
Rose, Jacqueline 16 n.
Ross, J. C. 35 n.
Ross, Marlon 131, 139–40, 145 n.,
194
Rousseau, George 94 n.
Rousseau, Jean Jacques 50
Rowe, Elizabeth 115–16, 119
Rowton, Frederic 196 n.
Rumbold, Valerie 88 n., 92 n., 93
Ruoff, Gene W. 135 n., 166 n.
Rymer, Thomas 37 n.

Sanders, Lloyd C. 109 n.
Sabor, Peter 63–4, 140 n., 141,
150 n., 157

Sappho 20, 35, 76–9, 197
Schellenberg, Betty A. 65 n., 159 n.
Schiebinger, Londa 10 n.
Schneider, David 8 n.
Schor, Naomi 90
Scott, Sir Walter 1–2, 37
edition of Dryden 1–2
relation to Austen 208–11
as son of Dryden 2, 4, 229
as son of Henry Fielding, 23, 229
Seidel, Michael 86 n.
semiotic 90
Seward, Anna 1–2, 194, 204
Shadwell, Thomas 23, 24 7, 37
Shakespeare, William 1, 4, 23, 37, 47,
106
as brother of ancient poets 133
as father of English dramatic
poets 22
as national playwright 5
place in line of poets 96, 98, 229
relation to Jane Austen 208–11
as son of mothers 97
Shelley, Clara Everina 128
Shelley, Elizabeth 98
Shelley, Harriet 128
Shelley, Mary 73, 119–20, 123–30
influence of 127
literary legacy from her father 120,
129
literary legacy from her
mother 119–30
on maternity and creativity 127–30
relationship with Percy Bysshe
Shelley 119–20, 123–4, 128
Frankenstein 125, 127–30
Rambles in Germany and Italy 125
Valperga 125–7
Shelley, Percy Bysshe 80
admiration for Mary
Wollstonecraft 123–4
relationship with Mary
Shelley 119–20, 123–4, 128
relationship with his mother 98–9

Shelley, Percy Bysshe (*cont.*)
  translates Bion and Moschus 98
  Adonais 80, 97–8
Sheridan family 99–101, 109–112
Sheridan, Alicia 100, 104, 109, 111
Sheridan, Betsy 100
Sheridan, Frances 46, 73, 99–114,
    202
  comic writing of, 112–14
  encouraged by Richardson, 110
  literary legacies of 101, 103–14
  manuscript play used by son 104–7,
    109
  praised by Johnson, 102
  relationship with son 101, 112
  in Sheridan family
    tradition 109–13
  as successor to Richardson 102
  The Discovery 100, 102, 110
  The Dupe 102, 113
  Eugenia and Adelaide 100, 110
  A Journey to Bath 102, 104–9
  Memoirs of Miss Sidney Bidulph 100,
    102, 103–4, 107, 110, 112
  Nourjahad 192
Sheridan, Richard Brinsley 17, 53, 67,
    99–114
  anxiety about plagiarism 107–9
  and comic vs. sentimental
    drama 112, 113–14
  encourages Burney to write for
    stage 47, 60
  as heir to male dramatists 109, 114
  literary inheritance from mother 73,
    100–1, 103–14, 172
  relationship with mother 101, 112
  in Sheridan family
    tradition 109–12
  The Rivals 103–8, 112
  A School for Scandal 108
Sheridan, Thomas 100, 101, 102, 106,
    110
Sheridan Le Fanu, Joseph 100
Sichel, Walter 112 n.

Simpson, Richard 228
Singer, Elizabeth *see* Rowe, Elizabeth
Siskin, Clifford 212
Sitter, John E. 96
Sidney, Sir Philip 73, 162, 184, 188
Skinner, Gillian 158 n.
Smith, Charlotte 194, 195–6, 215
Smollett, Tobias 50, 52, 106
Southey, Robert 167
Stael, Germaine de 206
  Corinne 206
Sterne, Laurence 148
social contract theory 132
Southam, Brian 227 n.
Southerne, Thomas 30, 33, 34, 38
Southey, Robert 167, 168
Spence, Joseph 45
Spenser, Edmund 1 n., 18, 133, 161
  place in literary line 229
  as son of Chaucer 18, 28
  The Faerie Queene 85, 161
spirit
  associated with men 17
spirit-matter hierarchy 11, 17, 26–8,
    47, 74
Stallybrass, Peter 91
Steele, Richard
  The Spectator 190 n.
Stepney, George 29
Sterne, Laurence 70
Stone, Lawrence 14 n., 158
Sulloway, Alison 214
Summers, Montague 41 n., 227
Swift, Jonathan 23, 92
  Battle of the Books 23–4, 85
  'A Beautiful Young Nymph going to
    Bed' 205
  'Corinna' 205
Swinburne, Algernon 37

Tate, Nahum 29
Taylor, Barbara D. 207 n.
Taylor, D. Crane 37 n.
Terry, Richard 5

Thaddeus, Janice Farrar 48
Thomas, Claudia N. 115 n.
Thomas, Elizabeth 46, 189, 205
Thrale, Hester 47, 52–3, 56–7, 65,
   153 n.
   patronage of Burney 60
Thrale, Hester 'Queeney' 57, 59
Tinker, C. B. 51 n.
Tomalin, Claire 214
Tonson, Jacob 88 n.
Trollope, Anthony 223 n.
Trotter, Catharine 39, 46, 190–1, 202
Tucker, George Holbert 214 n.
Tuite, Clara 212
Turner, Mark 8 n.
Twain, Mark 227

Vargo, Lisa 125
Virgil 21, 27, 43, 80
   as father of Roman poetry 22
   Aeneid 23–4, 25, 32, 83
Virgin Mary 74

Wakefield, Gilbert 97
Wall, Wendy 123 n.
Warburton, William 82
Ward, Charles E. 29 n.
Warner, William 51 n.
Warton, Joseph 96
Watkins, John 111
Weldon, Fay
   Letters to Alice 228
West, David 25 n.
Westcomb, Sophia 154 n.
White, Allon 91
William III 37
Williams, Aubrey 83, 85 n.
Williams, Carolyn D. 43 n.
Winn, James A. 25 n., 29 n., 32
Winstead, Karen A. 75 n.
Wolfson, Susan J. 185, 206
Wollstonecraft, Mary 4, 73, 119–30
   and idea of matrilineal
      inheritance 121

literary legacy to Mary
   Shelley 119–30
relationship with daughter Fanny
   Imlay 121–2
Elements of Morality 124
An Historical and Moral View 124
Letters from Norway 121–2, 124
Mary, a Fiction 124
Maria; or, the Wrongs of
   Woman 122–3, 124
Original Stories from Real Life 121
Ten Lessons 123
Thoughts on the Education of
   Daughters 121
A Vindication of the Rights of
   Woman 120–1, 125, 127, 130,
   155
Woolf, Virginia 210, 211
   A Room of One's Own 210, 213
Wordsworth, Dorothy 164–87
   as link to nature 167–8, 173, 184
   and literary ambition 164–5,
      185–6
   relations with Coleridge 134–6,
      165–9, 171–3, 175–6, 186–7
   relations with William
      Wordsworth 134–6, 164–5,
      167–73, 175–87
   sense of self 185–6
   writing style, 170–2
   'Floating Island at Hawkeshead' 186
   'Irregular Verses' 185
   Journals 134, 164, 169, 170–2,
      177–81, 186
   Narrative of George and Sarah
      Green 164
Wordsworth, Jonathan 176, 183 n.,
   184 n.
Wordsworth, William 16, 131,
   164–87, 189, 218
   and femininity 173
   marriage, 134, 164, 177, 182
   and masculinity 167, 173
   relation to Milton 133, 174, 183

Wordsworth, William (*cont.*)
  relations with Coleridge 134–6,
    165–9, 172–6, 182–7
  relations with Dorothy
    Wordsworth 134–6, 164–73,
    175–87
  relationship with his mother 166
  relationship with nature 165,
    166–8, 183
  and transcendence 172, 173, 184
  'Alice Fell' 177
  'Beggars' 177–80
  'Expostulation and Reply' 169
  'Home at Grasmere' 176, 183
  'Immortality Ode' 165
  'Lucy' poems 175
  Lyrical Ballads 133, 135, 169, 170,
    179

'Michael' 171
'A Night Piece' 171
The Prelude 17, 165, 166, 175,
  183–4
The Recluse 173–5, 176, 182–3
'The Sparrow's Nest' 181, 183
'The Tables Turned' 169
'Tintern Abbey' 167, 181, 183
'To a Butterfly' 180–1
'To My Sister' 169
'To a Small Celandine' 181
Wright, Frances 120
Wycherley, William 34, 109, 114

Young, Edward 133, 163
  *Conjectures on Original
    Composition* 133